ALAN MOORE

GREAT COMICS ARTISTS SERIES

M. Thomas Inge, General Editor

ALAN MOORE

COMICS AS PERFORMANCE, FICTION AS SCALPEL

Annalisa Di Liddo

UNIVERSITY PRESS OF MISSISSIPPI
JACKSON

www.upress.state.ms.us

Designed by Peter Halverson

The University Press of Mississippi is a member of the
Association of American University Presses.

Copyright © 2009 by University Press of Mississippi
All rights reserved
Manufactured in the United States of America

Detail from "The Reward of Cruelty." *From Hell,*
chapter 9, page 16 (excerpt). © Alan Moore and Eddie
Campbell. All Rights Reserved. Image reprinted here
with permission.

First printing 2009
∞
Library of Congress Cataloging-in-Publication Data

Di Liddo, Annalisa, 1977–
  Alan Moore : comics as performance, fiction as scalpel
/ Annalisa Di Liddo.
    p. cm. — (Great comics artists series)
  Includes bibliographical references and index.
  ISBN 978-1-60473-212-2 (cloth : alk. paper) — ISBN
978-1-60473-213-9 (pbk. : alk. paper) 1. Moore, Alan,
1953——Criticism and interpretation. I. Title.
  PN6737.M66D5 2009
  741.5'973—dc22   2008038646

British Library Cataloging-in-Publication Data available

CONTENTS

PREFACE AND ACKNOWLEDGMENTS

Why a book about Alan Moore?

When we talk about comics, it is practically impossible not to recall our childhood and adolescence, for it is there that most of us first came into contact with them. I am no exception to this rule, but I was born and bred in a small Italian town, so the story of my approach to the medium is certainly different from the experience of the average English-speaking comics reader. Nevertheless, Alan Moore played an important role in this story.

As a child I read avidly. Anything would do: fairy tales, adventure books, edifying young adults' novels. I read a lot of comics, too, especially Mickey Mouse and many Italian kids' comics. The ones I loved most were the tales of the good-natured devil *Geppo* by Pier Luigi Sangalli, and *Pinky the Rabbit*, a surreal, cynical strip (oddly, published in the Catholic children's magazine *Il Giornalino*) by Massimo Mattioli, who I later came to know as a key figure in the Italian underground movement. As an adolescent I turned to reading classics, then fantasy and gothic novels; I came across science fiction, and veered toward horror through the popular Italian comic book character *Dylan Dog*. I continued liking comics but gave my reading preferences to prose. I was not that interested in getting to know more about the strange world of sequential art. In my hometown a few miles from Milan there were no specialty stores, so the only comics I got to see were the ones I could find at newsstands—where the international selection was rather poor—or the secondhand Disney comics I occasionally bought at bookstalls when I was on holiday at the seaside with my family. My schoolmates did not seem peculiarly keen on the medium; my feeling toward comics remained one of mild curiosity, and my relationship with them a solitary one, albeit sometimes shared with Valentina, one of my older sisters. Then, one day, Valentina found that there was a comics section at our small public library and came home with two books: Frank Miller's *Ronin* and a dog-eared, battered copy of the collected edition of Moore and Gibbons's *Watchmen*.

Two very different books, but both extremely challenging reads. In particular, I remember lying on my stomach on the floor of my parents' living room, my back slightly aching because I had been there for hours, unable to stop reading *Watchmen*, carefully trying not to tear its creased pages. I felt intoxicated; I had never seen anything like that before. Curiosity changed into irrepressible enthusiasm with every turn of the page. That was the beginning of a very long journey: I started reading any comic book I could find, from Tezuka Osamu's *mangas* to American superheroes. I discovered Art Spiegelman, Winsor McCay, Andrea Pazienza, and much else. But thoughts of *Watchmen* never left me, and together with searching for whatever comics I could find, I began a systematic quest for Alan Moore's books. When I grew older and went to university, I chose contemporary English literature as my major. I took advantage of my first scholarship to spend some time in the U.K. and research material for my M.A. thesis about Angela Carter; I also seized the occasion to ransack London's comics shops and take the English-language versions of Moore's works home with me. It was 2000, and *From Hell* had just been published as a collected edition. I went back to Italy and brought the book to my would-be Ph.D. tutor, Professor Carlo Pagetti at the University of Milan, telling him that something really big was going on in there, and that I wanted to know more about it. Two years later, I started my Ph.D. in English literary studies with Moore's work as the main topic of my dissertation. My Ph.D. is now over, but it gave me the opportunity to make reading and teaching comics my regular job for a while.

Many people deserve my heartfelt thanks for accompanying me along the way, even up to the writing on this page.

For mentorship at the University of Milan, my tutors Mario Maffi and Carlo Pagetti. For guidance and patience as I was preparing this manuscript, Walter Biggins and Seetha Srinivasan.

For challenging conversations and advice about writing, Nicoletta Vallorani and Simona Bertacco at the University of Milan, Shelley Hornstein at the University of York (Toronto, Canada), and Oriana Palusci at the University of Trento. I owe special thanks to Jeet Heer for his precious suggestions about the title of this book, and for asking me thought-provoking questions. For counseling about research and for welcoming me at the Cartoon Research Library in Columbus, Ohio, Lucy Shelton Caswell; for publishing my first article in the United States, *International Journal of Comic Art* editor John Lent.

Last but not least, I should thank Maria Carla, Enrico, and Giuseppina Rusconi for assiduous moral support, and Martina Treu and Giovanni Nahmias for friendship and inspiring exchange. A special appreciation goes to my family, in particular to my sister Valentina—my all-time favorite fellow comics reader—for going to the public library that day a few years ago. For encouragement, help of all sorts, and boundless trust, Carlo Cardelli is unrivalled. And of course I thank my parents, who gave me the chance to pursue my studies in the first place, and who this book is dedicated to:

Sergio ed Enrica, questo libro è dedicato a voi.

ALAN MOORE

INTRODUCTION

This book is an examination of some motifs and concerns in the work of British author Alan Moore (1953–). It stems from a long-cultivated interest in comics as a medium, which I was lucky to turn into the object of my Ph.D. studies at the University of Milan, Italy. Criticism about Moore's work has been abundant so far, and it has been lately revived by the appearance of the three volumes of *Lost Girls*, the result of sixteen years of work with artist and partner Melinda Gebbie. Significant contributions toward an analysis of his wide artistic output have appeared in several publications—from the *Comics Journal* to the *Journal of Popular Culture*, from the *International Journal of Comic Art* to *Extrapolation*—and on specialized web magazines such as *NinthArt*, *ImageTexT*, and *Image and Narrative*. The web teems with interviews, YouTube videos, specially dedicated websites, and annotations to several works, from *V for Vendetta* to *Top Ten*, to the script for the *Watchmen* film that was never made by Terry Gilliam (even though rumor has it that Zack Snyder has been shooting his own adaptation from it). Independent director Dez Vylenz recently released a double DVD called *The Mindscape of Alan Moore*, featuring a lengthy documentary interview of the author plus extra conversations with scholar Paul Gravett and with Moore's co-authors Gebbie, Gibbons, Lloyd, O'Neill and Villarrubia. In short, the amount of commentary on Moore's work is colossal and scattered over several media, ranging from academic essays and high-quality journalism to hagiographic fan sites. A few books have been entirely dedicated to him: two annotated bibliographies—Lance Parkin's 2001 *Pocket Essentials* booklet and Gianluca Aicardi's 2006 *M for Moore*—and three companions to single works: *Kimota! The Miracleman Companion*, published by George Khoury in 2001, and two volumes of annotations to *The League of Extraordinary Gentlemen* compiled by Jess Nevins in 2003 and 2004. Three collections of miscellaneous essays have been published: *The Extraordinary Works of Alan Moore*, edited by

George Khoury; *Alan Moore: Portrait of an Extraordinary Gentleman*, edited by Gary Spencer Millidge and smoky man, both released in 2003; and *Watchmen. Vent'anni dopo* (*Watchmen: Twenty Years Later*), edited by smoky man and published in 2006. The broad scope of these three collections certainly is their credit, but their all-too-celebratory character sometimes results in deficient critical attitude. Hence, in an age when comics criticism has finally been (almost) fully legitimized by the academia, and comic books and graphic novels often appear in syllabi both at high schools and at universities, the need for a more systematically critical study of Moore's work is clear.

Nevertheless, this book by no means claims to be a comprehensive analysis of Moore's wide artistic production in the field of comics, prose, and performance. If anything, it can be defined as an attempt to map out one of many routes into the work of a writer and artist whose importance and influence have now been recognized worldwide, but whose complex aesthetics and cultural discourse have not yet been thoroughly examined. As my research and reading proceeded, I realized that trying to encompass all of Moore's works in a single analysis would bring me either to write a ten-volume treatise or to compile a fifty-page annotated bibliography. Considering that the former possibility was quite far-fetched and beyond the scope of a Ph.D. grant, and that the latter was doomed to superficiality, I opted for a different approach. Therefore, I selected only a few of Moore's works and tried to build a consistent argument about what I identified as some core aspects of his production. When an author is so prolific and encyclopedic in both style and content, selectivity becomes crucial for the scholar to avoid shallowness or stereotype.

The method employed in this study is as hybrid as the medium it is devoted to: a form of expression as mixed and heterogeneous as comics—"a wandering variable," as Charles Hatfield defined it (*Alternative* XIV)—cannot but be open to assorted critical approaches. In my work, certainly because of my own taste and academic education, but also—and maybe most of all—because of the inborn characteristics of Moore's narrative, I mainly use the tools of literary and cultural studies. Therefore, Mikhail Bakhtin, Gérard Genette, and Northrop Frye meet the modern and postmodern perspectives of Fredric Jameson, Linda Hutcheon, of cultural analyst Raymond Williams, and of specialized comics studies scholars such as Charles Hatfield, Roger Sabin, or Geoff Klock. It is always worth stressing the point that other methods of inquiry could have been possible; what I chose is only one of the many ways of approaching the multifarious universe of sequential art.

A few words about the title of this book might be helpful to understand my argument. It mentions a sentence from the *From Hell* scripts where Moore describes the result of his work with Eddie Campbell as "the post-mortem of a historical occurrence, using fiction as a scalpel" (Moore, *From Hell: Compleat Scripts* 337). In my study I argue that fiction is not just the scalpel the author uses to dissect the Ripper mythology in this graphic novel, but also the tool he employs to deconstruct, manipulate, and reassemble the forms of tradition and narrative both in literature and in comics, thereby raising crucial issues in Western—and above all English—culture, politics, and identity. The scalpel metaphor is effective in drawing our attention to the distinctive deconstructive quality of Moore's narrative, which over the years has become increasingly influential in his thinking, and in step with his later interests in performance and in the retrieval of both individual and collective memory as related to specific physical locations.

As one can notice from the above lines, I have called *From Hell* a graphic novel. There are precise grounds on which the term can be considered appropriate when referring to some of our author's works, and I am going to explain them in the course of this introduction. In order to do so, it is necessary to offer an overview of the term and of the different uses to which it has been subjected over the years. The definition of what a graphic novel may be, and above all the question whether this label really is needed, has been crucial since the term started to catch on in the mid-seventies, even though it actually had been first used by U.S. publisher and importer of European comics Richard Kyle in 1964 (see Gravett 8). As Rob Vollmar observed in 2003, "no one emerging idea has had quite the catalytic effect as that of the graphic novel. . . . Yet, for all the glory and critical attention paid to its essential contribution to the evolution of comics, there is a scarcity of accord on what a graphic novel might actually be . . . and while few critics are willing to allow the question 'What is a graphic novel?' to pass without sharing an opinion, no one definition offered has been accepted as authoritative by the others in such a fashion that it is not still a necessity for each individual critic to state their own, localized definition in order for the conversation even to begin" (Vollmar, "Discovering Part 1"). The controversy between the supporters of the term and its detractors involved both the critics and professionals of the comics medium. While the former often opted to endorse the soundness of the definition, the latter just as often embraced a more pugnacious attitude, especially in reaction to the rise in the comics market that followed the publication of the so-called Big Three (Sabin, *Adult Comics* 87) in

1986: Art Spiegelman's *Maus I*, Frank Miller's *Batman: The Dark Knight Returns*, and Alan Moore and Dave Gibbons's *Watchmen*. As Sabin recalls, those three long and demanding comic books revived the idea of using the term graphic novel—which, as we will see, had been promoted by Will Eisner in 1978—and started a process of rediscovery for comics which, with the aid of a good amount of media hype, soon turned into a fashion.

Many publishers took advantage of the propitious moment by seizing the opportunity to reprint low-quality works, or simply to repackage older series into book editions with restyled covers in order to sell them as representatives of the brand-new comics sensation. This is why Art Spiegelman, for example, was so skeptical of the term. In a talk he gave at the Yale Graphic Design Symposium in 1986, Spiegelman dismissed the graphic novel as a whim of the industry, doomed to short duration: "[Comic books] were dubbed graphic novels in a bid for social acceptance (personally, I always thought Nathanael West's *The Day of the Locust* was an extraordinarily graphic novel, and that what I did was... comix). What has followed is a spate of well-dressed comic books finding their way into legitimate bookshops. Sadly, a number of them are no more than pedestrian comic books in glossy wrappings" (Spiegelman, *Comix* 81). Shortly afterward, *Comics Journal* curator Robert Fiore, together with colleague Gary Groth, wrote an introduction to a book dedicated to the best authors of the 1980s, and he too manifested his doubts about the usefulness of the label: "A 'graphic novel' is a long comic book. The term is essentially a reflection of the industry's yearning for unearned status. Rather than improving the image of comics by improving comics themselves, it tries to enhance its status through semantic jiggery-pokery. Throughout most of the world, a comics story or collection of stories in book form is referred to as an album" (Groth and Fiore 5). Fiore's opinion shares Spiegelman's polemic tone but actually manages to highlight one of the main grounds for use of the term: the attempt to lend dignity to a medium that, for a mix of historical and cultural reasons, was long considered a negligible by-product of mass culture or a heap of lowbrow publications good for thick-headed adolescents.[1]

On the contrary, using such an expression as "graphic novel" strived for the recognition of comics as a complex, meaningful narrative form, which had to be considered as good as any other artistic expression. This was what Will Eisner meant when he brought the term into the spotlight as he tried to promote his long comic books, in particular *A Contract with God* (1978). Despite the ambiguity—given the fact that *Contract* was actually a collection of short stories—the expression soon became common in the market and therefore at least partially owes its success to Eisner, who, unlike Spiegelman, remained one of its strenuous defenders. He explained that the graphic novel is a "true literary form . . . with its own code of communication" (Eisner, "Address") and that "if a comic is a melody, a graphic novel can be a symphony" (qtd. in Sabin, *Adult Comics* 235).[2] Comic book artist Eddie Campbell, who also worked with Moore on several occasions, is another author who devoted some time to reflection about the issue. This is what he declared in his *Alec: How To Be an Artist* in 2001: "Graphic novel. It's a misnomer, of course, but then so is 'comic book.' It has been lately discarded in some circles, but it will be a thing, like the sales receipt for a shirt, that you throw out and then find you're going to need" (120). Campbell thus somehow recognized the plausibility of the term, even though in his later, definitely ironic "Graphic Novel Manifesto" he regarded it as much abused, underscoring that "publishers may use the term over and over until it means even less than the nothing it means already" ("Graphic Novel") and thus taking a far more polemical stand toward the issue.

While Moore's own stance will be dealt with in chapter 1, we will now move on to review the considerations offered by comics scholars over the years. Many critics have now recognized the possibility of the existence of a graphic novel tradition, but their definitions of the term tend to lack in homogeneity and are therefore suggestive of the indeterminacy that still characterizes this field of study. Paul Dawson, who at the University of Manchester in the early nineties became the first British professor to hold an entire course dedicated to the graphic novel, acknowledged the convenience of the term but also expressed his doubts about applying the word *novel*—with all its implications of the literary canon—to such a hybrid, unstable medium as comics: "the assimilation of comics to the novel is tempting, because it offers a way to domesticate a form which we are still struggling to understand adequately" (qtd. in Sabin, *Adult Comics* 247). Belgian professor Jan Baetens strongly advocated for the graphic novel: he devoted a whole conference to it at the University of Leuven in May 2000 (the proceedings of which were published in the volume *The Graphic Novel*, 2001). Yet Baetens too saw terminological trouble, especially in the use of the adjective *graphic*, which emphasizes the idea of visuality in British English but tends to acquire the meaning of "hyperdescriptive" in American English. In his view, the result is that in the United States, "graphic" is used to characterize a certain type of hyperrealist prose (and it is probably in this sense that Spiegelman referred to *The Day of the Locust* in the quotation reported above), and that therefore the graphic novel is meant above all as a narrative where the visual aspect is marginal to the literary one, thus tending more to become a sort of illustrated story. By contrast, in Europe authors give preference to the pictorial quality of narrative, Baetens claims, and consequently build their stories by laying emphasis on the visuals. It must be said that, although it worked with the examples provided by Baetens at the time, this notion appears too restrictive nowadays; it is enough to think of U.S. artist Chris Ware's *Acme Novelty Library* or *Jimmy Corrigan: The Smartest Kid on Earth* (2000) to find a case for primarily visual narratives, where stories are constructed by experimenting with the layout of the page.[3] Geographical and linguistic matters surely carry significant weight, but the trouble with the definition of the graphic novel goes far beyond them.

Scholar and cartoonist Robert C. Harvey was also involved in the debate. He manifested his mistrust of the term, but the reasons he advanced were somewhat unclear. In his *The Art of the Comic Book* (1996) he calls non-serial narratives "comic books" and employs the term "graphic novel" only to indicate texts that somehow go back to the origins of the comics medium: "Perhaps the graphic novel is no more than a revival of comics in their most primitive form. Perhaps there is nothing new except what has been forgotten. In form, most early specimens of the graphic novel were distinguished from the ordinary comic strip or comic book by the presence of narrative text accompanying sequential pictures. These graphic novels look remarkably like the prototypical comic strips of the nineteenth and early twentieth centuries—parades of panels with text underneath. . . . The form may be strikingly similar, but the elements of that form function in markedly different ways whenever all the resources of the graphic novel are brought into play" (106–7). Harvey then proceeds to examine the specific features of the graphic novel by using two works by Gil Kane as examples: *His Name Is . . . Savage* (1968) and *Blackmark* (1971). From Harvey's point of view, Kane's work differs from mid-nineteenth-century strips such as those of Rodolphe Töpffer (1799–1846), which consisted of images accompanied by captions (and which Harvey considers as the illustrious precursors of modern comics), because "narrative text, spoken words, and pictures . . . are carefully integrated, each in its way conveying to us a portion of the information we need to understand what has happened, none revealing in itself the whole story. . . . The chief elements of the medium are artfully deployed, the import of each element supporting that of the others to create an impression that no single element by itself could create" (111–13). This definition is certainly correct, and yet Harvey limits its usage to Kane's work without clearly explaining why and without providing any further examples. He adds that works like Eisner's *A Contract With God* or *A Life Force* (1983) do not fit his definition of the graphic novel because their structure is too conventional—but he then dismisses the topic in the space of a paragraph, without specifying where Eisner's conventionality resides and without examining in detail the difference between Gil Kane's graphic novels and any other existing comic books. He ends up reaching a hasty conclusion that distinctions are always ephemeral, that the term has been deprived of its meaning by the market, and most of all that "the graphic novel as I've been discussing it virtually disappeared" (117). Today the latter statement appears honestly questionable, for Harvey's book does not take into consideration a wide array of comics published in the eighties and the nineties (and not only at the hands of Moore): many of them meet the requirement that "narrative text, spoken words, and pictures . . . are carefully integrated" (111), thus easily refuting his final stance.

A further step toward the conception of the graphic novel as it is now meant is represented by Roger Sabin, who, in his 1993 essay *Adult Comics*, claims that its existence is an unquestionable fact. He classifies three types of graphic novel depending on productive and publishing modalities, but all three share being equipped with a coherent, organic narrative motif. When a graphic novel comes out as a single book—and is thus produced more or less in the same way as traditional prose novels—it belongs to the first type (see 234). Sabin is right in distinguishing this category, but we must add that this kind of publication is something of a rarity: creating a novel-length comic book is a very long process, and sending it into stores without serializing it beforehand puts considerable financial pressure on both publishers and authors. It is not an impossible goal, as Charles Hatfield notes (see *Alternative* 161–62) by providing examples like Howard Cruse's *Stuck Rubber Baby* (1995), Raymond Briggs's *Ethel and Ernest* (1998), or Joe Sacco's *The Fixer* (2003); but it is extremely difficult to attain.

Serialization, on the contrary, is safer for publishers and allows authors to be paid as they go. Going back to Sabin, the second and third type of graphic novel he identifies are both published in serial form. Type two is the graphic novel that is distributed in installments and only later collected into a book edition (as happened with nineteenth-century novels), but that is structured as a self-contained narrative from the very start; a contemporary example could be Canadian artist Chester Brown's comic strip biography of Métis leader Louis Riel, serialized by Drawn and Quarterly between 1999 and 2003, and published as a book in the latter year. Type three is actually the most problematic kind of graphic novel as Sabin defines it, for it is represented by the so-called "section of a comics continuity" (235). From the point of view of narrative structure, it could be compared to a soap opera, in that the episodes it collects are part of a longer and potentially everlasting series. But despite coming from a long, as yet unfinished sequence, this kind of graphic novel is organic enough to amount to a self-standing narrative entity. On one hand, works belonging to this type seem to erase the boundary between series and novel, thus threatening to invalidate the previous definitions. On the other, this distinction is acceptable when we think of examples such as Moore and O'Neill's *The League of Extraordinary Gentlemen* (which will be dealt with in the following chapters); this work has been collected in two independent book editions, even though they are part of a series that Moore himself describes as potentially endless (see Khoury, *Extraordinary* 182).

Beyond classification and controversy, the most important notion for the purposes of this book is that the graphic novel is a narrative where word and image are bound in indissoluble cooperation (hence the term *graphic*) and where the final result is "longer than usual, . . . with a thematic unity" (Sabin, *Adult Comics* 94). Thematic unity is a crucial element, the importance of which has often been played down in the course of the debate. What makes the difference between a graphic novel and a comic book is less the length of the work (for how many pages really make it possible to say that a book is a novel?) than the presence of one or more adequately developed motifs that build up the core of the narrative. The graphic novel is a composite, well-organized structure whose construction implies careful textual design on the part of the author(s). This basic element makes the difference from the pure iteration of the adventures of one or more characters. Rob Vollmar and Paul Gravett have satisfactorily highlighted this aspect by stating that the graphic novel must be "written with the larger structure of the work in mind and allowed for the length of the segments to be dictated by the story instead of by serial format demands" (Vollmar, "Discovering Part 3"), and that it must tell "a solid, self-sufficient tale" (Gravett 9).

However, the most exhaustive recent considerations about the topic were provided by Charles Hatfield's book *Alternative Comics* (2005). In his stimulating study, this American scholar underscores aspects that had been neglected or too hastily dealt with in previous examinations. He claims that, despite its ambiguities, the graphic novel has established a solid position within the market that it would be inappropriate to ignore—but also that one must be careful when using the term, because it "unfortunately tends to hide the complexity and precariousness of comics publishing, obscuring the long form's dependence on the serial" (155). As noted above, the graphic novels Sabin includes in the first type—the ones directly published as book edition—are the exception to the rule. Most graphic novels get into the stores as a series of episodes because it is the only way to make them financially sustainable, both for the publisher and for the author(s). This risks hindering the progress of comics that are meant to work as a big, single story, because both narrative rhythm and the readers' expectations can be damaged by fragmentation into installments. However, serialization can affect the graphic novel in several interesting ways: it inspires authors to painstaking care of structure via thematic repetition; allows them to get reader feedback; and most of all, if the creators have control of the narrative, they can use serialization to emphasize features of plot and structure, thus making the reading experience more powerful (for examples and further analysis of these aspects, see Hatfield, *Alternative*, especially 152–62). Provided we remember that not all authors are capable of reaching the latter effect, and that most comic books represent self-contained cases due to the inherent flexibility of the medium, I agree with Hatfield in believing that the term graphic novel is acceptable as long as we carefully contextualize it: "we need to know where these works come from, and what conditions enable and constrain their production. We also need to know what readerly habits and expectations shape their reception" (162).

Having said that, why does it make sense to refer to certain works by Alan Moore as graphic novels? The preceding overview has shed light on the fact that the graphic novel has made a name for itself both in the market and in the field of criticism. Therefore, my current use of the term does not come from a longing for status or legitimization. The point is simply that the comics by Moore this book deals with (which shortly will be introduced) match the characteristics of thematic unity, large structure, and cohesiveness mentioned above. Most of them also feature novel-like length, such as the massive narratives of texts like *From Hell* or *Promethea*. On top of that, Moore long ago decided not to draw his comics, but to devote himself to meticulously writing and planning his works, producing impressive amounts of pages of descriptions and suggestions for the artists with whom he collaborates (an aspect that will be touched on in chapter 1). Indeed, he defines himself as "primarily a writer" (Khoury, *Extraordinary* 195), and he is very much a *literary* writer who often refers to, and plays with, the tradition of prose literature, as will be shown throughout the following chapters by explaining his use of intertextuality (see ch. 1) and by placing him into a cultural context he shares with other contemporary novelists (see conclusion). These elements, and his recent choice to devote more of his time to prose than to comics scripting, confirm that the connection with traditional novel writing is more evident in Moore's production than in many other comics creators' work. In his case, the expression "graphic novel" is appropriate because it conveys the balance between the weight of the literary tradition and the equally important visual aspect of his works. For all his appreciation of literature, we will see that Moore makes it very clear that the medium of comics has unique qualities, and that making the most of those qualities—the interaction of word and image—is what has interested him throughout the greatest part of his career.

Yet, the title of this book does not call Alan Moore a graphic novelist. Doing so would actually be limiting and therefore inadequate. Instead, the title refers to Moore's comics as performance. Not all of Moore's works are graphic novels: he also created strips (like his early *Maxwell the Magic Cat*), cartoons, serializations, and single comic books. He wrote poetry and prose. He acted in performances and recorded CDs. He is definitely more than just a graphic novelist. For this reason, the best term I could come up with to describe him (and again I have to say thanks to Jeet Heer for suggesting it) is "a performing writer." We will see that there is more to the adjective *performing* than just the denotation of a writer who is also active as a theatrical performer. But I am jumping to my conclusion. Let us briefly outline the chapters of this book.

Chapter 1 considers Moore's "aesthetics of comics" by examining his 1986 manifesto *On Writing for Comics*, and by reflecting on his peculiar approach to scripting and to relating with the artists he chooses as co-creators for his works. Again the concept of the graphic novel will be explored, with special reference to the author's awareness of his own literary influences and approach to writing, and to his simultaneous belief in the unique value that characterizes the blending of the verbal and the visual in comics. The chapter then studies the author's strongly intertextual narrative strategy, which allows him to playfully manipulate both the literary tradition and the tradition of comics, and to metafictionally call into question the validity of his own narrative, thus constantly endowing it with multiple layers of reading and possibilities of interpretation, which are always emphasized by the polysemic complexity of the interaction between word and image. We will focus on literary intertextuality and on the rewriting of genres and narrative formulas, drawing examples from *V for Vendetta*, *The League of Extraordinary Gentlemen*, *From Hell*, and a brief look at the controversial *Lost*

Girls, published in 2006 after sixteen years of work with Melinda Gebbie (and further examined in chapter 4). We then highlight the intertextual manipulation of the comics tradition by focusing, as a case study, on the hackneyed but nonetheless unavoidable topic of superhero comics and their revisiting, mainly dealing with *Miracleman* and with milestones *Swamp Thing* and *Watchmen*.

The following chapter is devoted to an examination of Moore's narrative structures, drawing on the Bakhtinian notion of the chronotope to study the way he experiments with time and space in a medium where these two elements are "one and the same," as noted by Scott McCloud (*Understanding* 100). We start by studying the relation between space—also intended as outer space—and time in *The Ballad of Halo Jones*, one of Moore's most critically neglected works. Structural and thematic features of the work will be considered, paying particular attention to its use of science-fiction conventions; the representation of the psychology of the protagonist both as a woman and as a sci-fi character; and the way the narrative is organized with a circular structure on both visual and verbal planes.

The space of the city and its expansion into historical and mystical time will be considered as lying at the core of *From Hell*. The movements of Dr. Gull through London, accompanied by the character's mystical insights, offer Moore and Campbell the possibility masterfully to play with the representation of space and time through verbal and visual interaction. Moreover, the somber portrayal of Victorian London that emerges from the contrast between the depiction of the affluent West End and the poverty-stricken scenery of the East End calls attention to the novel's teeming narrative universe, whose dense network of characters is not unlike the one created by Charles Dickens in his 1865 novel *Our Mutual Friend*. Finally, we will consider how the strong metafictional slant of *From Hell* (in particular as regards the second appendix to the novel) opens the Ripper mythology out to infinite possibilities of fictionalization and interpretation by simultaneously keeping it isolated in the impenetrable circle of an irretrievable and perhaps nonexistent historical truth.

Finally, chapter 2 focuses on *Promethea*, a revolutionary work in which Moore explodes the very notion of chronotope by undoing space and time in favor of an absolute "space-time of the imagination," where narrative becomes a site for reflecting on the process of artistic creation. Some basic elements about Moore's magical turn and the way it has informed the very organization of this work are introduced, thus providing a series of examples of the visual/verbal experimentation accomplished by the writer and his co-authors, and of the way such experimentation blends with Moore's usual intertextual and quotational strategies. The idea of circularity is here maintained and yet simultaneously disrupted in favor of the concept of a fluid, harmonious space-time where meta-fictional reflection once again is called for, and where imagination and artistic creation become apparent as mankind's most powerful resource—with comics being the most innovative result, provided they are ready to undergo radical change.

Such a stance clarifies that Moore's narrative, despite being overtly meta-fictional, resists withdrawal into itself and opens out onto precise historical, social, and cultural issues. Chapter 3 moves from concerns of narrative structure and organization to more tangible facts by explicitly stressing the connection between Moore's works and their historical, cultural, and political context. We focus on the author's attitude toward English identity, and the crisis it has undergone in the twentieth century, by examining his stand on issues such as imperial legacy—especially in its ethnic and gender implications—with particular reference to the characters from *The League of Extraordinary Gentlemen*. The most significant character in the novel seems to be Mina Murray, one based on a revisiting of her *Dracula* namesake and revealing of the attention Moore pays to female characters, as already seen in the depiction of the prostitutes in *From Hell*, of *Halo Jones*, and of the revised superheroine *Promethea*. Margaret Thatcher's politics, in which gender trouble was also ingrained, are an essential feature of twentieth-century English identity whose consequences on Moore's narrative will also be considered. We take examples from *V for Vendetta* and from the long poem *The Mirror of Love*, where the issue of gender is more specifically explored with reference to Thatcher's repressive, homophobic politics. Another important aspect of the Thatcher years, social decay, is then scrutinized as it appears in the committed commentary provided by such works as *Skizz*, and by the two existing episodes of the unfinished but still valuable graphic novel *Big Numbers*. Both works focus on issues of unemployment and the lack of welfare funds that characterized England in the 1980s.

Our considerations then move to the strong sense of place that again emerges from *Big Numbers* and from *Voice of the Fire*, Moore's only prose novel so far. By drawing a parallel with Raymond Williams's *People of the Black Mountains*, we reflect on the importance of Williams, a key figure for English culture, in the development of Moore's vision.

While each of the above-mentioned chapters covers three or more of Moore's works on the basis of a common topic, chapter 4 is dedicated to a single graphic novel. *Lost Girls* deserves separate treatment for at least two reasons: first, because it was only released in 2006, sixteen years after its first page was created, and thus we are still in the process of absorbing it in order to locate its place in Moore's output; and second, because it differs considerably from the author's previous works—or better, because it shares many topics and stylistic features with but diverges from them in that it is not entirely successful. After reviewing the considerable controversies generated by the problematic genre the novel belongs to—pornography—we examine *Lost Girls* in terms of both style and content to find out which elements work and which do not. Intertextuality is analyzed by exploring the thick fabric of verbal and visual quotations woven by the authors and made particularly sophisticated by Gebbie's drawings, which are replete with allusions and pastiches that recall other artists' work. Circularity, thematic repetition, and verbal/visual puns are considered, concluding that in narrative terms the book is weakened by an excess of schematism and technical tricks.

The subsequent section of the chapter involves the way space and time are manipulated, arguing that Moore and Gebbie create a "chronotope of sex" that, while functional to their discourse on the nature of imagination, fails to adequately prop the story and thus partially collapses. Lastly, we consider the political aspects of *Lost Girls;* the authors' discourse on gender; the portrayal of sexuality; and the subversive potential of pornography. Drawing inspiration from a parallel reading of two works by Angela Carter—*The Infernal Desire Machines of Doctor Hoffman* and *The Sadeian Woman*—we argue that, even though it is flawed in narrative and crushed by excessive formalism, *Lost Girls* is successful at least in its attempt to become an arena for discussion on the representation and problematic social perception of sex.

Finally, we draw conclusions from our journey into Moore's production by identifying him, as anticipated above, as a truly performing writer, with special reference to his performances and to the deep-rooted theatrical quality of his writing. The sum of the characteristics of Moore's work as they are outlined in this study ultimately place him in a specific context he shares with certain twentieth-century British authors, with particular emphasis on the connection between his work and books by the likes of Angela Carter, Iain Sinclair, and Peter Ackroyd. Nevertheless, what makes Moore's production unique is the way he uses the comics medium.

I hope my book can prove to be an (admittedly partial) answer to the need for inquiry into the wide realm of Alan Moore's art, and perhaps become a starting point for further questions and concerns, thus paving the way for new perspectives in the critical analysis of his work.

A NOTE ON EDITIONS, PAGINATION, AND ELLIPSES

For the sake of convenience, in this book I usually refer to Moore's works in their collected editions (save exceptions like *Big Numbers*, which only came out in two issues). When pagination is present, it is sometimes consecutive, and sometimes not, for in many cases it starts all over again at each chapter. Whenever books are not paginated, I have tried to obviate the difficulty by personally counting the pages and allocating them hypothetical consecutive numbers. Original ellipses from quoted material are represented by unspaced dots [...]; editorial ellipses are marked with spaced dots [. . .].

CHAPTER 1

FORMAL CONSIDERATIONS ON ALAN MOORE'S WRITING

This chapter examines some of Moore's works in terms of form and structure, aspects of his aesthetics that are crucial to the extent that, in the opinions of a few critics, they turn into an obsession in his latest enterprise *Lost Girls* (only hinted at here but better explored later in this book). Most of Moore's comics start from an intertextual assumption: a quotation, or an allusion to an existing character, a distinctive genre, or a particular work. They are built on a proper web of references that are not only mentioned or suggested but challenged and recontextualized in order to convey new meanings. Thus transcended, intertextuality is stripped of the status of mere formal device to become a proper narrative motif. These pages are devoted to the study of the various ways in which the author practices intertextuality, indeed one of his key strategies. But in order to proceed with this analysis, we need to begin with Moore's own elaboration of the basic concepts of the aesthetics of comics.

THE LANGUAGE OF COMICS AND THE AESTHETICS OF THE GRAPHIC NOVEL

Moore first preferred to skirt the problematic issue of use of the term "graphic novel" and kept his distance from the debate by simply asserting, together with other fellow artists and writers, that the graphic novel is actually nothing new but that the term works very well from the commercial point of view: "['graphic novel'] is just a handy, convenient marketing term that can be used to sell an awful lot of the same old crap to a big new audience" (Groth, "Big Words Pt 1" 71). More recently, the author declared that a possibly better term could be "graphic story" (Kavanagh), even though he ultimately seems to have accepted the usage of graphic novel (see Baker 23) in compliance with the current custom, for in late 2007 he admitted that "there's something quite interesting going on in comics at the moment, which is that it seems that the respectable book publishers are moving in. . . . [T]he comic book form—the original pamphlet form—is probably on its way out, and it means that trade paperbacks and graphic novels will become more the norm. . . . I think that the whole of comics could be moving into some new territory, which would hopefully throw off a lot of the dross of comics' origin" (Amacker, "Opening the Black Dossier Part 2").

However, Moore's earlier refusal to recognize the graphic novel as a self-standing literary category contrasted with his short programmatic essay *On Writing for Comics*. This treatise was featured in *Fantasy Advertiser* between August 1985 and February 1986, published again in the *Comics Journal* in 1988, and reprinted as a revised edition in a booklet released in 2003. Although presented as a quick reference manual for young comics scriptwriters and not as a proper piece of criticism, the essay nevertheless allows us not only to understand the author's aesthetical orientation but also to appreciate his deep connection with prose. As the concluding part of this book will show, this link has recently become more overt and has been put into practice in the novel *Voice of the Fire* (1996), the work-in-progress *Jerusalem,* and the future project *Grimorium* (see Santala); but its role in Moore's artistic production has been prominent from the start. In *On Writing for Comics* the author highlights his belief in the unique expressive skills of comics to construct far-reaching, innovative fictions, but the comparison he chooses when appraising narrative density and originality is the complexity of prose. Moore draws inspiration from the tradition of the novel, in order to revisit it and to convert its most interesting peculiarities into visual communication. Despite his admiration for some of his predecessors in comics, Moore asserts that most of his artistic and cultural points of reference come from the tradition of English and American prose. This stance was already apparent in an interview he gave in 1984, two years before publishing the first version of the booklet: "I suppose one major point is that in writing comics I don't really absorb too much influence from the comics that I read unless it's something inexpressibly brilliant. . . . Mostly I'd say that my influence comes from novels that I read or the occasional film that I see. If anything, I'd say that what I'd like to do as a writer is to try and translate some of the intellect and sensibilities that I find in books into something that will work on a comics page" (Burbey, "Alan Moore" 78–79). Moore mentions a wide array of texts and authors, both classic and contemporary, as his favorites, and the multiple intertextual references that pervade his work (an aspect that will be dealt with in the following sections) show how eager and omnivorous a reader he is. His interests span from antiquity to Jacobean theater, from experimental to formulaic and genre fiction; he pronounces his enthusiasm for Norse sagas, Arthurian legends and the story of Robin Hood, Shakespeare, fantasies by Mervyn Peake, science fiction, ghost and horror stories from M. R. James to H. P. Lovecraft, Ray Bradbury, Michael Moorcock, J. G. Ballard, and John Sladek (see Baker 19); he appreciates William Faulkner and Truman Capote, but also Angela Carter, Dorothy Parker, Stephen King, Harlan Ellison, Iain Sinclair, Derek Raymond and especially William Burroughs (see Sharrett 13).[1] Of course he also recalls reading, as a young boy, a fair quantity of comics, from common British strips of the 1960s to American superhero and underground magazines, and he does not fail to state his admiration for the genius of Winsor McCay (see Baker 64).

According to Moore, being a strong reader is essential for the process of cross-fertilization (see 68) that lies at the core of a good writer's activity. Knowing literature in all of its varieties—both traditional and contemporary narratives, be they in prose, poetry, or comics form—will allow the artist to approach his/ her own context, and to pursue the vital aim of adjusting the form of his/her art to the continuous changes that contemporary society is exposed to. In this perspective, the notion of relevance grows to be essential for Moore: "It becomes more of a problem to create work with any relevance in the rapidly altering world in which the industry and the readers that support it actually exist. By 'relevance' . . . I mean stories that actually have some sort of meaning in relation to the world about us, stories that reflect the nature and the texture of life in the closing years of the twentieth century" (Moore, *Writing* 2). If the script has no relevance to the current cultural context of the society where it is produced, there is no way to make the comic book more interesting or effective, no matter how sophisticated its visual qualities can be; but one of the basic tools for the writer to attain current relevance is actually turning to the past for knowledge and inspiration—hence the importance of tradition.

Moore's view is not dissimilar from the theories presented by T. S. Eliot in *Tradition and the Individual Talent*. In this 1919 essay, Eliot explained that focusing on the present implies being aware of the tradition of the past; therefore, the artist must be endowed with a sharp historical sense, which "compels a man to write not merely with his own generation in his bones, but with a feeling that the whole of the literature of Europe from Homer and within it the whole of the literature of his own country has a simultaneous existence and composes a simultaneous order. This historical sense, which is a sense of the timeless as well as of the temporal together, is . . . what makes a writer most acutely conscious of his place in time, of his own contemporaneity" (Eliot 38). Moore's perspective is evidently close—if not indebted—to Eliot's, except that, as his work shows, our author clearly conceives of tradition as something that includes not only prose and poetry but also music, cinema, and of course comics (also see Baker 68). Moore refers less to the literary tradition in a canonical sense than to culture, seen as both literature and other manifestations. He is more likely to see culture as a total way of life, in tune with the views offered by Raymond Williams, who was active as a cultural and social commentator in Britain from the sixties onward and who exerted a remarkable influence on Moore's own critical consciousness, as this book will discuss later.[2]

Before turning to his close examination of comics scriptwriting, Moore devotes a few lines of his 1986 pamphlet to offering some introductory considerations on writing in general. He claims that the written word is the primary vehicle for the ideas that underpin comics narratives, and that it clearly comes before the pictures. Therefore, awareness of the practice of writing is the most important element the comics author must accomplish: "the way we think about the act of writing will inevitably shape the works we produce" (Moore, *Writing* 2). Moore's interest in the practice of writing arose in his early childhood reading (see Campbell, "Alan Moore" 3) and gradually evolved into a consistent aesthetical project. It is significant that, right after his first experiences as a comic book artist, Moore decided to stop drawing in order fully to devote himself to scripting; the crucial significance of the written word was thus made clear at the very start of his career. Fascination with the power of words became a stronger influence on Moore's work as the years passed, culminating in his decision to dedicate a substantial part of his time to studying occultism and magic. From the early nineties onward, these elements have wielded significant influence on his production and experimentation, both in comics (especially *Promethea*, 1999–2005) and in prose (*Voice of the Fire*, 1996). Moore's reflection on the supremacy of language as the primary instance of representation—which eventually led to the multimedia performances that are briefly dealt with in the concluding pages of this book—results in his view of the word as the first step in all creative and cognitive acts. Yet, if words are the starting point of creation, our author does not deny the irrepressibly visual nature of comics. On the contrary, he states that what interests him most is exactly the specificity of the medium, whose unique characteristic is that of using an "underlanguage" (Sharrett 13), that is, an alternative idiom to common language, which results from the inter-action between two codes: the iconic and the verbal. His production certainly owes much of its appeal and effectiveness to this awareness, and to his conse-quent careful balancing of the constituents of the medium. Written words surely constitute the basis of the narrative, but as Moore works towards achieving the underlanguage of comics, those words are made anomalous, hybrid, somehow already "graphic." It must be said that the very term *underlanguage* may actually prove debatable, for the prefix *under-* could imply that the language of comics is secondary, or inferior, to conventional language. However, considering Moore's discussion of the potentialities of comics in his essay, it is unlikely that he had such a theory in mind. He probably used "underlanguage" for lack of a better term. His scripts bear no trace of any sense of inferiority toward language as it is more commonly meant; they are massive outpourings of words whose purpose, as we will see, is to become the primary channel for visualization.

Moore's activity as a scriptwriter—as opposed to writer-and-artist—is not an isolated example, for there are several approaches to the creation of comics. Some writers provide their artists with a schematic, boiled-down script; others prepare a more accurate version, complete with sketches or thumbnails for the artist to begin drawing while the writer refines the text. Another possibility is the so-called Marvel style, where the illustrator provides the scriptwriter with a rough framework for the narrative and the text is written in a later phase (Bissette 333; for the characteristics of Marvel publications, also see Daniels). An interesting example of hybrid scripting is provided by the *Sandman* series (con-sisting of seventy-five episodes published between 1988 and 1996, now collected in ten volumes) by English author Neil Gaiman, who hired several different art-ists when creating its episodes. He developed a peculiar synergy with illustrator Dave McKean, who also joined him on later projects. Gaiman asserted that the comic books emerged from his long conversations with the artist, which were later transcribed "in some strange bastard form that only myself and McKean could understand a word of. The script would be completely meaningless to anyone else" (Wiater and Bissette 192).[3]

Moore's scripts represent a unique case, because his method stands out from most scriptwriting practices. The tools that enable us to speculate about his creative process are the many interviews he and his collaborators have given and the three books where his scripts were officially published: the above-mentioned *From Hell: The Compleat Scripts* (1994) and the so-called "absolute editions" of the two *League of Extraordinary Gentlemen* graphic novels (2003 and 2005). The

preliminary phase of the work consists in dialogue and exchange of ideas between Moore and the artist, who define the characters' essential traits, together
with the general structure and style of the text. This often happened through
direct contact or through correspondence, the latter especially in the eighties,
when our author began publishing his books in the United States usually without leaving his home in Northampton, England (see Thompson 100–101). He
still resides in Northampton, and when this phase does not take place through
personal contact he usually relies on extensive phone calls or his fax machine.
The preliminary outline of the work is sketched, followed by proper elaboration
of the script, which Moore usually writes in detail, including a wide range of
precise indications for the artist. Such instructions are sent out as the scripting
proceeds (implying a rapid working process, considering the pressing timeta-
bles of serialization), often with Moore directly addressing his collaborator. The
script for the first volume of *The League of Extraordinary Gentlemen* begins with
Moore speaking to Kevin O'Neill in the same lighthearted, mock-Victorian
tone that characterizes the narration: "Page 1, Panel 1. Right, Kevin, here we go.
Starch your collar and tighten your corset. We have a six-panel page to open
with" (Moore, *League I: Absolute* 5).

Unlike Gaiman's scripts, which are conceived as a private communication
between him and the artist that might be incomprehensible to an external reader, Moore's texts are hyperdescriptive and already "visual" due to their richness
of detail. The volume that collects the scripts for the prologue and first three
chapters of *From Hell* is more than 300 pages long, while the sixteen chapters of
the graphic novel amount to about 450 pages: on this basis, we can presume that
the whole script could cover about 1,200 pages. The *Watchmen* script, too, was
very long and dense; Dave Gibbons recalls receiving a 101-page fascicle just for
the first chapter, which would come out as an installment of about thirty pages.
As a consequence, he had to number each sheet and highlight Moore's several
sets of indications in different colors, in order to work with such an imposing
amount of information (see Stewart, "Pebbles" 97–103).

Moore's scripts do not provide artists only with the words they should set
into the balloons and with the necessary technical suggestions about perspective
and angles, or about the positions of objects and characters in each panel. The
author also enters historical notes, commentaries, and descriptions of the possible sounds and smells one might have found on the scene. He voices his characters' thoughts even when they are not meant to appear in writing on the page.
He describes what nuances colors might have, even if the work is to be printed

in black and white. In short, he fills the script with all the details that, though unwritten and undrawn in the final version, are necessary for the artist to fully understand the atmosphere that is to characterize the comic book. (Moore abandoned this custom to turn to the thumbnails method in the creation of *Lost Girls*, which took place over several years spent in close contact with co-creator Melinda Gebbie. The resulting work diverges considerably from his previous output, but for reasons that cannot be put down only to the scripting process. This issue is investigated in chapter 4.)

His scripts, then, appear almost as separate works and can be viewed not only as preliminary versions but as autonomous, parallel texts to the comic books. As Rich Kreiner wrote in his review of *From Hell: The Compleat Scripts*:

> There's an inextinguishable, headlong precision, an apologetic pan sensual pungency utilized to establish mood, action, and motivation. No visual artist could possibly reflect constructions like these in their totality or their subtlety. As conceived, these scripts require the delicate facial expressiveness, the richness, clarity, and control of Vermeer (but not his spartan composition), the careful design and balanced draftsmanship of Mondrian (but not his chilly choice of abstraction over representation), the facility for detail of Bosch (but not his quirky, narrow emotional pitch), and the visceral wallop of Francis Bacon (sans his overt flamboyance). . . . Beyond what the comic accomplishes, the scripts, in giving us what Moore specifically wrote, offer an irreplaceable and invaluable testimony not just to what was said but what was meant. (58–59)

It would be legitimate to infer from such commentary that, given the size and scope of Moore's scripts, the visual artist's participation in the creation of the work is reduced to the minimum. However, Kreiner underlines that the bulk of Moore's *From Hell* scripts does not lessen Eddie Campbell's contribution to the final result. Campbell helped Moore structure the work and carried out geographical and historical research about Victorian London; most of all, he painstakingly selected and assessed the most useful indications in the script and transposed them onto the page, trying to meet the author's requests but nonetheless managing to preserve the distinctive qualities of his own style. Apart from the example of *From Hell*, Moore himself has always insisted on the collaborative nature of the creation of comics, a process based on a "meeting of minds and meeting of sensibilities" (Wiater and Bissette 165), which he considers one of the features that made him focus his attention on the comics medium instead of traditional prose. The author describes his approach to scripting as indissolubly connected to the characteristics of the artists he works with, who inspire and shape his writing from the outset (also see Khoury, *Extraordinary* 83–97 and 173–93). The aim of his scripts is less to impose his narrative vision by force than to give those who provide the illustrations a series of possible hints, which they are free not to follow if they do not deem them proper:

> I make suggestions as to the camera angles, the lighting, the background, the mood, sometimes the colour, the posture, and the body language. I try to put everything in there. But I make sure that the artists know that if they've got a better idea, they're free to use it. After all, they've got better visual imaginations than me. I provide them with a springboard, so if they're facing a blank sheet of paper . . . they've got somewhere to start. . . . I put a real burden on them. But now I've learned to gear my stories to an individual artist's strong points. I'd like to make one thing very clear. It annoys me when people talk about "Alan Moore's *V for Vendetta*" or "Alan Moore's *Marvelman*," and I'm not going to enjoy "Alan Moore's *Swamp Thing.*" I can't claim to be an individual artist in my own right. The end result, the strip you see on the page, is the meeting between me and the artist. That's where the creation is. . . . I don't consider my stories more important than the art. It's got to be equal. (Lawley and Whitaker 25)

Notwithstanding the nature of the scripts that, as noted above, might suggest a nearly full predominance of Moore's part in the construction of the work, evidence provided by his own words, and especially by those of his collaborators, lays emphasis on the process of cross-fertilization (see again Wiater and Bissette 165) between the imagination of the writer and that of the artist. At the end of such a process, it is not always possible to establish who the authorship of certain ideas belongs to; the creation of a comic book thus exists as an organic, almost alchemical act, which is in itself hybrid and not entirely definable.[4]

The most exciting expressive potentialities of the language of comics originate exactly from the crossbreed nature that has characterized the medium from its very conception; for this reason Moore gives prominence to the necessity to avoid tracing the aesthetics of comics back to literature or cinema all the time. These forms of expression share some features with comics and often offer fascinating terms of comparison, curious tips, or useful technical vocabulary. Nevertheless, the qualities that make comics unique, and that come in fact from their hybrid condition, are far worthier of notice: "What it comes down to in comics is that you have complete control both of the verbal track and of the im-age track, which you don't have in any other medium, including film. So a lot of effects are possible which simply cannot be achieved anywhere else. You control the words and the pictures—and more importantly—you control the interplay between those two elements. . . . There's a sort of 'under-language' at work here, that is neither the 'visuals' nor the 'verbals,' but a unique effect caused by a com-bination of the two" (Wiater and Bissette 162–63). This combination of words and pictures allows for an infinitely flexible relationship between them to be established, according to the way they are used; it enhances the "restless, polyse-miotic character" of the medium (Hatfield, *Alternative* XIV). For example, the author might take advantage of the possibility to manipulate the time of narra-tive by peculiarly orienting the reader's attention on the page, or he might play with the juxtaposition of seemingly unconnected words and pictures, whose association will only become clear in the following pages. Moreover, the very fact that the image is static—and not moving—makes it possible for the reader to go back to examine it as many times as s/he wants. The page can thus be loaded with nearly subliminal details that become appreciable only after read-ing the comic several times (see Moore, *Writing* 41). Moore conflates the hybrid language of comics with the novelistic patterns he draws inspiration from, and it is from the same models that he picks up the idea of constructing extended nar-ratives: his works tend to feature complex, overarching structures that survive the fragmentation into single episodes made necessary by serialization and that, as chapter 2 will show, are usually characterized by recurring circularity. The narratives resulting from this process are far from the formulas and oversimpli-fications comics were sometimes subjected to in the past (see 29).

But let us now examine the textual strategy Moore most often makes use of: the re-elaboration of genres, especially through the composition of a thick web of intertextual references that underlie his fictions.

THE REWRITING OF LITERARY SOURCES

The presence of intertextuality in Moore's work—be it in the form of quotation, allusion, parody, or, as happens most often, the revisiting of well-known works or patterns—is pervasive and results in an incessant, vigorous re-elaboration of textual practices. Intertextuality permeates Moore's oeuvre in all its facets and covers not only the domain of literature but cinema, music, popular culture, and, last but not least, comics. The considerations offered in this section and in the following one deal with the references to the literary and to the comics tradition, as they are the two prevailing intertextual strands in the writer's dense narrative universe. However, even limiting the field of analysis to these two categories, it is impossible for this book to offer an exhaustive inventory of the connections the author creates. Complete sets of annotations to references do exist (such as Madelyn Boudreaux's online notes to *V for Vendetta*, or Jess Nevins's two books about *The League of Extraordinary Gentlemen,* plus other annotations one can easily find by searching the Web), and they represent excellent companions to Moore's work. I will only offer a few significant examples in order to show how the considerable use of quotations or allusions, and above all the superimposition and combination of them, can constitute an effective strategy leading to both narrative resignification and formal experimentation.

The first instance I examine is that of *V for Vendetta*, which is further analyzed in chapter 3. Moore created it in collaboration with David Lloyd and published it between 1981 and 1989; it then came out as a book edition in 1990. Together with *Marvelman* (later renamed *Miracleman*, which will be briefly considered in the following section), *V* constitutes Moore's first attempt in the field of the graphic novel. It is a dystopian fiction set in a hypothetical 1997, a time when the U.K. is governed by a fascist regime whose institutions are strongly reminiscent of the anti-utopias created by George Orwell in *1984* (1949) and by Ray Bradbury in *Fahrenheit 451* (1953). The setting is made more alienating by the fact that, in contrast with the external appearance of the city (which is marred by the invasive presence of governmental mass control machinery), the indoor environments and atmospheres of this fictional future are rather old-fashioned, for they were made to recall the look of pulp magazines from the 1930s (see Moore, "Behind the Painted Smile" 269). Besides this, the protagonist, an anarchist terrorist simply called V who is busy contrasting the fascists through a series of attacks, wears a mask that resembles the distinctively English face of Guy Fawkes and starts his offensive against the established authorities exactly on November 5, the day when Fawkes tried to put the Gunpowder Plot into practice in 1605.

Moreover, as Carter Scholz effectively remarks, V speaks in blank verse (see especially 61), just like the personae from the Jacobean revenge plays the novel hints at through the leitmotiv of vengeance and through his disguise: "Still, all in love and war is fair, they say, this being both, and turn-about's fair play. Though I must bear a cuckold's horns, they're not a crown that I shall bear alone. You see, my rival, though inclined to roam, possessed at home a wife that he adores. He'll rue his promiscuity, the rogue who stole my only love, when he's informed how many years it is since I bedded his" (Moore and Lloyd 201). V's language is interspersed with literary references that appear directly in verbal form, or both verbally and visually. A demonstration of the first instance is the considerable presence of Shakespearean quotations, the use of which can give rise to different interpretations, as always happens in intertextual practice; extrapolating sentences from their earlier context in order to graft them into a new one makes them resonate with new, different meanings while retaining the halo of what they were originally meant to convey. The most remarkable example stands out in the initial pages of the novel, on the occasion of V's first appearance: young Evey, a destitute sixteen-year-old, decides to turn to prostitution for a living, but unfortunately approaches a plainclothes policeman as her first customer. The man attacks her and threatens to arrest her; he then changes his mind and summons his brutal colleagues, who seem about to gang-rape the poor girl. The situation reverses as V appears all of a sudden and rushes to her aid. Before dazing the policemen with tear gas, he recites a passage from *Macbeth*, Act I, scene 2. He repeats the words with which the wounded captain praises Macbeth's military valor in front of King Duncan: "The multiplying villanies of nature / Do swarm upon him—from the Western Isles / Of kerns and galloglasses is supplied, / And fortune in his damned quarry smiling, / Showed like a rebel's whore. But all's too weak, / For brave Macbeth—well he deserves that name!— / Disdaining fortune, with his brandished steel / Which smoked with bloody execution, / Like valour's minion / Carved out his passage till he faced the slave, / Which ne'er shook hands nor bade farewell to him" (Moore and Lloyd 11–12; for the original passage see Shakespeare 977 Act I, II, vv. 11–21). The most direct message of the words V pronounces while carrying out Evey's rescue is to make his heroic stature clear: heedless of danger like Macbeth, he attacks the villains and saves the girl.

But the quotation also suggests other things: in the repressive, dystopian world of *V for Vendetta*—which the author overtly defines as a representation of the possible consequences of Thatcherist ideology on England (an aspect dealt with in detail in chapter 3)—the great Shakespearean tradition has been erased, and the bard's voice can be heard only through the hero, who has preserved its memory. The result of this removal is that the literary tradition cannot be understood. The insensitive agents of the Finger (such is the name of the state police in *V*, where the totalitarian government is spoken of as a huge, all-controlling body) comment on V's words by saying: "FIRST POLICEMAN: Who's he? SECOND POLICEMAN: I dunno. Must be some kinda retard got out of a hospital" (Moore and Lloyd 12). It is impossible not to perceive a touch of irony—if not outright parody—in the choice of this quotation. The language of Shakespeare, here, is ultimately only good for a madman's mouth, and *Macbeth*, with its allusions to the motif of insanity, is the ideal source for shaping the protagonist of *V*, for lunacy is indeed brought into play. Despite V's undeniable charm, his idealism often appears to border on madness, as shown in another episode of Shakespearean memory: before committing another terrorist attack, he has a conversation with the statue of Justice by providing both the questions and the answers. When the bizarre dialogue ends, V hands the statue a heart-shaped box while declaring he has repudiated Justice to turn to a new lover called Anarchy. Afterwards, V observes the fire he has started and repeats the words that Henry VIII, in Shakespeare's 1613 play *All Is True*, tells Anne Boleyne after choosing her as his partner in dancing: "O beauty, 'til now I never knew thee" (41; for the original passage see Shakespeare 1201 Act I, IV, vv.76–77). Again, Shakespeare's words are separated from their original dramatic context and resonate with V's distorted, paranoid view, where beauty comes to reside in destruction.

In his reworking, Moore also seems to be suggesting a parody of the immoderate use that contemporary culture sometimes makes of Shakespeare by arbitrarily reshaping his language, and by reutilizing it almost as if it were a plain repository of catchphrases good for talking big in a variety show. V himself is aware of this, and therefore he explains to Evey:

> Ha ha ha ha! Melodrama, Evey! Isn't it strange how life turns into melodrama? That's very important, to you, isn't it? All that theatrical stuff. It's everything, Evey. The perfect entrance, the grand illusion. It's everything... and I'm going to bring the house down. They've forgotten the drama of it all, you see. They abandoned their scripts when the world withered in the glare of the nuclear footlights. I'm going to remind them. About melodrama. About the tuppenny rush and the penny dreadful. You see, Evey, all the world's a stage. And everything else... is vaudeville. (31)

Here, too, V quotes the English bard by repeating the famous motto: "All the world's a stage / And all the men and women merely players" from his 1600 play *As You Like It* (Shakespeare 638 Act II, VII, vv. 139–40). The whole world is a stage, then, or even better, the world is a huge vaudeville show: V pronounces

Fig. 1-1. V's library in *V for Vendetta*,
page 18 (excerpt). © DC Comics.

these words while he replaces his cloak and Guy Fawkes mask with a merry
cabaret artist's outfit, complete with striped jacket and bow tie. The emphasis in
V for Vendetta on the theatrical aspects of existence, together with Shakespearean
quotations and the topic of comedy and show, curiously anticipates the theme
that English writer Angela Carter (1940–1992) would develop in her last novel, *Wise Children* (1990). Her twin protagonists Dora and Nora Chance, two
vaudeville actresses and dancers, tell the stories of their adventurous lives,
which are spangled with quotations, manipulations, and above all distortions
of Shakespeare's words (see Webb 279–307). *V for Vendetta* and *Wise Children*
are very different in tone, but this common motif calls important attention to
Moore's connection with Carter's poetics, which must be kept in mind; besides
acknowledging her as one of his literary points of reference, Moore shares some
of her views in terms of both critical stance and thematic choices. The points of
contact between these two artists emerge on several occasions that will be dealt
with in the course of this book.

Apart from Shakespeare, *V* overflows with other quotations, also in visual
form; an example is the protagonist's hiding place, which is crammed with books,
playbill posters, and records—all of which have been strictly forbidden by the
regime. Its shelves are crowded with books by ever-present Shakespeare, Thomas
More's *Utopia*, Karl Marx's *Capital*, Thomas Pynchon's *V*; then the *Odyssey*, the

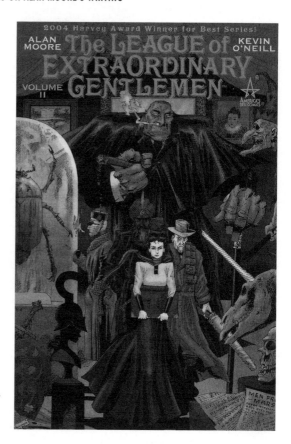

Fig. 1-2. *The League of Extraordinary Gentlemen*: the cover of volume II. © Alan Moore and Kevin O'Neill.

Divine Comedy, Gulliver's Travels, Don Quixote and Dickens's *Hard Times*. Much in the same way, the walls are covered in posters from movies such as *The Son of Frankenstein, Murders in the Rue Morgue* featuring Bela Lugosi, and *White Heat* featuring James Cagney, which can be seen as alluding to V's vicissitudes as they include monsters and outsiders, gangsters and murderers (see fig. 1-1).

Last but not least, V's figure hints at several comic-book characters, too. For example, he shares many of his attributes with superheroes: he wears a mask, moves at an almost unbelievable speed, and chooses as a sidekick a young helper he instructs as his possible successor. In the latter case Moore revises the tradition, because V's sidekick is Evey, a young woman and not a male adolescent (an idea that Frank Miller would also later utilize in creating a female Robin in his version of *Batman*), and because her process of education is not made explicit till the end: only after V's death does she understand her role. The mixture of literary, cultural, and comic book references that underlie V's character emerges from the list Moore himself provided when the novel was being serialized: "Orwell. Huxley. Thomas Disch. *Judge Dredd*. Harlan Ellison's '"Repent, Harlequin!" said the Ticktockman.' 'Catman' and 'Prowler in the City at the Edge of the World' by the same author. Vincent Price's *Dr. Phibes* and *Theatre of Blood*. David Bowie. The Shadow. Nightraven. Batman. *Fahrenheit 451*. The writings of the New Worlds school of science fiction. Max Ernst's painting 'Europe after the Rains.' Thomas Pynchon. The atmosphere of British Second World War films. *The Prisoner*. Robin Hood. Dick Turpin . . ." (Moore, "Behind the Painted Smile" 270).⁵ All of these elements, or inspiring macrotexts—to which critic Rob Rodi adds *Le Fantôme de L'Opera* (1911) by Gaston Leroux (see "A World Saver" 52)—form a thickly stratified basis of archetypes and genres that results in a dense narrative landscape. The allusions and quotations are open for the readers' detection—but the amount is overwhelming, and their nature is re-elaborated and reshuffled to such an extent that an estranging, almost whirling effect of polysemy is guaranteed.

This mechanism is even more powerful in the more recent *The League of Extraordinary Gentlemen* (1999–2003), made in collaboration with Kevin O'Neill (assisted by Bill Oakley and Ben Dimagmaliw). The story of the Gentlemen was serialized and later collected in two separate volumes, which resume and develop the adventures of the same characters but which constitute separate narrative entities. The same will happen for their follow-ups, of which there are at least two: *The Black Dossier*, released in 2008, and *The League vol. III*, which at the time of writing of this book is still due for publication. In the *Gentlemen* stories the intertextual process becomes even more overt and pervasive than in *V for Vendetta*. The difference between the two consists not only of a larger amount of quotations in *The League*, but most of all in their more markedly ludic quality. This feature is also mirrored by the lighthearted, sometimes parodistic tone of the narration and, in visual terms, by the deliberately caricatural nature of the characters' looks (see fig. 1-2).

It is no accident that Moore chose to work with Kevin O'Neill, who, together with Pat Mills, previously authored *Marshal Law* (1987), a series where an S&M-looking vigilante persecutes and kills superheroes. Intertextual practice here is so enveloping that Moore himself has defined the adventures of the Gentlemen as a "literary connect-the-dots puzzle" (Khoury, *Extraordinary* 182). The target of the author's textual manipulation, this time, is especially the Victorian literary imagination. The characters are a group of famous protagonists from the tradition of late-nineteenth-century romance: Mina Murray

Fig. 1-3. Mock-Victorian advertisements in *The League of Extraordinary Gentlemen*, volume II, page 158. © Alan Moore and Kevin O'Neill.

from Bram Stoker's *Dracula* (1897); Allan Quatermain, the hero from H. Rider Haggard's colonial novels, such as *She* (1887); Captain Nemo from Jules Verne's *Twenty Thousand Leagues Under the Sea* (1870); Hawley Griffin, from H. G. Wells's *The Invisible Man* (1897); and last but not least, R. L. Stevenson's Dr. Henry Jekyll (from *The Strange Case of Dr. Jekyll and Mr. Hyde*, 1886), who of course turns into Mr. Hyde at the right moment. The colorful group of personages is summoned by Queen Victoria in order to fight the perils that threaten the nation and the empire: the evil Fu Manchu in volume I and the Martian tripods first created by Wells in volume II (again, I recommend Nevins, *Heroes and Blazing,* for a full account of literary references). The two novels unleash a barrage of direct and indirect quotations, both verbal and visual, touching both "highbrow" literature and popular genres and crossing over the borders of the English tradition. In these works Moore mixes and parodies adventure novels, scientific romances, steampunk fiction, erotic narrative, and much else, and he does not fail to pay tribute to cinema by hinting at James Bond movies.

Moreover, the two collected editions of the *League* are equipped with appendixes. The first volume offers the fake reprint of a Victorian magazine called *The Boys' First-Rate Library of Tales*, including the short prose story "Allan and the Sundered Veil" (see Moore and O'Neill, *League I* 161–84), which features Allan Quatermain as its protagonist and is enriched by some extra pages with games and puzzles for young boys. The second volume is accompanied by parodies of Victorian advertisements (see fig. 1-3) and by a mock-erotic postcard; moreover, it includes the substantial "New Traveler's Almanac" (see Moore and O'Neill, *League II* 159–206), which collects Mina Murray's travel annotations and the reports written by the Gentlemen's predecessors in the Crown's intelligence service ("Prospero's Men," and another group captained by Lemuel Gulliver in the eighteenth century).

It is interesting to consider the response that the success of the two *Gentlemen* graphic novels triggered in the world of comics fandom. Thanks to the above-mentioned Jess Nevins, a webpage listing the intertextual references of the novels was created while they were being serialized. The page was open to anyone who wanted to add extra information to what Nevins had already published. This operation resulted in the publication of two sizeable companions to the novels, *Heroes and Monsters* (2003) and *A Blazing World* (2004). *The League of Extraordinary Gentlemen* is a significant piece of work that confirms Moore's use of literature as an inexhaustible repository of stories. As the author pronounces in an interview, "We've certainly got stories that could take the *League* up to the 30th century and beyond, because the thing about literature and the world of literature is that it extends in the future as well as the past" (Khoury, *Extraordinary* 182).

The Victorian imagination plays a leading role in another work by Moore, even though its narrative modalities are quite different from those of the *League*. *From Hell: A Melodrama in Sixteen Parts*, created with Eddie Campbell, is a massive reassessment of what Moore himself unhesitatingly defines as a proper mythology (see Moore, *From Hell: Compleat Scripts* 9–16 and 337–40): the fabric of narratives that has developed around the Jack the Ripper crimes since they took place in late-nineteenth-century London. Before creating *From Hell*, Moore and Campbell carried out extensive research, which is corroborated by the substantial notes and bibliography section they placed at the end of the novel, and decided that they wanted their work to be an unconventional Ripper

narrative. The result is a subversion of traditional whodunnit fiction: who the
culprit is is clear from the beginning. Freemason and royal doctor Sir William
Gull is revealed as the Ripper—and as the instrument of the Crown's schemes—
in chapter 2, and is shown carrying out his first killing in chapter 5. The inves-
tigative plot and the description of the police searching for the killer are but
a pretext for the author to expose the darkest aspects of Victorian culture and
society: "*From Hell* is the post-mortem of a historical occurrence, using fiction
as a scalpel. . . . Though it concerns itself with a notable and historic mystery,
it does not attempt to be a 'Whodunnit?' so much as a 'Wha'happen?' . . . In
one sense we are not at all concerned with whether he 'dunnit' or not. What
we are more interested in is the attempt to examine in detail the anatomy of a
phenomenal human event" (*From Hell: Compleat Scripts* 337–38).

Deconstruction of the patterns of detective fiction allows Moore and
Campbell to invest the narration with a series of symbolic interpretations
and critical considerations, the most relevant of which is the depiction of the
Victorian Age as the cradle of fantasies and concerns that would surface in the
twentieth century. The interplay of allusions and intertextual references is highly
refined; the tight net of historical, geographical, and popular records—the so-
called "Ripperology"—to which the authors allude is re-energized by the direct
quotations that open each chapter, which suggest symbolic readings of the events
or offer new interpretations of information taken from the historical records
of the time. Thus, chapter 14—which involves a mystical vision that precedes
Gull's death in which the doctor meets the Masonic deities he worships—opens
with a long quotation from the short story *Le Horla* (1888) by French writer
Guy de Maupassant. Its initial lines can be read as an anticipation of the events
that take place in the chapter; indeed, they help the reader liken Gull to some
monstrous, supernatural creature: "Dead? Perhaps. Or perhaps that body of his,
through which the light of day could pass, was impervious to the means of destruction which kill our bodies? Suppose he was not dead? . . . Perhaps only time
alone has power over that Invisible and Fearful Being" (Moore and Campbell,
From Hell ch. 14, 0). A longer set of quotations opens chapter 6, which follows
the vicissitudes of Scotland Yard inspector Abberline as he grapples with the in-
vestigations of the Whitechapel murders. The quotations can be traced to several
sources: many existing essays about the Ripper, Abberline's own police records,
and a few newspapers of the time (see ch. 6, 0).

Visual quotations are just as thickly embedded into the text: an example can
be the reproduction of the painting *Blackmail (or Mrs Barrett)* by Walter Sickert

Fig. 1-4. "The Reward of Cruelty." *From Hell*, chapter 9, page 16 (excerpt). © Alan Moore and Eddie Campbell. All Rights Reserved. Image reprinted here with permission.

that appears at the beginning of chapter 2 (0), just before the pages where the character of Sickert is shown as he paints Mary Kelly's portrait. Another striking case of visual quotation, in chapter 9 (16), is the reproduction of an engraving by William Hogarth titled *The Reward of Cruelty,* depicting a gruesome autopsy. Hogarth's original intention was apparently that of satirizing the medical class, although, as Moore remarks in a note (see Appendix I, 31), many expert "Ripperati" claim that it depicts a Masonic ritual, thus explaining why the incisions reproduced in the picture are so similar to the ones performed by Jack the Ripper on his victims' bodies. The presence of this visual quotation in the chapter definitely grabs the reader's attention: it is first placed behind the back of Netley, Gull's coachman and accomplice, who is explaining to the doctor that he has not yet managed to locate the last victim. When the conversation is over, the page closes with a single, wordless panel entirely filled by a larger reproduction of the etching (see fig. 1-4), thus anticipating the final, savage autopsy Gull/Jack is about to perform on Mary Kelly's corpse.

The last example I briefly mention before moving to the reassessment of the superhero tradition is *Lost Girls*, which Moore began in 1989 in collaboration with his partner Melinda Gebbie and which underwent an endless row of publishing vicissitudes (see Khoury, *Extraordinary* 154–58) before finally being published as a three-volume edition in summer 2006. In this graphic novel, Moore and Gebbie turn to the genre of pornography to tell the story of three women who meet in an Austrian hotel in 1914. The three protagonists make friends and tell each other how they discovered and then explored sex in their youth. Their stories turn out to be sexualized reinterpretations of well-known masterpieces of children's literature: sophisticated Lady Alice Fairchild[6] is the now grown-up protagonist of Lewis Carroll's *Alice's Adventures in Wonderland* (1865) and *Through the Looking Glass* (1871); strait-laced, bourgeois Mrs. Potter is Wendy from J. M. Barrie's *Peter Pan* (1904); while lively country girl Dorothy comes straight from L. Frank Baum's *The Wonderful Wizard of Oz* (1900). Apart from these fundamental references, the novel is extremely thick with allusions and quotations that, as always, transcend the purely literary and cross over into other fields. This mechanism is here so exaggerated that the book becomes a catalog of Moore's intertextual and structural strategies, thus ultimately crushing its own narrative substance. However, given the peculiar nature of *Lost Girls* and its departure from the bulk of Moore's other works, I leave further considerations for the fourth chapter of this book, where this aspect will be considered in detail along with other features of the novel.

REVISITING THE SUPERHERO TRADITION

As noted above, Moore's intertextual practice involves not only the field of literature but also the tradition of comics, which is revisited and rewritten in several ways. In Moore's vast bibliography, the genre he has most frequently reworked is the superhero narrative, which for cultural and historical reasons has occupied a privileged position in comics all over the world from a very early moment in the development of the medium (for a few notes with respect to this, see Klock and Benton, *Superhero Comics*). This section examines the textual practices Moore used to manipulate the stylistic features of superhero narrative from the early eighties onwards. The process reached its apex with *Watchmen* (1986–87) and continued with the somewhat mannerist development of more recent projects such as *Supreme* or the *America's Best Comics* line (with the exceptions of *Promethea* and *The League of Extraordinary Gentlemen*), which will be considered further on in this section. Moore's superhero comics are usually included in the category of "revisionary superhero narrative," a rich current that came into being thanks to Frank Miller and to Moore himself, and that was later joined by several other authors. It is important to notice, as Geoff Klock readily remarks, that the term *revisionary* is not connected to the common meaning of revisionism as it is used, for instance, in the context of historical studies. The word here must be interpreted in its affinity with Harold Bloom's idea of a "strong poetic revision through misprision. . . . What should be emphasized in the use of the word *revisionary* is not 'revise' but 'visionary'" (qtd. in Klock 16; Klock's italics).[7] Klock observes that superhero comics are structured on a few basic motifs that have been repeated over and over for more than sixty years. In this framework, reinterpretation in the form of intertextual play becomes indispensable for the survival of the genre (see 13), and thus represents an unavoidable necessity for the contemporary authors who, like Moore, feel the need to find a place for their own voice and identity in the context of tradition.

The shift that lies at the core of Moore and Miller's revisions—characterization of the superhero as a neurotic, fragile individual, endowed not only with great strength but also with human weakness—is not an original creation of these two authors. The protagonists of *The Fantastic Four* (created by Stan Lee and Jack Kirby in 1961) and of *The Amazing Spider-Man* (who stemmed again from Stan Lee's prolific imagination, this time together with Steve Ditko, in 1962; for considerations of both series, see Daniels, *MARVEL*) had been presented from the start as far from the monolithic certainties and optimism that distinguished golden-age superheroes like Superman; they were compelled to face anxieties and moments of crisis, and were in step with the moods and concerns of the second half of the twentieth century. But the narrative potential of the cracks surfacing on the mask of the superhero is brought to its extreme consequences in Moore's production. He creates fresh characters and revisits existing ones, retaining some of the features of the original models but at the same time further developing their personalities, bringing out their dark side and sometimes pushing them to the verge of psychosis. The latter aspect allows for critical reflection on the figure of the superhero, on the ideologies conveyed through the filter of fiction, and most of all on the legitimization of the ethics of vigilantism that surfaced between the 1970s and 1980s, especially in big metropolitan contexts in the United States. Such ethics massively spread both in the comics and in the movie production of those years. In comics its success was bound to characters like *The Punisher* and *Judge Dredd*. Inspired by the character of the *Executioner* from Don Pendleton's pulp novels, the Punisher appeared in a few *Spiderman* issues beginning in 1974, and became the protagonist of his own series in 1986. As his name makes clear, this character is a crude, reactionary vigilante (see Di Nocera 152–55 and Goulart, *Comic Book* 285). *Judge Dredd*, the merciless avenger of Mega City, was created by John Wagner and Carlos Sanchez Esquerra. He made his first appearance on the pages of British magazine *2000 A.D.* in 1977; he later became the protagonist of a movie where his part was played by Sylvester Stallone (1995). In the field of cinema, vigilantism was upheld by the extreme popularity of characters like Paul Kersey, whose role was played by Charles Bronson in *Death Wish* (1974); policeman 'Popeye' Doyle from *The French Connection* I and II (1971 and 1976); and Inspector "Dirty Harry" Callahan, played by Clint Eastwood in a series of five films that began with *Dirty Harry* (1971) and concluded with *The Dead Pool* (1988). All of these elements added up to turning the figure of the superhero into a repository for reactionary, diehard power fantasies of judgment and vengeance.

Moore reassesses this pattern and projects its many possible faces onto several characters. Some of his superheroes (like the Comedian from *Watchmen*, or Batman in *The Killing Joke*) do show the traits of the vigilante, but the weakness that lies under their shield is always brought to light. Most of them, while having their distinctive features, share the motif of existential unease and a considerable drive toward introspection. Between 1982 and 1985, on the advice of Derek Skinn (who was then in charge of *Warrior* magazine), Moore resumed the figure of Captain Marvel from the fifties and turned him into *Marvelman*, later renamed *Miracleman* due to copyright trouble (see Khoury, *Kimota!* and Smith). He told his version of the Miracleman story for three books before the character was handed over to Neil Gaiman. Miracleman's vicissitudes anticipated the complex development of the superhero characters that would be later created for *Swamp Thing* and *Watchmen*: the hero is now devoid of the innocence and naivety that distinguished him in his early days, but too human to embrace para-fascist ethics and become a Punisher. In Moore's creation, journalist Mike Moran suddenly—and only accidentally—remembers he is a superhero. He then realizes that he has not only been endowed with extraordinary powers, but that his very identity has been altered, too: malicious scientist Gargunza,[8]

Fig. 1-5. Swamp Thing. From
Saga of the Swamp Thing,
page 60. © DC Comics.

secretly hired by the British government to kidnap orphaned Moran in his early childhood, had him go through a series of experiments in the eloquently named "project Zarathustra." A superhuman *Doppelgänger* was thus created, ready to materialize in Moran's body whenever he, thanks to some sort of posthypnotic condition, pronounces the word "Kimota!" (see Moore and Davis, *Miracleman I*). Through this narrative turn, Moore questions the character's positive, stabilizing function. Moran is depicted in the context of his everyday life and of an uncertain, difficult relationship with his wife—that is, in his human aspect; nevertheless, awareness of his powers brings him to meditate on his nature and to acquire mixed feelings of compassion and contempt toward the human race. In short, his character represents Moore's first attempt to deconstruct the superhero and to turn him into a melancholy, disillusioned figure who is far removed from the peace of mind of earlier times. In the case of *Miracleman*, this difference is made clear on the graphic level too, because the protagonist's body is slender and thin, his muscles and frame surely less marked than those of canonical superheroes (see Lawley and Whitaker 13).

The results of Moore's reworking of the superhero pattern can be appreciated even better in *Swamp Thing*, which was originally created by Len Wein and Berni Wrightson for *House of Secrets* magazine in 1971. In the first version of the comic, the protagonist is biologist Alec Holland, who is busy working on a scientific project aimed at solving the problem of famine in the world. Holland dies in an explosion, caused by evil conspirators who place a bomb in his laboratory in the swamps of Louisiana, and is turned via chemical reaction into Swamp Thing, a horrid creature—even though pathetic in its monstrosity—who comes back from death in order to take revenge on its killers. The character's popularity declined shortly after the first issues were published; the starting idea was probably not too original and too similar to the already trite model of Frankenstein's monster (see Daniels, *DC Comics* 160–61). When Moore agreed to work on the character in the early eighties—primarily with the already mentioned Steve Bissette and John Totleben—he gave rise to a very successful series, which was published between 1983 and 1987. The new graphic layout he worked out with the two artists was meant to reflect the vibrant proliferation of the plants and animals of the swamp through intricate lines, lush colors, accurate backgrounds, and peculiar lettering (see fig. 1-5).

Moore decided to preserve the character's physical look, but he modified a crucial aspect. In his first issue, "The Anatomy Lesson" (see Moore, Bissette, and Totleben, *Saga of the Swamp Thing* 13–35), the seemingly inanimate body of Swamp Thing is retrieved for an autopsy. We thus discover that Alec Holland was not transformed into a monster; the scientist is dead and the swamp that ate up his corpse has somehow formed an entirely new creature, a sort of vegetable puppet that believes it is a man even though it has never been one: "Alec Holland is already dead. His body goes into the swamp along with the formula that it is saturated with. And, once there . . . it decomposes. A patch of swampland like that would be teeming with micro-organisms. It wouldn't take long. . . . Those plants eat him. . . . They eat him . . . and they become infected by a powerful consciousness that does not realize it is no longer alive! . . . We thought that the swamp thing was Alec Holland, somehow transformed into a plant. It wasn't. It was a plant that thought it was Alec Holland!" (23–24). Thanks to this device, Moore can leave behind the obsolete pattern of the bloodthirsty monster so typical of horror comics and have the character shift onto another level. He

Fig. 1-6. Swamp Thing materializes from a rose. From "Natural Consequences," in *Swamp Thing: Earth to Earth*, page 39. © DC Comics.

eliminates the monster's excessively pathetic traits and tries instead to examine its vegetable nature more in detail, as he explains in an early interview: "What I wanted to do was try to come at it from a more hard science fiction angle, investigate the possibilities of his being a plant. . . . In the future, what we can do is to try and examine him. . . . there's a lot of things about a plant that supply you with story ideas, things we can slowly and gradually explore. We want to explore his psychology, his emotions, his physiology" (Thompson 100, also see the 1984 *Comics Journal* special issue dedicated to *Swamp Thing*).

After this transformation, the dreadful swamp-bred hybrid becomes a peculiar mystical creature that, thanks to its vegetable identity, can perceive the vital pulse of the earth and of the natural world. Swamp Thing is thus endowed with a proper "pantheistic consciousness" (Di Nocera 146, my translation) that urges it to fight against the threats of growing industrialization and uncontrolled urban expansion. As Swamp Thing develops the awareness of its ability to enter a state of communion with the environment, it becomes a sort of green superhero, the incarnation of the primeval force of the elements, ready

Fig. 1-7. Some of the characters from *Pogo*. From *We Have Met the Enemy, And He Is Us*, page 119 (excerpt). © Walt Kelly.

to rebel against man's violent invasion of natural spaces. For example, in an episode called "Natural Consequences," the creature manifests itself in Gotham City—which is of course Batman's metropolis, here used as an emblem of the decay of American cities—in order to reunite with the beloved Abigail Cable, who is considered a madwoman and has been taken to court because of her relationship with the monster. Swamp Thing, who can go anywhere on Earth by moving through the fibers of the vegetable world, breaks out in the asphalt jungle of Gotham and materializes from a rose (see fig. 1-6). Then it starts to accuse the inhabitants of the city in a language that reflects its peculiar qualities, for its balloons are always filled with dots; Moore thus underlines that his protagonist leads a vegetable existence, tuned on the slow rhythms of nature and not on the neurotic pace of human beings: "Hear this... men of this city. I have tolerated... your species... for long enough. Your cruelty... and your greed... and your insufferable arrogance... you blight the soil... and poison the rivers. You raze the vegetation... till you cannot... even feed... your own kind... and then you boast... of man's triumph... over nature. Fools, if nature were to shrug... or raise an eyebrow... then you should all be gone" (Moore, Bissette, and Totleben, *Swamp Thing: Earth* 42).

The reworking of narrative motifs Moore put into practice in *Swamp Thing* is not limited to the reassessment of the character. The conventions of superhero and horror comics are manipulated, too, and once again this is done through intertextual practice. The quotation of Gotham City mentioned above is an example; an even more effective one is that of the episode called "Pog" (1985), where the swamp briefly hosts an invasion by a group of tiny aliens. The figures

Fig. 1-8. The aliens in "Pog." From *Swamp Thing: Love and Death*, page 145 (excerpt). © DC Comics.

of the invaders are clearly modeled on the protagonists of Walt Kelly's strip *Pogo*, first published in 1946, where the small opossum Pogo lives in the Okefenokee Swamp with his friends Albert the Alligator, Howland Owl, and the turtle Churchy La Femme. Pogo and his comrades speak their own peculiar language and constitute a proper social and political microcosm that the strip explores with irony (for further information I recommend Norman Hale's 1991 book *All-Natural Pogo*). In "Pog," Kelly's characters become extraterrestrial creatures that have been evicted from their own swamp, which they call "the Lady" (Moore, Totleben, and Bissette, *Swamp Thing: Love* 144). Their planet has been usurped by an evil breed of violent, polluting creatures who do not respect the environment and have thus compelled them to roam across outer space in search of a new home (see figs. 1-7 and 1-8).

The meeting with Swamp Thing is peaceful, but the little alien alligator is killed by his ferocious Louisiana cousins; besides, after watching a few humans buying hot dogs at a booth by the bayou, the visitors feel they have to leave: "Oh, no. Not here as well. . . . They can't own this lady, too! We were going to be happy here," exclaims Pogo's little double from outer space (156). With this episode of *Swamp Thing*, Moore pays tribute to an older comic strip that belongs to a very different genre but that shares the setting of the swamp and above all its critical and debunking disposition, which highlights—among many other topics—the issue of man's relationship to the ecosystems of the earth, for Kelly's environmentalist stance was quite evident. Indeed, in his introduction to a 1972 collection of *Pogo* strips, Kelly wrote: "The big polluter did not start out with smokestacks. He didn't start pumping gunk into the waters of our world when he was six years old. He started small. Throwing papers underfoot in the streets, heaving old bottles into vacant lots, leaving the remnants of a picnic in the fields and woodlands. Just like the rest of us. . . . Man has turned out to be his worst enemy" (10).

The hybridization of *Swamp Thing* with the world of *Pogo* also offers the opportunity to experiment with new linguistic formulas; Moore replaces the original dialects of Kelly's characters with a slang of his own creation. Here is how extraterrestrial Pogo speaks to Swamp Thing: "I knew you wouldn't be antagravated. You're made out of the same ingreenients as the Lady. You must be her guardiner, or such. I configure we must have startlized you as much as reviceversional. I whish I could explacate, but I don't squeak your linguish, so... what are you droodling?" (151). The aliens' tongue affectionately plays with Swamp Thing's vegetable nature, which is highlighted by terms like "ingreenients," which stems from mixing "ingredients" and "green," and "guardiner," which includes both "guardian" and "gardener." In *Swamp Thing*, the ironic distortion of language matches the deformation of the graphic sign, which also becomes almost parodistic because of the excess and redundancy that constitute its most prominent features. Through the emphasis on the deformation and metamorphic quality of the protagonist and of the narration in general, Moore turns *Swamp Thing* into a metaphor of comics themselves, for they appear as an indefinite, sometimes shapeless creation, which is nevertheless equipped with an extraordinary ability to absorb the stimuli of the surrounding environment, finding sustenance in its own continuous remixing and in the reassembling of disparate elements.

However, the work that left Moore's deepest mark on the tradition of superhero comics probably remains *Watchmen* (1986–87). Even though decades have passed since this graphic novel was first published, and even though Moore's journey through the reconfiguration of superhero characters continued later, *Watchmen* remains a most significant work for contemporary comics criticism. Its relevance has also been confirmed by Geoff Klock, who has placed it (together with Miller's *Batman: The Dark Knight Returns*) at the end of the hypothetical second phase of the development of superhero comics, the so-called Silver Age that started in the 1960s. According to Klock, the Silver Age is now over, thanks to the evolution of contemporary comics productions; yet, it must be acknowledged that these two graphic novels undeniably influenced all of the works that were published after them. With a convincing comparison, Klock quotes a sentence by Alfred North Whitehead according to which the whole of the European philosophical tradition is made of footnotes to Plato's thought, and claims that in the same way, the superhero comic narratives of the last two decades are a row of annotations to Moore and Miller's work (see Klock 3). *Watchmen* is an extremely intricate and layered text, which here will be taken into consideration only as regards the aspects we need for our survey of Moore's narrative techniques and intertextual strategies.

The title of the novel itself stems from an intertextual reference and marks the central critical perspective of the work. At the end of the twelfth and last chapter, an epigraph from Juvenal's *Satires* appears: "Qui custodiet ipsos custodes? Who watches the watchmen?" (Moore and Gibbons ch. XII, 34). *Watchmen*, then, was born out of the will to revise the very presuppositions of superhero fiction and to use them to organize a renovated narrative that would offer fresh considerations on the contemporary context; in Moore's words, "We produced a moral and political fable that used the icons of superhero adventure fiction to make its point" (Sharrett 16–17). In the book's scary alternative America, Richard Nixon is in his third term of office, the States have won the Vietnam war, and most of all they have become the greatest power in the world thanks to Doctor Manhattan, a scientist turned immortal after a laboratory accident, who can freely manipulate the atomic composition of bodies. The masked superheroes that form the team of the Watchmen are far from being positive figures. On the contrary, they immediately appear ethically ambiguous or, in some cases, corrupt.

It is important to note that in *Swamp Thing* and the later *Batman: The Killing Joke* (1988) Moore elaborated on preexistent characters, while here he and Gibbons created fresh characters, even if they were rather openly inspired by a superhero team from Charlton Comics.[9] This offered considerable advantage for the author, as he was not forced to deal with a known prior continuity that would compel him to preserve the peculiar features of the preexisting work. His freedom in characterization choices was thus safeguarded, and the lack of limitations allowed Moore to handle the characters as daringly as he pleased—in this case, to turn them into a group of semi-archetypal figures whose features represent in various ways the several facets of the superhero pattern he wanted to deconstruct. Every protagonist of *Watchmen* is thus an independent, fully formed figure that nevertheless rests on a net of intertextual references. For example, as noted by Klock, the filthy Comedian looks exactly like the naive Captain America would had he witnessed the horrors of Vietnam (see 66). Rorschach, the anarchic, brutal, mad outsider—who, in his madness, respects a scary but consistent moral code—is a sort of Punisher, a supervigilante whose

Fig. 1-9. Sally Jupiter and her Tijuana Bible. From *Watchmen*, chapter II, page 8 (excerpt). © DC Comics.

ethics are rigid and saturated with violence like those of Miller's Dark Knight; but his words also recall the desperate lyrical force of Georg Büchner's *Woyzeck*, the philosophical speculations that serial killer Carl Panzram wrote in his diaries in the 1930s, and the notes that David Berkowitz—also known as Son of Sam, the killer of several New Yorkers in 1976 and 1977—gave the police as he was arrested (Moore seemingly turned some of those very notes into pages of Rorschach's diary; see Sharrett 9). The figure of Batman, too, is brought to mind: Dan Dreiberg, also known as Nite Owl, owns a subterranean shelter filled with technological devices, even though in his everyday life he behaves more like the mediocre white collar Clark Kent (Superman), for he is obsessed by a tough inferiority complex. A counterpart to the rich businessman Bruce Wayne/Batman is actually embodied by Adrian Veidt/Ozymandias, who aspires to become a modern Alexander the Great and who resembles Superman because of his Antarctic refuge—his personal version of the Fortress of Solitude, where his pet companion is the genetically modified lynx Bubastis instead of Krypto the dog. This staggering mechanism of incessant intertextual referencing is the tool Moore uses to consciously problematize the narrative and ethical principles that have shaped superhero narrative over the years. Besides, it must be remarked that the intertextual web of *Watchmen* does not only include allusions and quotations from the traditions of superhero comics, literature, and music, that echo in the chapter titles or in the sentences that conclude them.[10] Moore embraces the wider world of comics history. For example, the aged superheroine Sally Jupiter keeps a few issues of a series of erotic comics that saw her as the protagonist when she was young and popular (see fig. 1-9), thus reminding the reader of the so-called 'Tijuana Bibles' that offered erotic parodies of historical or fictional characters (from Hitler to the Marx Brothers, from Betty Boop to Little Orphan Annie, or Mickey and Minnie Mouse), which circulated mainly in the United States between the 1930s and the 1950s (see Skinn 26–27).

However, the most substantial allusion to the history of comics emerges from the *mise en abyme* Moore operates by grafting a "tale-within-the-tale" into the novel. The narrative fabric of *Watchmen* is interspersed with pieces from a horror comic book (entirely invented by the author) called *Tales of the Black Freighter*, which appears in chapter III in the shape of a magazine read by a kid, and which accompanies the main narrative as far as chapter XI. *Tales* tells the story of a castaway who has survived a frightening attack from a pirate ship that will eventually turn out to be an infernal vessel loaded with damned souls. He tries to go back to the harbor of his hometown, fearing it is going to be the target of the next ruthless assault. He travels alone on a raft he builds using the swollen and decaying bodies of his fellow navigators; then, after the long, desperate trip has practically made him crazy, he reaches the city, believing it has already fallen under the siege of the enemies. He wants to kill the pirates who have presumably massacred his family and taken abode in his house but, blinded by madness, he does not realize that the pirates are not even there. He ends up killing his wife and children as they lie fast asleep in their beds. Suddenly aware of his crime, he goes back to the shore and sees the pirate ship, which is now coming close to the coast, waiting for him to join its damned crew:

> Where was my error? The freighter was heading for Davidstown. It should have already arrived. My deduction was flawless, step by step... Pausing, . . . I raised my head... and saw her. She seemed to be waiting, not hovering to strike... Gradually, I understood what innocent intent had brought me to, and, understanding, waded out beyond my depth. The unspeakable truth loomed unavoidably before me as I swam towards the anchored freighter, waiting to take extra hands aboard. There'd been no plan to capture Davidstown. What could a mortal township offer

Fig. 1-10. "Tales of the Black Freighter." From *Watchmen*, chapter III, page 2. © DC Comics.

those who'd reaped the wealth of the Sargasso? . . . They'd come to Davidstown to wait until they could collect the only prize they'd ever valued, the only soul they'd ever truly wanted. (Moore and Gibbons ch. XI, 13)

This story-within-the-story, which echoes literary reminiscences of Coleridge's *Rime of the Ancient Mariner* (1834), Poe's *Manuscript Found in a Bottle* (1833) and *A Descent into the Maelstrom* (1841), and Brecht's *Dreigroschenoper* (1928), counterpoints and comments on the plot of *Watchmen,* for the main storyline of the graphic novel is ultimately based on Adrian Veidt's insanity. Veidt is sure the Earth is on the verge of a nuclear conflict and thinks he can ward it off by fashioning and actually carrying out a fake alien invasion, which is supposed to unite the world's main powers against a common enemy. The result is a slaughter of devastating proportions that takes place in the last chapter of the book. The parallel commentary provided by *Black Freighter* is made particularly effective by the way Moore and Gibbons take advantage of the juxtaposition of words and pictures. The panels from the *mise en abyme* are sometimes inserted into the main story to alternate with it (see fig. 1-10); at other times only the captions from the pirate tale—which the reader easily recognizes, because they seem written on ancient parchment, in tune with the genre—are placed alongside pictures that are actually part of the main story, and that describe the events occurring while the kid is reading his comic book. This happens, for instance, in chapter VIII, where a panel shows the streets of New York, the outward tranquility of which actually conceals the degradation and the violence of metropolitan gangs. The caption of the panel comes from *Tales of the Black Freighter* and reports the protagonist's thoughts about the quiet streets of Davidstown as they are filled by the horrid invaders he is so afraid of (see fig. 1-11).

The prose article that concludes the fifth chapter of *Watchmen* also requires our attention in this discussion: a fictional text about the success of the *Tales of the Black Freighter* comic book. Moore uses the names of real authors and publishers in it, such as Gil Kane and Julius Schwartz, but the article comes from an imaginary volume, which the author, of course, mentions as if it were a real reference book: "*The Treasure Island Treasury of Comics,* New York, Flint Editions, 1984" (ch. V, 29). Besides offering elucidations about the narrative structure of the story-within-the-story and about the literary quotations it features, the text calls to memory the great popularity of the horror comics—and in particular the ones dealing with pirates—published by William Gaines's E.C., whose logo is also reproduced within the article. It is easy to understand that Moore is

Fig. 1-11. Word-and-image interaction in
Watchmen, chapter VIII, page 3 (excerpt).
© DC Comics.

playing again with comic book history. In the fictional universe of *Watchmen*, the theories by psychiatrist Fredric Wertham that ultimately led to the collapse of E.C. (for details see Nyberg, Barker's *A Haunt of Fears*, and Lent) have been totally uninfluential: "Unsurprisingly, as one of the few companies to anticipate the coming massive boom in pirate-related material, E.C. Comics flourished and their hold upon the field remained unchallenged" (Moore and Gibbons ch. V, 29). The irreverent, subversive comics that, in reality, were unjustly eradicated as a result of the wide diffusion of Wertham's theories, still circulate in the world of *Watchmen*. As for superhero comics, we can guess that they must have almost disappeared from that world, for they have been replaced by the gadgets and publications created after the living heroes—which, incidentally, are distributed by one of Adrian Veidt's companies. Another prose insert shows some of the documentation connected to Veidt's business activities, including a series of dolls that reproduce Rorschach, Nite Owl, and Veidt himself, and an ad for the "Veidt Method for physical fitness and self-improvement" (ch. X, 29–32).

The example of *Tales of the Black Freighter* thus effectively illustrates Moore's narrative strategy, which comprises many of the categories that French literary scholar Gérard Genette defines as the components of *transtextuality*, "the textual transcendence of the text" (Genette, *Paratexts* 20). If we use Genette's terminology, the insertion of the pirate tale in *Watchmen* embraces several textual practices, in particular: 1) "pure" intertextuality, which is given by the presence of quotations and by the allusions to E.C. Comics; 2) archtextuality, by the use of the horror genre and its patterns; 3) paratextuality, by the juxtaposition of images and captions that seemingly belong to different fields; and last but not least, 4) metatextuality, which is given by the fact that the text provides a commentary on itself. It is worth remarking on that while these components do not usually appear together in a single work of literature, all four are simultaneously present in *Watchmen*. Because Moore and Gibbons make the most of the underlanguage of comics (as seen from the examples mentioned above), it is through the synergy of visual and verbal elements that their work achieves such an impressive degree of transtextuality.

From the late nineties on, Moore's intertextual practice in superhero comics became more intense and resulted in such works as *Supreme* (created in collaboration with Rick Veitch and other artists, and later collected in two volumes: *Supreme: The Story of the Year* in 2002, and *Supreme: The Return* in 2003), and the project *America's Best Comics*. A refashioning of a character created by Rob Liefeld, in Moore's version Supreme knows he is a superhero, and is aware that as such he has been represented in several ways throughout the years. The books are thus packed with fake *Supreme* stories from the fifties and sixties, which eventually represent a playful metanarrative reflection on the endless resurrections of the figure of the superhero (see Klock 110–11).

America's Best Comics was published between 1999 and 2005 in installments featuring episodes from several serializations. Its characteristics are suggestive of the moment Moore was going through at that time: he had completed *From Hell*, was trying to complete *Lost Girls*, and had published his first prose novel. *America's Best* was a lot of work, and it was also Moore's main source of income in a time of transition; he was moving fast into his new interest in magic, and thus into a new phase in his creative life. The resulting level of production is uneven. Many of the *ABC* series look like a sort of lighthearted interlude where the author playfully re-elaborates conventions and masterly displays his skills: *Tom Strong*, which focuses on a *Doc Savage*–like protagonist; *Top 10*, which is set in a police precinct and is a sort of comic book version of the *NYPD* TV series; and *Tomorrow Stories*, a parodistic collection of subseries called *Cobweb*, *Greyshirt*, *Jack B. Quick*, *First American*, and *Splash Brannigan*. The mannerist quality of many of these episodes gives the impression that Moore considered them a sort of formal exercise to be dutifully performed while he concentrated his efforts on fewer important elements, which he developed in works such as *The League of Extraordinary Gentlemen* and *Promethea*. The latter are part of *ABC* too, but despite sharing their frequently playful atmosphere with the other serializations, they are the sites for Moore seriously to explore themes like identity and magic.

The author's tendency to structure his work through quotations is exaggerated to the extent that one might think of the technique of pastiche, which, according to Fredric Jameson, constitutes one of the main limits of postmodernism, for it risks becoming a jumble of references that ultimately result as an end in themselves (see Jameson, *Postmodernism* 1–54). However, even if *ABC* and *Supreme* sometimes cross over into pure genre play, and are often marred by an excess of schematism (the same element, as chapter 4 will show, that flaws *Lost Girls*), they are not entirely devoid of cultural relevance: they represent a continuation, if lighthearted, of the reflection on superhero ideology (for further reference see Klock 98–121, and *Comic Book Artist* special issue 25). In varying degrees, therefore, Moore's works are always anchored to contemporary historical, social and cultural context. I would argue that Moore's intertextuality is less definable as pastiche than as Bakhtinian heteroglossia (or plurivocality) and dialogism (Bakhtin 55), or even as historiographic metafiction. As described by Linda Hutcheon, this term defines deliberately diverse narrative forms that are open to the multiplication of interpretative levels, where self-reflexivity and intertextuality do not deprive the past of its possible significances and do not disconnect it from the author's context, because "to re-write or to re-present the past is . . . to open it up to the present, to prevent it from being conclusive and teleological" (Hutcheon, *Poetics* 209). The following chapters examine the specific Moore works in which this process of dialogism, or historiographic metafiction, is best expressed. It is certainly true that Moore has many irons in his fire: genres and intertextual references, together with the new meanings his reworking endows them with, turn into a magmatic, all-inclusive narrative substance that would risk becoming too vague and slippery if not disciplined by the author himself. Perhaps this is why Moore imposes strong, precise structures on his works in order for them to attain cohesion and consistency—hence his manipulation of the basic structural coordinates of narration (space and time) and his tendency toward narrative circularity. Both of these aspects are analyzed in chapter 2.

CHAPTER 2

CHRONOTOPES
Outer Space, the Cityscape, and the Space of Comics

This chapter examines two core aspects in Moore's work—space and time—and, more specifically, the fusion and dynamic relationship that occurs between spatial and temporal dimensions. In dealing with this issue I use the term *chronotope*, and in doing so refer to Mikhail Bakhtin's collection of essays *The Dialogic Imagination*, in which the Russian scholar defines the substantial interconnection between space and time as the organizing center of the novelistic form. Bakhtin focuses on the "representational" (250) significance of this interconnection, which provides space and time with narrative substance. Even though Bakhtin's studies originally had nothing to do with the comics medium, his observations interestingly acquire a peculiar resonance if applied to it, for he discusses the importance of chronotopes in the novel in terms of narrative "visibility" (247). The hybrid, verbal/visual nature of comics, and the fact that narratives appear as sequential actions on the space of the page, make the space-time connection even more palpable than it appears in the prose novel.

When Will Eisner published *Comics and Sequential Art* in 1985, he dedicated a section to timing issues (see 25–37) and mentioned Albert Einstein and the theory of relativity in order to account for the variety of representational and time-manipulating techniques comics can take advantage of through the distribution of panels on the page. Eisner probably did not think that Bakhtin could be involved in comics criticism; however, Scott McCloud's later theories resound with the Russian scholar's words even more clearly. McCloud's remarks draw attention not only to the relationship of interdependence between space and time in comics, but also to the problematic nature and remarkably expressive potential of that very relationship: "In learning to read comics we all learned to perceive time spatially, for in the world of comics, time and space are one and the same. The problem is, there's no conversion chart . . . So, as readers, we're left with only a vague sense that as our eyes are moving through space, they're also moving through time—we just don't know by how much. . . . [Have you] ever noticed how the words 'short' or 'long' can refer to the first dimension or to the fourth? In a medium where time and space merge so completely, the distinction often vanishes" (McCloud, *Understanding* 100–102). Since the sequencing of panels articulates the temporal progression of the narrated incidents, McCloud points out, comics not only generally conflate space and time but uniquely manage to represent the past, the present, and the future in the same compositional unit, the page itself (see 104). The following sections contend how Moore creates different kinds of chronotope in his works, with particular reference to *The Ballad of Halo Jones*, *From Hell*, and *Promethea*.

THE CHRONOTOPE OF SCIENCE FICTION: *THE BALLAD OF HALO JONES*

The Ballad of Halo Jones, one of the most critically neglected works in Moore's abundant output,[1] was drawn by Ian Gibson and serialized in the British weekly magazine *2000 AD* between 1984 and 1986; it was later collected in three books and finally into a single volume in 2001. Moore had seemingly planned to create nine books and to bring the character to eighty years of age, but Halo's adventures came to an end in Book 3. *Halo Jones* is a science fiction graphic novel that derives a great deal of its narrative and iconographic conventions from classic sci-fi narratives such as the estranging, futuristic setting; the presence of aliens, androids, and mutants and their respective languages; and the motif of the journey into outer space. However, most of those conventions are significantly renovated and subverted. Consider the protagonist's character: Halo is an eighteen-year-old woman living on the Hoop, an immense circular tunnel where the U.S. institutions from the fiftieth century have decided to relegate the unemployed. Welfare services are at their minimum, and the Hoop's population can barely survive, trapped as it is between fits of depression and outbreaks of social tension. The representation of an oppressive, authoritarian society is indeed a leitmotiv of anti-utopian and science fiction narratives; nevertheless, contrary to the requirements of the sci-fi or adventure comics heroine *à la* Wonder Woman, Halo's distinguishing trait is her absolute normality. She has no special powers to aid her, and she is neither stunningly good-looking nor outstandingly clever. Moreover, a traditional heroine would just as traditionally demand a sidekick or a fellow adventurer, but Halo always ends up being utterly alone. If her cyberdog Toby is to be considered her sidekick, his behavior is decidedly different from that of Krypto, Superman's loyal four-legged friend: Toby eventually turns out to be a dangerous murderer, and Halo is compelled to kill him. Here is how the protagonist is described by Dr. Brunhauer, the character who tries to reconstruct the story of her existence, and who thus becomes the author's alter ego: "You see, I've spent 15 years researching this woman—and you know what I've found out? It's this . . . She wasn't anyone special. She wasn't that brave, or that clever, or that strong. She was somebody who felt cramped by the confines of her life. She was just somebody who had to get out. And she did it! She went out past Vega, out past Moulquet and Lambard! She saw places that aren't even there anymore! And do you know what she said? Her most famous quotation? 'Anybody could have done it'" (Moore and Gibson 59). Halo is just a girl like any other, or an Everywoman of future times, as the reader can infer from her last name 'Jones'—which, however, sounds paradoxically unusual in the distorted world of the year 4949, especially if compared to the names of other characters, such as her friends Brinna Childresse-Lao and Rodice Andelia Olsun, or the cetacean navigator Kititirik Tikrikitit. Halo's special nature originates exactly from her "sheer ordinariness" (5), which becomes the reason for the sort of mythical fabric that eventually envelops her figure.

Some parts of her life are told through a *mise en abyme* (the story-within-the-story) that redoubles the narration into two levels. At the beginning of the second book, the plot moves from Halo's fiftieth-century vicissitudes to one of the lectures the above-mentioned Dr. Brunhauer gives at the Institute for Parahistorical Studies on an unspecified planet in 6427 (see 55);[2] we discover that Halo was involved in a series of historical events, but also that information concerning her is inexplicably poor or inconsequential. Thus, her character is shrouded in an aura of mystery that, over the years, has turned her into a fabulous figure, ranging from the marvelous traveler to the treacherous space criminal—the object of legends and popular ballads—(hence the title) or of improbable academic publications such as "*The Halo Jones Myth in Modern Concordian Folklore* by Van Eyck" (55). Thanks to the professor's explanations, the reader is enabled to understand a good amount of the estranging elements s/he encountered in the first book and to place the protagonist's figure onto a double level of interpretation: she is an anti-heroine, a plain and common

Fig. 2-1. Rodice and her Zenade. From *The Complete Ballad of Halo Jones*, page 27 (excerpt). © Rebellion.

woman (hence her last name) but also a shifty, irretrievable figure who cannot be restored by means of traditional historiography—or rather, not even by means of fictional historiography—and who is ultimately only outlined by the shroud of legendary stories surrounding her (hence her first name).

As in every narrative universe created by Moore and his collaborators, the conventions and intertextual references the world of *Halo Jones* rests on are refashioned according to the modalities of recontextualization examined in chapter 1. Quotations and references mostly contribute to the consolidation of the sense of estrangement of the text and to the representation of a neurotic and distorted future world, where the traces of what the twentieth (or twenty-first)-century reader recognizes as 'reality' are at times identifiable, at other times quite feeble. For instance, the success of TV soap operas that were popular in the 1980s seems unchanged. Brinna, Halo, and her friend Toy watch them keenly, even though these are no conventional soaps but sci-fi "holo-soaps" (16), where characters materialize on an electronic platform in the form of holograms.

In most cases the words and ways of the past have changed to such an extent that their original meaning is blurred. When Halo and her friend Rodice set out in search of basic supplies, they have to arm themselves and devise a safe way through the Hoop in order to avoid being attacked by the dangerous gangs that often raid it. Rodice's remark highlights the reader's sense of linguistic estrangement: "I've got six zenades and a sputstik. Plus, our route's figured exactly! We'll be able to dodge any drangsturms" (19). Of course, neither protagonist is aware of the original meaning of the phrase *Sturm und Drang*, which has undergone a considerable transformation in the world of the future, even though it has generally retained its connotation as something linked to the commotion of feelings. The meaning of the word *zen* and its connection to the philosophy of ascesis and inner peace has been disrupted in the same way, for the object Rodice calls a "zenade" is actually a powerful weapon that ironically compels the aggressor to abandon himself or herself to a deep meditative state. This reversal is stressed by the presence of a caption (see fig. 2-1) providing definitions for both "zen" and "zenade" in the top left corner of a panel entirely filled by Rodice's angry face and by her hand holding the weapon.

The estrangement of *Halo Jones*, especially in the first chapters of the graphic novel, is conveyed both by the representation of the sci-fi landscape of the Hoop and of the spaceships that hover above it, and by the argot used by its inhabitants, which puts the reader's ability to decode language to the test. The very first page of the story begins with the words of the celebrity radio speaker Swifty Frisko, which sound like a parody of the slang and acronyms commonly used by radio newscasters:

> Dataday, day-to-day, making a pact with the facts... I'm Swifty Frisko, hi! Algae Baron Lux Roth Chop: will he, won't he? Is intervention his intention? Over to Jazz Firpo at Chop Towers in Pseudo-Portugal... "Lux Roth Chop, will you make a bid to save the E.S.S. Clara Pandy from the dissembler yards?' 'Probably not.' Hmm... Sounds like "Wait and see" from the L.R.C.! I'm Swifty Frisko, here's today traffax... Expect ozjams around East-Am for the next hour, cloudniks, as the E.S.S. Clara Pandy is floated in to the Manhattan Platform. (6–7)

The radio news program allows Moore to introduce the reader into the narration *in medias res*, as often happens in other estrangement-based texts; for example, in the opening lines of George Orwell's *Nineteen Eighty-Four* (5), the ceaseless flow of the news about industrial progress under Big Brother's dictatorship spurts from an unstoppable radio set, as occurs in Moore's own *V for Vendetta*, which was overtly inspired by Orwell's novel. In the same way, the sci-fi classic movie *2001: A Space Odyssey* (1968) by Stanley Kubrick opens with

Fig. 2-2. Hokusai Katsuhika's *Mount Fuji as Seen from Kanagawa (or The Wave),* painted between 1826 and 1833.

a long digression about the dawn of mankind and the lunar base, but right afterwards the viewer is told about the voyage of the spaceship *Discovery* toward Jupiter by the news. Interestingly, the opening news in *The Ballad of Halo Jones* also provide information about a glorious spaceship—the *Clara Pandy*—which is heading toward destruction, just like Kubrick's *Discovery.* The world of the future, then, is represented from the start as an entirely entropic one. The journey into outer space will provide Halo neither with a happy career nor with any opportunity for human relations, as her friend Rodice foretells when the girl declares her intention of fleeing the Hoop: "Forget it, girly. Even if you do get out it's no good... 'Cause no matter how far you get, they'll fetch you back here and bust you to pieces. Just ask Clara Pandy" (Moore and Gibson 11).

In the estranging universe of *Halo Jones,* the remains of the old cultural tradition appear every now and then, but no one is capable of identifying or understanding them anymore. For instance, in the last part of the novel Halo—now a warrior on the planet Moab—is puzzled by the bizarre puritan doctrine professed by the natives. To her, their unknown religion counts just as much as the platoon's popular superstition according to which Mona Jukes, the most naive and unprepared among the soldiers, is supposed to possess some power which allows her to survive any kind of battle: "They [the Moabites] all carry

Fig. 2-3. The "Hoopflex." From *The Complete Ballad of Halo Jones*, page 25 (excerpt). © Rebellion.

this black 'book' thing full of violent, frightening stories, long since banned on Earth. Apparently, they take their name from some ancient tribe. This tribe were descendants of Lot. Lot was some guy whose wife turned into a pillar of salt because she looked back at something or other. I guess everybody has to believe something. Around our new barracks, a lot of people have started believing in Mona Jukes" (157). In a world where books no longer exist and where almost nobody ever writes (as underlined by general Luiz Cannibal a few pages before the novel's conclusion, "Writing. Sergeant Jones? How very extraordinary. Only one being in a thousand still writes, did you know that?" 180), biblical allusions mingle with the dryness of youthful language, thus generating a pervasive leveling out of the past. This is most effectively represented in the so-called "Hoopflex" (25), the moment occurring every day at 5 p.m. when the Hoop opens to let a huge wave pass by. The conformation of the wave—which would actually destroy the whole Hoop were its way blocked—clearly reminds us of the famous *Mount Fuji as Seen from Kanagawa* (or *The Wave*) from *Thirty-six Views from Fuji* (ca. 1826–1833) by Japanese painter Hokusai Katsuhika (1760–1849) (see figs. 2-2 and 2-3). The wave passes through the open Hoop, comes into sight for a quick instant and soon disappears in the muddy waters that surround the huge metal ring, thus epitomizing the destiny of cultural tradition in the world of the future. The traces of past culture peep out for a fleeting moment, only to be immediately engulfed by the chaotic jumble of signs, stimuli, and pieces of information that throng the space of the fiftieth century. In this sense, the wave that crosses the Hoop acts as a metaphor of postmodern storytelling, of its instability and heterogeneity.

Let us now examine the novel's chronotope more closely. One way in which *The Ballad of Halo Jones* is emblematic of Moore's narrative technique is the presence of a circular structure, which is both conceptually and graphically made apparent in the text. The first circle the reader encounters is the above-

Fig. 2-4. Circular structures in *The Complete Ballad of Halo Jones*, page 22 (excerpt). © Rebellion.

mentioned Hoop, the huge, ring-shaped tunnel floating on water off a place called Manhattan, which could be a futuristic, decayed version of present-day New York. The Hoop is equipped with several ramifications, in their turn provided with small appendixes. The life of the great tunnel's occupants mirrors its shape: it is repetitive and monotonous, and it offers no chance for change. This condition is also visually highlighted by the outline of round corridors that almost always stand out in panel backgrounds, and by the presence of other recurring round elements in the pages (see fig. 2-4).

Exasperated by her circumstances, Halo decides to try her luck and board the *Clara Pandy* as a hostess on the occasion of the last voyage of the old and sumptuous spaceship. Jobless again in 4951, Halo starts to wander; she travels to Proxima IV, Vescue, Pwuc, and other planets, all of which invariably appear as entropic worlds that tear apart the protagonist's innocence and shatter her hopes for the future. Years and years in the woman's peregrinations are compressed in about four pages, concluding that, "Records of her movements over the next few years are incomplete, yet reveal a pattern of increasing desperation . . . as if she were pacing the galaxy, trying to get out. . . . She was a woman with no money, no hope of ever affording the journey beyond the confines of the galaxy she'd been born to. She was twenty-nine years old . . . and she was stranded. She'd escaped the Hoop to find a bigger prison waiting outside" (114–15). Halo's state of mind is reminiscent of the disenchantment that overcomes the Swiftian traveler Gulliver after his disastrous journeys; or better still, it evokes the Spanish traditional literary figure of the picaro, a humble-born character whose primary need is survival—finding something to eat and staying out of trouble—in a society that favors only a privileged few (see Del Monte and Rico). Halo may be seen as a postmodern Lazarillo de Tormes, then, and fiftieth-century outer space may well mirror early-seventeenth-century Spanish society: the protagonist is precluded from enjoying any real freedom of action, and her wanderings are entirely pointless—just sterile roaming on desolate planets, with a backdrop of existential pessimism rooted in the author's criticism of contemporary culture and society. As chapter 3 will point out, in Moore's case the reference is a critical vision of the English society of the 1980s, and especially of the politics of Margaret Thatcher's conservative government.

It is only at the end of Halo's stay on Moab—her last stopover, and the setting for some of the most interesting developments in the narration—that she recovers her ability to act and that the novel heads toward its conclusion (one that is of a problematical and unresolved kind). On Moab, the circle of Halo's existential vicissitudes is finally closed. The space of the planet is a specular reflection of her place of origin, and it is no accident that Moore and Gibson dedicate more or less the same number of pages (barely forty) to both settings. Moreover, the most directly recognizable feature of the planet is that it is "a tunnel society, shut away from light. It reminded [Halo] of the Hoop" (115), even though there the existence of galleries is dictated not by the necessity to hide the unemployed and more marginalized fringes of society but by the need for survival: Moab's gravity requires that people wear special suits they can only safely get out of in the army tunnels. Gravity affects Moab to such an extent that the temporal dimension is also squeezed: when Halo, now a mercenary, spends her first five minutes in the Crush (166), the most dangerous war zone on the planet, she feels she is moving in slow motion. In the first five pages of the chapter, every seemingly endless minute is spread out onto an entire page, each organized as a composition of extremely detailed panels where suspended bullets hover beside the static figures of the women soldiers, frozen in the slowing down of time; the characters' thoughts crowd the captions. In order to take in all these words and details, the reader is compelled to slow down his/her reading pace and experience the slowness of the Crush.

After the first five minutes spent fighting, Halo goes back to the gravity-safe tunnels and finds that two months have elapsed. Distorted temporality, life in the oppressive suits, and the repetitiveness of the actions of the women's mercenary army turn Moab into the site of total estrangement, both for the protagonist and for the reader: "I've been fighting in the Crush for two days now. I've been fighting in the Crush for six months. We go through the shield doors, scream and run around and shoot things for five minutes, then come out to find a month has elapsed outside. Like Sergeant Wo says, it passes the time. My body-clock feels messed up. . . . The worst thing was emerging to find I'd missed my birthday, by two weeks. I'm thirty now, but I don't remember it happening. Never mind. I'll have better luck when I'm thirty-one, in three days' time. I've been fighting in the Crush for two days now. I've been fighting in the Crush for six months. I'm not crazy . . . but I'm working on it" (171–72). The abrupt iterative rhythm of Halo's diary entries (the phrase "I've been fighting . . ." is repeated several times) proceeds at the same rate as the pressing repetition of the panels that depict the soldiers exiting the base to enter the Crush, and then coming back. Information about the passing of time is provided not only by Halo's diary, but also by the aspect of the guard sitting beside the tunnel entrance: his beard and hair grow more and more, while the sprouts in a vase on his desk turn into a full-grown plant (see fig. 2-5). Moab's temporal deceleration becomes as disheartening as life on the Hoop; within a few "days" Halo finds she is now thirty-three, and after her last battle she goes back to the tunnels only to discover that the war has been over for weeks.

Almost as if the unnatural space-time of the Crush had granted her enough time to ponder her condition, Halo decides to flee from the disarming planet. While she steals a spaceship and takes off in the last panels of the novel, time goes back to its regular beating, pulling back like a piece of elastic, or like the spider web that used to imprison the heroine in her dreams at night (see 185–86). However, this is no reconciliatory ending: the character's movements through space and time—in particular on planet Moab, but also during the other stops in her journey—define a circular route where Halo does not physically go back to her starting point, but where she remains psychologically stuck, filled with the same perception of the insecurity of her own existence and with the same need to be "just out" (190); what is more, she is now aware that her innocence is irretrievably lost. None of the locations Halo visits is suitable for permanence;

Fig. 2-5. In and out of the "Crush." From *The Complete Ballad of Halo Jones*, page 171. © Rebellion.

even the opulent spaceship *Clara Pandy*, where the protagonist initially feels reasonably unworried, is exposed at the end of the novel as the site of ruthless general Cannibal's obscure war schemes. Every movement in the space and time of *Halo Jones* ratifies the ineluctable disintegration of the protagonist's innocence, and her subsequent rejection of the characters and places she encounters. Moore and Gibson set up a permeable text—both a sci-fi novel organized on defamiliarization processes, and therefore "a privileged site for critical thought" (Kneale and Kitchin 4), and a graphic novel, a text by nature hybrid and open to contamination—against an impermeable character, for Halo's psychology is made increasingly impenetrable as she proceeds in a journey that makes no progress, but that only increases her condition of isolation and apathy.

In a sense, Halo is the polar opposite of the protagonist in Scottish writer Naomi Mitchison's 1962 novel *Memoirs of a Spacewoman*, also an account of the journeys of a female traveler in outer space. But while interstellar travel, for Mitchison's spacewoman, constitutes the utopia of a space-time of communication and empathy with the inhabitants of the universe (in this regard see Armitt and Donawerth), the space and time Halo sails across shape a geography of disillusionment and incommunicability. More than subscribing to Mitchison's utopian vision, Moore's approach seems to be in tune with the alienation processes that corrode J. G. Ballard's characters; the sterile outer space Halo travels in might be a projection of the British author's inner space, which in turn mirrors the sclerotic nature of contemporary sensitivity. Let us not forget that the unfruitfulness of the landscapes and experiences Halo faces can surely be assessed from a sexual point of view. Again, whereas Mitchison's spacewoman Mary reaches the climax of her empathetic practices by welcoming an alien graft into her body, Halo, despite meeting a few friends over her journeys, is totally unable to establish any considerable sentimental or sexual bond save for a short, ambiguous relationship with general Cannibal, the menacing, tusked humanoid she eventually kills in order to escape from Moab. Her mind's closure is mirrored by her body's ultimate refusal of human relations—a body that ends up facing the experience of monstrosity and derangement, thus once again appearing close to the typical issues of Ballard's aesthetics (for Ballardian leitmotifs see Lockhurst and Gasiorek).

The Ballad of Halo Jones thus offers a dystopian, disjointed, crumbling universe—one enclosed, however, by a meticulous narrative organization that, as this section has argued, eventually closes up like a circle. This novel, then, effectively represents the narrative strategy conjectured by Moore in his programmatic essay *On Writing for Comics*, where several possible textual layouts are suggested, stating that the ideal choice is "the basic elliptical structure, where elements at the beginning of the story mirror events which are to happen at the end, or where a particular phrase or a particular image will be used at the beginning and the end, acting as bookends to give the story that takes place in between a sense of neatness and unity" (Moore, *Writing* 15). Moore, then, theorizes consistent, coherent, well-proportioned narrative structures, as if the only possible way for the author to shape an otherwise chaotic, decaying world were to filter it through a thick network of recognizable references—in spite of the fact that intertextuality and genre conventions end up underscoring their own pointlessness and paradoxical inscrutableness—and to aim at establishing narrative balance through a sound plot where each element fits into its own place, like a piece in a jigsaw puzzle. Through different modes, the same mechanism is triggered in other works, as the subsequent sections of this chapter will show.

THE URBAN CHRONOTOPE: *FROM HELL*

The first chapter of this book offers some considerations as to the sophisticated intertextual play that provides a backdrop for *From Hell: Being a Melodrama in Sixteen Parts*, co-authored by Eddie Campbell and published between 1989 and 1999. This section is devoted to analysis of the other great frame of reference underpinning this graphic novel, that of the cityscape. In its intent to use fiction as a surgical instrument to dissect Victorian culture, *From Hell* can also be interpreted as a homage to London and its many facets, from the city's architectural monuments to the dreariest East End streets, which Eddie Campbell's panels represent with an almost photographic meticulousness. As literary scholar Franco Moretti observes, space has played a crucial role in the development of novelistic narrative: "specific stories are the product of specific spaces, . . . and . . . *without a certain kind of space, a certain kind of story is simply impossible*" (100; Moretti's italics). The existence of *From Hell* as a novel would thus be impossible without the presence of the city of London, which pervades the narrative like a proper character. In the eyes of Sir William Gull, the city is a real and tangible body, but also a mystical and allegorical entity. In the fourth chapter of the novel, entitled "What doth the Lord require of thee?" Gull leads his coachman and accomplice Netley along a time-consuming route through the streets of the city and uses architecture as a means to legitimate the insane Masonic mission he is going to perform. In his words, the texture of the city becomes a majestic work of art, a literary text that must be mystically read and interpreted: "GULL: Take this city, in itself a great work, you'll agree: a thing of many levels, and complexities. How well do you know London, Netley? NETLEY: Like the back o' my hand, sir. GULL: Ha ha! As grubby, certainly, but London's more besides: it too is a symbol, history and myth. . . . Do you begin to grasp how truly great a work is London? A veritable textbook we may draw upon in formulating great works of our own! We'll penetrate its metaphors, lay bare its structure and thus

Fig. 2-6. Gull's hand moves across London in *From Hell*, chapter 4, page 19 (excerpt). © Alan Moore and Eddie Campbell. All Rights Reserved. Image reprinted here with permission.

come at last upon its meaning. As befits great work, we'll read it carefully and with respect" (Moore and Campbell, *From Hell* ch. 4, 6–9).

Over the long coach journey, the two characters visit the places where Gull believes he will find traces of the great Masonic layout of London as they are outlined by the locations of the city's obelisks and of the churches designed by seventeenth-century architect Nicholas Hawksmoor. As the space of London is crucial for the development of this narration, Moore and Campbell use the journey with the uncouth Netley as an expedient to have the character of Gull give an erudite lecture about its urban landscape, with which the reader is quite familiar by the end of the chapter. Gull and Netley leave from King's Cross and go across Battle Bridge, where according to the Freemasons, the male principle of the Sun triumphed on the matriarchy of Boudicca, queen of the Iceni and a great enemy of Rome. They then head for Essex Road and London Fields, the location of Druidic rituals, and follow their route to observe the obelisks of Bunhill Fields cemetery—where William Blake is buried—and of Old Street. The journey goes on to Northampton Square and to the Hawksmoorian church of St. George Bloomsbury, and then as far as Earl's Court, where the doctor and the coachman stop for a break. Before they go on, Gull unfolds a map of the city and marks the previous stopovers in pencil, thus starting to outline his crazy vision of history together with the route of the journey (see fig. 2-6). About a third of the panel is occupied by the balloon filled with the litany of Gull's topographic indications, while the doctor's body does not even appear and is reduced to a hand moving a pencil on the map. Moore and Campbell thus underline the oppressive presence of the city, which invades almost all of the space the panel offers to the reader, as if Masonic London itself were guiding a weak-willed hand along the mazy lines of its streets and boroughs.

Gull and Netley set out again from the famous obelisk called "Cleopatra's Needle" and then descend Waterloo Bridge in order to reach Lambeth and Elephant & Castle; they go up toward the Tower and then swerve to the east as far as Limehouse and the Isle of Dogs. They go back again toward Christ Church Spitalfields, in the heart of Whitechapel, and finally reach St. Paul's Cathedral, the destination of their intense coach ride and, in Gull's view, the ultimate demonstration of the supremacy of the male principle over the female one. Indeed, the cathedral was supposedly built on the remains of an ancient temple dedicated to the cult of Diana and architecturally organized in such a way to tie down the power of the ancient goddess into a more stately, virile building (see ch. 4, 35). Gull unfolds the map of London again and completes the outline of the route of the journey, helped by Netley. St. Paul's now appears as the center of a pentacle, which, according to Masonic belief, consecrates the power of the male principle and decrees the final submission of the feminine. The page (see fig. 2-7) presents a grid of nine panels organized on two diagonal lines. The pentacle is drawn along the diagonal that from the top right corner reaches the bottom left one, while the other diagonal shows Netley's response to Gull's folly: the coachman approaches the doctor in the first panel, focuses on the pentacle in the central one, and runs away feeling sick in the bottom right panel, which is the last on the page. The rigorous geometrical structure of the page mirrors the precision of the morbid calculations Gull uses to foster and justify his insanity, thus making the representation even more powerful.

By eliminating the prostitutes who threaten the Crown's reputation and by soaking the streets of London with their blood, the doctor believes he will per-petuate the violent submission of femininity the Freemasons hope for, and fol-low the inevitable pattern of history—a pattern Gull perceives as clearly written into the macrotext of the urban landscape: "You see? Your destiny's inscribed upon the streets wherein you grew . . . Our story's written, Netley, inked in blood long dry . . . engraved in stone" (37–38). Gull's speech is made even more eloquent by Campbell's managing of page layouts: the last page of the chapter, where only the aforementioned phrase "engraved in stone" appears, is filled by a single image representing the city as a colossal dark mass where the dome of St. Paul's is silhouetted against the sky. The centuries of history and myth Gull condensed into the time of an exhausting coach trip—which eventually bewil-ders the reader as much as Netley, who ends up feeling sick—now materialize

Fig. 2-7. Gull's crazy conception of his Masonic trip in *From Hell*, chapter 4, page 36. © Alan Moore and Eddie Campbell. All Rights Reserved. Image reprinted here with permission.

into shapes and become the body of the city; a hard body made of stone, and yet a mighty, pulsating, almost living entity.

This is not the only passage where Gull refers to the city as a body. A few pages before the conclusion of the chapter, the doctor reports the legends about Boudicca and recounts her terrible vengeance against the Romans with these words: "She gathered the Iceni, howling to her mother goddesses for vengeance, and burned London to the ground, its gutters heaped with steaming heads. She left a stripe of ash, a cold black vein in London's geologic strata, token of a woman's wrath" (8). In the same way, when Gull visits Christ Church in Spitalfields together with his friend James Hinton in chapter 2, he explains how Masonic architects used to design their buildings "borrowing proportions from God's Temple, the human body" (ch. 2, 14).[3] But while the body of the city can be read, interpreted, and mapped in clear lines, the female bodies of the Whitechapel prostitutes are seen by Gull as mysterious, uncontrollable, and subversive; they are threatening, disorderly bodies, and therefore represent too great a danger to the status quo the doctor has vowed to defend.

Gull's distorted and mythologizing interpretation of urban space also affects his equally hallucinatory relationship with time, which (starting with chapter 4) surfaces more and more manifestly as his madness intensifies. The doctor's vision of time is prefigured during the above-mentioned dialogue with Hinton: "HINTON: You know, Gull, this puts me in mind of some theories that my son, Howard, proposed to me. They suggest time is a human illusion . . . that all times co-exist in the stupendous whole of eternity. He hopes to publish a pamphlet one day. GULL: Indeed? And how shall this pamphlet be entitled? HINTON: 'What is the fourth dimension?' . . . An invisible curve, rising through the centuries. GULL: Can history then be said to have an architecture, Hinton? The notion is most glorious and most horrible" (14–15). Not only does Gull interpret every material sign in the world around him as a symbol to be fitted into the eternal dimension of the Masonic historical pattern, but he also acquires some mysterious visionary power that enables him to open up gashes into the future, especially during the ritual moment of murder. Shortly before he kills Annie Chapman, the doctor glances at an illuminated window and, for an instant, sees a man pulling the curtains, a TV set and an electric bulb behind his back; before the setting goes back to 1888, Gull and the man exchange a frightened stare (see ch. 7, 24). Likewise, after massacring Kate Eddowes's body, Gull disappears from Netley's sight for a second and triumphantly raises his arms to the sky in front of a twentieth-century skyscraper (see ch. 8, 40).

Gull's hallucinations reach their climax in two other episodes. First, the killing of Marie Kelly, followed by the dissection of her corpse, fills thirty-one of the thirty-four pages of chapter 10. The first temporal entity to be manipulated, then, is that of the reader, who is compelled to closely watch the tortures Marie's body is undergoing as they are represented in every detail; panel breakdown slows down, and the slaughtering lasts much longer in comparison with the previous murders. The reader is turned into an obscene voyeur and is invited to attend the scene in real time, as in the case of the dazing coach trip of chapter 4. While Gull horrifyingly mutilates the woman's body, he projects himself into the future again, first in a lecture hall where he explains how to carry out a post-mortem, and then into a modern office. The imperturbability of the employees—who cannot perceive his presence—shocks him: "Where comes this dullness in your eyes? How has your country numbed you so? Shall man be given marvels only when he is beyond all wonder?" (ch. 10, 21). Frightened by such obscure circumstances, Gull turns back to Marie's dead body and hugs it in a panel that condenses both present and past space and time in a single unit, for a computer screen is depicted in the background (see fig. 2-8). In the following panels, the doctor catches a glimpse of a near-future episode—the madhouse nurses bent over him—and in three instances he seems to cross the borders of the page to reach the present of the reader, whom he stares at directly, almost in an accusation of voyeuristic connivance (see ch. 10, 11, 13 and 15; on voyeurism in *From Hell*, see Alaniz, "Into Her Dead Body").

The second episode takes place when the dying Gull performs his last mystical voyage and materializes in several places and historical moments in the form of a blood rain, fire, or a disembodied ghost. He visits both William Blake, thus providing him with a revelation he will then reproduce in his painting *The Ghost of a Flea* (see ch. 14, 17), and Robert Louis Stevenson, who draws inspiration for *The Strange Case of Dr. Jekyll and Mr. Hyde* from him. These are the words the late Victorian writer uses to describe his frightening vision: "I... I had a dream. Awful. . . . Th-the man. The man in my dream. I must write it down. He was a doctor. A doctor with the soul of a terrible beast inside him" (15). In the future, Gull reaches Netley, then the Scottish serial killer Ian Brady, and a Yorkshire family—presumably the family of Peter Sutcliffe, later known as the Yorkshire Ripper; Moore thus conjectures a meeting between the Ripper spirit and two of its dreadful successors.[4]

In Gull's last vision before he dissolves into eternity, he makes out a woman with her daughters. He does not recognize her, but she perceives his pres-

Fig. 2-8. Past and present melt in Gull's savage ritual. *From Hell*, chapter 10, page 22 (excerpt). © Alan Moore and Eddie Campbell. All Rights Reserved. Image reprinted here with permission.

ence and exorcises his baleful power: "And as for you, ye auld divil, I know that you're there, and ye're not havin' these. Clear off now wit' ye. Clear off back to Hell and leave us be!" (23). According to the caption on top of the page, the scene is set in Ireland in the early twentieth century. The woman's three daughters are called Katey, Lizzie, and Polly, like three of Jack's victims. The background is finally clear and sunny, in contrast with the ink-suffocated panels that depict Whitechapel. It seems that Marie Kelly is still alive and has fulfilled her dream of going back to her home country; maybe the woman Gull slaughtered in her room at Miller's Court was not Marie after all, but one of the friends she often gave hospitality to. Campbell's closely woven lines blur the women's facial features throughout the novel and thus enable Moore to create a narrative twist where Marie's character is saved—at least in fictional terms, as the author himself asserts (not without some irony) in the last notes of the first appendix to the novel: "These final pages are invented, and the cryptic scene upon page twenty-three must go without an explanation for the moment. Work it out yourself" (Appendix I, 42). In the following note, the author actually justifies the plausibility of his hypothesis: "Oh, and concerning that scene on page twenty-three of chapter fourteen: it might be worth pointing out that, according to *The JTR A-Z*, Marie Kelly was known by various nicknames that included Ginger and Fair Emma. Just in case that helps. Beyond that, it only remains for me to thank you for your patience and wish you all a safe and pleasant night. Your friend, Alan Moore, Northampton, England, May 1996" (42).

Fig. 2-9. Parallel awakenings: Dr. Gull and the miserable East End women. *From Hell*, chapter 5, pages 4–5. © Alan Moore and Eddie Campbell. All Rights Reserved. Image reprinted here with permission.

The reflection on the fictional nature of the attempt of historical reconstruction in *From Hell* will be examined later in this section. But let us now go back to the specifically spatial dimension of the representation of London. Throughout the novel, the British capital appears not only as the city of monuments and of Hawksmoor's religious architecture; it is also a maze of sordid alleys, especially represented by the Whitechapel slums, which were very densely populated by the people Charles Booth labeled as "vicious" and "semi-criminal" in his 1889 *Descriptive Map of London Poverty* (qtd. in Moretti 76, 136). Indeed, Whitechapel's miserable lanes become the theatre for the Ripper murders. Its soot-blackened buildings and its overcrowded streets serve as a counterpoint to the majestic geography of West End monuments and avenues. The West End palaces and clean church façades clash with the images of the East End, which look dark and grimy even when the scene is set in broad daylight; Campbell's substantial superimposition of lines covers the buildings, the paving, and the sky, sometimes filling even the backgrounds and making them almost indecipherable. This antithesis becomes strikingly evident in chapter 5, whose initial sequence is organized on cross-cut panels depicting the morning awakening of Gull in his room, and of a group of indigent women presumably accommodated in some free house. The Gull panels are painted in watercolor and toned down in soft black and white, in sharp contrast with the scratched inks characterizing the representation of the women, which make the panels look almost like excerpts from a lithograph (see fig. 2-9). Yet, despite their poverty, the slums of London teem with life and character; in their vivacity and diversity, the slums—and not the affluent monumentality of the West End—-ultimately lie at the core of the peculiar fascination with late Victorian London that captivate not only Moore but other contemporary writers and artists who, just like him, have recently reappraised the "narrow but imaginatively inexhaustible map of Spitalfields" (Brooker 118).[5]

Depiction of Moore and Campbell's city is not confined to streets and façades but includes dark interiors of the pubs where the prostitutes meet, their bare rooms, editorial offices of the gutter press that capitalizes on the killer's unknown identity, and the Scotland Yard premises; it embraces the royal residences, Gull's aristocratic abode, and inspector Fred Abberline's middle-class dwellings. It is an all-embracing, heterogeneous landscape that—much in the same way as in Charles Dickens's *Our Mutual Friend* (1865), which too is an exploration of late-nineteenth-century London life—connects the East and West Ends through a network of spaces, characters, and relationships (see Moretti 75–140 and Wolfreys). Moreover, there's a further, ironic resemblance between Dickens's novel and *From Hell*: again, as Franco Moretti maintains, the Dickensian novel deluges the reader with information about the urban space and the characters that move in it, like mosaic tesserae in search of their proper location. The organizing principle of such bulks of information and such movements eventually turns out to be blood—the tight weave of family relationships, kinships, and associations that connects people, which Moretti illustrates by means of eight London maps with the locations of the novel's characters (see 125–28). Similarly, the world of *From Hell* seems to be organized by blood—that of the illegitimate heir to the Crown to whom Annie Chapman gives birth, which initially triggers the serial killing, but most of all the very visible blood of the Ripper's victims, whose arrangement on the streets of Whitechapel is represented in a provided map (Moore and Campbell, *From Hell* Appendix I, o).

In *From Hell*, Moore's choice to use the aforementioned principle of circular narrative structure is made clear both by quotations interspersed in the narrative and by authorial speculations in the second Appendix to the novel. We thus find a sentence from Charles Hoy Fort's 1931 book *Lo!*[6] right before the Prologue,

In 1994 the *Complete History of Jack the Ripper* is published. Its author, Philip Sugden, arguably provides the most compendious and level-headed work yet. Even so...

The sheer exhaustive excellence of Sugden's research highlights an impending crisis in the field. The fractal shape known as Koch's Snowflake provides an illustration.

Koch's Snowflake begins with an equilateral triangle, which can be contained within a circle, just as the murders are constrained to Whitechapel and Autumn, 1888.

Next, half-sized triangles are added to the triangles' three sides. Quarter-sized triangles are added to the new shape's twelve sides, and so on.

Eventually, the snowflake's edge becomes so crinkly and complex that its length, theoretically, is INFINITE. Its AREA, however, never exceeds the initial circle.

Likewise, each new book provides fresh details, finer crennelations of the subject's edge. Its area, however, can't extend past the initial circle: Autumn, 1888. Whitechapel

Fig. 2-10. Koch's snowflake in *From Hell*, Appendix II, page 23 (excerpt). © Alan Moore and Eddie Campbell. All Rights Reserved. Image reprinted here with permission.

which reads "One measures a circle, beginning anywhere" (Prologue, 0); similarly, in Appendix II, as the author metanarratively reflects on the process of creation of *From Hell*, he writes: "Koch's snowflake begins with an equilateral triangle, which can be contained within a circle, just as the murders are constrained to Whitechapel and Autumn 1888. Next, half-sized triangles are added to the triangle's three sides. Quarter-sized triangles are added to the new shape's twelve sides, and so on. Eventually, the snowflake's edge becomes so crinkly and complex that its length, theoretically, is infinite. Its area, however, never exceeds the initial circle. Likewise, each new book provides fresh details, finer crenellations of the subject's edge. Its area, however, can't extend past the initial circle: Autumn, 1888. Whitechapel. . . . Koch's snowflake: gaze upon it, Ripperologists, and shiver. . . . The actual killer's gone, unglimpsed, might as well not have been there at all" (Appendix II, 23; see fig. 2-10).

The novel is permeated with awareness of its own purely fictional nature and of the impossibility of adding or discovering anything new about the story of Jack the Ripper. Nevertheless, within the circumscribed space of fiction lies the possibility of crafting a universe where stories, relationships, and social and cultural connections can be created, as demonstrated by the previous examples and by the way Moore tries to associate the Ripper mystery with a wide range of historical figures and events, such as the painter Walter R. Sickert (1860–1942), whose character is instrumental in starting the plot of the novel; the "Elephant Man" John Merrick (see ch. 2, 23–24); or the episode of Buffalo Bill's arrival in London (see ch. 4, 14–16). Within the same fictional space it is possible to provide the Ripper's final victim with a means of escape. Once again we face a circle that contains a potentially infinite, multi-faceted structure, a well-defined macrocosm that embraces a myriad of diversified microcosms. As Moore observes in an interview, "The Whitechapel murders took place over a finite period of time and claimed a finite number of victims. . . . [But] as more detail becomes apparent with closer and closer examination, so too does the 'surface' of the narrative become more crinkly, prickly, and fractal. The perimeter of the story starts to extend towards infinity. The space and time needed for each episode expands" (Sim, "Correspondence Part I" 313). This quotation is peculiarly apropos to conclude this section and move on to the following one. Indeed, *Promethea* is a work where the author carries his narrative play with time and space to extremes, together with his search for radically innovative results in terms of interaction between written word and graphic sign.

THE CHRONOTOPE OF THE IMAGINATION: *PROMETHEA*

Promethea, a graphic novel Moore created with the aid of several collaborators—mainly J. H. Williams III and Mick Gray, plus others—was first serialized from 1999 in the *America's Best Comics* line and later collected in five volumes between 2000 and 2005 (which I use as reference here instead of recurring to single issues, whose availability has been scarcer). It is an extremely demanding and not unproblematic work that perhaps would be better served by a more extensive separate treatment. Even so, this graphic novel is worth considering in the present essay for two reasons at least: first, because of the radical formal experimentation carried out by Moore and his co-authors; second, because of the importance of the authorial reflection on the use of space and time, which here undergoes further evolution.

As a preliminary remark, it must be noted that *Promethea* is a doubly hybrid text in that, besides being a graphic novel, it is also a mystical and philosophical treatise that introduces Moore's theories about cosmic order and the principles of the Jewish Kabbalah. As previously stated, the British author started his systematic study of magic disciplines in 1993, with particular reference to occult scholars Aleister Crowley (1875–1947) and Austin Osman Spare (1886–1956), the use of the Tarot deck, and the Kabbalah. According to the latter, the universe is organized in ten *Sephira*—or spheres—that form the Tree of Life, which, in turn, constitutes a conceptual map of the human soul and therefore, on a cosmic level, of existence as a whole (see Sim, "Correspondence," especially Parts 2 and 3). In Moore's view, esoteric practitioners become aware of the configuration of the Tree and gain access to an area of consciousness the author defines as Ideaspace, an immaterial dimension acting as repository for both individual fantasies and the collective imagination: "Ideaspace, a kind of medium or field or space or dimension in which thoughts occur. I believe this space to be at least in part mutual, rather than discrete, which is to say that I believe that this 'space' impinges to some degree upon all consciousness and that it is co-accessible" (Sim, "Correspondence Part 1" 315). *Promethea* is first of all Moore's means of expressing these theories, which shape the protagonist's character and the sequence of her exploits. Nevertheless, this work is also an adventure narrative that shares and refashions the superhero tradition.

For some, *Promethea*'s narration leans excessively toward the theoretical front, and as a consequence the plot is too flimsy and based only on a succession of substantially uninteresting philosophical and religious disquisitions: "Much of what he [Moore] is saying would be dismissed as the ramblings of a nutter if it weren't coming from somebody whose contribution to comics has (deservedly) earned such immense respect from the audience. *Promethea* isn't trying to impose its views on anyone, but if like me you take it all about as seriously as the flat Earth theory, and you're not interested in the displays of technique for its own sake, the book's appeal is pretty limited" (O'Brien, "Magical Mystery"). O'Brien is not entirely wrong if we consider that the Kabbalistic theoretical descriptions sometimes make the narrative pace heavier and that some of Moore's considerations can sound hazardous to many ears. However, this graphic novel features several interesting elements not confined to graphic experimentation— which, anyway, is never displayed for its own sake. This section will argue that, despite the prominence the authors attach to abstract and Kabbalistic aspects, *Promethea* is also the tale of a superheroine and a self-reflective deliberation about the power of narration, the role of the artist, and the modes of representation of comics.

The text opens with a two-page prose essay signed by Moore about the mythical figure of Promethea, accounting for the woman warrior's first appearance as a nymph in an eighteenth-century long poem by one Charlton Sennet, whose dates of birth and death are provided to add to the veracity of the article. According to the text, Promethea's character later appeared in Margaret Taylor Case's early-twentieth-century comic books; then, it resurfaced in the twenties and thirties in *Astonishing Stories,* a popular series of short fantasy novellas illustrated by Grace Brannagh (see Moore, Williams, and Gray, *Promethea Book 1,* 5). The heroine's latest adventures took place in the comics created by William Woolcott and then by Steven Shelley, who died in 1996. This short but very detailed text is clearly a fictional construct meant to introduce information about the character before the actual story starts. Here Moore is using one of his favorite narrative devices—the creation of a fictional "document" within the plot, which he previously experimented with in *Watchmen*—and also playing with quotations and intertextual references. As Geoff Klock correctly observes, the names Moore chooses for his fake *Promethea* authors recall those of some superhero comics creators, such as Margaret Brundage, William Moulton Marston—who fathered *Wonder Woman*—and Grace Gebbie Drayton (see Klock 112). Two further references are particularly evident: Mary Wollstonecraft Shelley (1797–1851), who wrote *Frankenstein, or, the Modern Prometheus* in 1818, and French feminist scholar Hélène Cixous, whose actual essay *Le livre de Prométhéa* (1983) is explicitly mentioned in the novel (Moore, Williams, and Gray, *Promethea Book 1,* 163). Of course, the reference to Cixous—a renowned theorist of the *écriture feminine* and the author of the well-known *Le rire de la Méduse* in 1975—is no accident, considering that female identity and writing are among the many motifs developed within this graphic novel.

The initial setting of the story is indicated as "New York, 1999 A.D." (12), the same year the actual serialization of the *Promethea* installments began. However, the representation of the city does not exactly correspond to late-twentieth-century New York City; instead, it re-creates the science-fiction imagery of the pulp magazines from the early years of the same century. *Promethea* often pays ironic, affectionate homage to such magazines by drawing on both their iconography—especially in issue covers—and their emphatic, often verbose language, as happens in Book Two when chapter six is heralded at the end of the previous episode as "the strangest comics-reading experience of the DECADE!" (*Promethea Book 2*, 132).

Another telling example is an episode from Book One: the protagonist Sophie and Promethea/Grace Brannagh are traveling together in the realm of Immateria, the world of individual and collective fantasy (the fictional equivalent of Moore's Ideaspace theory). There they meet Marto Neptura, an imaginary writer used as a figurehead by several *Promethea* pulp authors in the 1920s. In the Immateria, Neptura's fantasies appear as the landscape of Hy Brasil, a land crammed with dangers and grotesque creatures—and pervaded by the pulp writer's presence to such an extent that his threatening, gigantic typewritten words are silhouetted against the sky. However, Promethea/Grace invites Sophie to mistrust bad literature and to ignore their enemy, who is only seemingly intimidating: "MARTO NEPTURA: Promethea. Think not that I do not SEE thou, little one. Neptura sees ALL! PROMETHEA/GRACE: Stupid man. It's 'thee,' not 'thou.' Hopeless without an editor! Oh, well. Let's go and make a few significant cuts in his major passages. . . . I said he was a writer, poppet. I didn't say he was a good writer. He repeats himself awfully" (*Promethea Book 1*, 158–59).

In *Promethea*'s New York, early-twentieth-century pulp imagination blends with the same century's later science fiction clichés: the metropolis is dark, dirty, filled with skyscrapers, rubbish, and big shining advertising placards—that is, some of its features are not too far from the current ones—but it is also equipped with flying taxis and other futuristic means of transport, and studded with TV screens where the "Texture" news bulletin (117) regurgitates a ceaseless flow of information. It is a dangerous, violent city, as the reader can infer from the constant presence of the police force and from the laughable Five Swell Guys, a superhero group (18) in charge of maintaining public order, and also a city troubled by a masked serial killer called The Painted Doll (148) and governed by a psychotic mayor with forty-two different personalities (117).

Such is the context in which the young student Sophie Bangs is preparing a paper about the figure of Promethea. As she tries to interview Steven Shelley's widow, she discovers Promethea is not merely a character or a fictional creation. She is indeed the purest of all fictions: she is the personification of imagination and of the ability to tell stories, and she materializes into those who are gifted with enough energy and sensitivity to conceive her in their fantasies. Promethea thus becomes a superheroine ready to help those who are in need and to fight against the forces of evil, which lie in constant ambush against her, for they consider the force of imagination as the most formidable resource of the human mind. Book One also shows us the ancient god Thoth-Hermes as he creates the first Promethea in history out of an orphaned Egyptian child left alone in the desert. He explains: "THOTH-HERMES: Only in my world, the Immateria, can I protect you... and there you would no longer be a little girl. You'd be a story. PROMETHEA: W-would I still be alive? Would I be able to come back and visit this world? THOTH-HERMES: You would live eternally, as stories do. As for coming back, well... sometimes, if a story is very special, it can quite take people over. We'll see. Come along" (29). The Promethea of 1999 is going to be Sophie, whose name clearly hints at the long journey into knowledge she embarks on as the story unfolds.

The young protagonist turns into Promethea for the first time in order to save the Shelley widow as she is attacked by a supernatural force. As soon as she incarnates into Sophie, Promethea announces that her metamorphosis will affect the space and time of the narration: "Now that I'm back, I have all the time there is in the world. Time... and the radiant, heavenly city" (39). Now that Promethea has come, the city becomes heavenly and time becomes eternal, for she—despite her ability to take bodily form—comes from the realm of ideas (the Immateria) and transcends the tangible world. After her transformation, Sophie/Promethea enters into a long apprenticeship in order to learn how to use her power: such is the narrative pretext Moore uses to insert some notions about magic into his text and, as previously mentioned, to offer a proper treatise on the subject of magic and esotericism. Sophie/Promethea's training period takes her to the Immateria, where she learns the structure of the universe through the precepts of those who acted as a vessel for the superheroine before her, the authors and artists—Grace Brannagh and others—who created her stories in the past by projecting their fantasies onto themselves or onto their beloved ones.

As imagination transcends space and time, it cannot but go beyond the borders of panels and pages, which is an essential aspect in *Promethea*'s narrative and visual organization. The space of the Immateria is a fluid, changing, perpetually evolving entity; its time seems eternally hanging. In order to provide all of these aspects with visual substance, the authors have often devised experimental formulas. *Promethea*'s pages seldom feature regular divisions into panels, for images freely come one alongside the other and are almost always spread in a continuum that covers two full pages, as in fig. 2-11. Another relevant feature of the illustration reproduced here is that a single color prevails: in step with the setting of Yesod (which, according to the Kabbalah, coincides with the sphere

Fig. 2-11. Loose page layouts and peculiar color palettes in "Moon River." From *Promethea Book 3*, pages 30–31. © America's Best Comics.

of the moon), the nuances of blue predominate in these pages and throughout the episode.

Moore and his co-authors indeed tried to match the parts dedicated to the various spheres to the dictates of Kabbalistic iconography: for instance, when the protagonist reaches the sphere of Geburah, which is similar to Mars and connected to the concepts of strength and war, the dominant color is red (see *Promethea Book 3*, 129–54). One of the most remarkable results of this effort is the representation of the sphere of Kether, the quintessence of divinity. According to the Kabbalah, its palette is supposed to feature the use of four colors: "White, Brilliant White, White-flecked with gold, and, most unhelpful of all, Brilliance" (Campbell, "Alan Moore" 23). Here the creators let the silhouettes of Promethea and her fellow traveler Barbara gradually emerge from the clean page and remain evanescent (see fig. 2-12). The nature of divinity, which encompasses all the stages of existence, is represented through the evolution of the two figures, who appear first as simple sketches irradiating from light on top of the page, and who gradually take more definite shapes and are matched by speech balloons.

The Promethea portrait that appears on the opening page of the chapter—originally the cover of the issue—is noteworthy as well: the protagonist is drawn in a way that openly recalls the works by the well-known Art Nouveau illustrator Alphonse Maria Mucha (1860–1926). This is no random encounter: Mucha—who exerted an influence on other comics creators, such as Terry Moore, William Kaluta, and Joe Quesada—had a penchant for representation of the female figure, which he often portrayed within allegorical contexts hinting at religious or mystical experience. He also paid particular attention to the use of color and to the possibilities of reproducing the effect of light on different kinds of surfaces (see Bollom and McKinney).

Another example of the authors' experimentation is found in an episode where Sophie carries out a part of her journey in the Immateria in the company of former Promethea Bill Woolcott. When the young woman is compelled to return to New York because of an imminent attack from the forces of evil, Bill/Promethea takes her along the path that goes back to the material world (see fig. 2-13). In order to represent the characters' gradual approach to the dimension of everyday life, here Moore is helped by digital photography and graphic design specialist José Villarrubia. Characters thus turn from comics to photographs, while the dialogue between Sophie and Bill/Promethea provides the reader with explanations about the process they are going through.[7]

Fig. 2-12. Promethea and
Barbara in the sphere of Kether.
From *Promethea Book 4,*
page 109. © America's Best
Comics.

Another example in this regard is an episode from Book Three. Here Sophie/
Promethea and Barbara/Promethea are in the sphere of Hod, which is connected to the planet of Mercury and to the faculties of language, magic, and
the intellect. As they discuss the notion of infinity, the two characters enter a
spatiotemporal loop and find themselves walking on a Moebius strip, the shape
that is the symbol for infinity in mathematics (see fig. 2-14). In order to follow
the route and the words of the two Prometheas, the reader must continuously
rotate the book; in the same way, the characters' words can be repeated over and
over, even though the top left and bottom right balloons serve as links with the
previous and following pages.

Apart from all possible value judgment about the mystical and philosophical discourse that underpins the novel, these examples suffice to prove that

Fig. 2-13. Sophie and Bill Woolcott turn real in *Promethea Book 2*, page 17. © America's Best Comics.

Promethea features more than one striking aspect both on technical and structural levels, and that graphic experimentation is not an end in itself but is always connected to the meanings implied by the manipulation of the chronotope. Here Moore does not feel the need to organize his fiction on a strict circular structure; he instead opts for fluid space and time, resulting in a ceaselessly evolving, metamorphic narrative continuum.

While some Kabbalah experts imagine the spheres in the Tree of Life as a complex of elements laid out in hierarchical order, Moore actually sees their arrangement as circular: "Rather than viewing it hierarchically as a structure with a top and a bottom, I see it as a map or circuit-diagram that connects two remote points (Ultimate God and the world of Matter) by the shortest possible route. The energy can flow either way, and the structure itself has no preference. Generally, we tend to think of the moon as being above the earth and the sun being above that (or, in Qabalah, of Yesod being above Malkuth, with Tiphareth above them both), but, in actuality, there is no 'up' or 'down' in space, nor, I believe, in the structure of the Otz Chiim [the Tree of Life]" (Sim, "Correspondence Part 3" 331). This is a metamorphic, unrestrained circle whose components move freely, in full harmony, just like the characters who move within the space and time of *Promethea* in a kind of cosmic dance. Such are the words Promethea uses to take her leave from the reader in the very last page of the graphic novel: "I've enjoyed our dance. You were the perfect partner, and I'm going to miss you. But spacetime is eternal, with everything in it. And you and me are always here, always now. You and me are forever" (Moore, Williams, and Gray, *Promethea Book 5,* 192). The novel's chronotope is let free to flow and change, to expand and fold back; *Promethea* thus ultimately acquires a metafictional status, too. A text whose protagonist is a story cannot but end up becoming a reflection on the ways stories are told and language is used.

As the heroine's caduceus (which refers to Mercury, the god of communication, and which appears in Promethea's hands from her first incarnation) indicates, one of the character's main qualities is her ability to understand and have a good command of any language. For instance, Promethea manages to release the streets of New York from a wicked computerized gelatin programmed to invade the city and choke its inhabitants. She plunges into the alien matter saying, "Come, then, synthetic one... let us reason together" (*Promethea Book 3,* 126–27) and begins uttering a long string of characters, numbers, and symbols—the language of computer programming—and succeeds in convincing the synthetic gel to disintegrate.

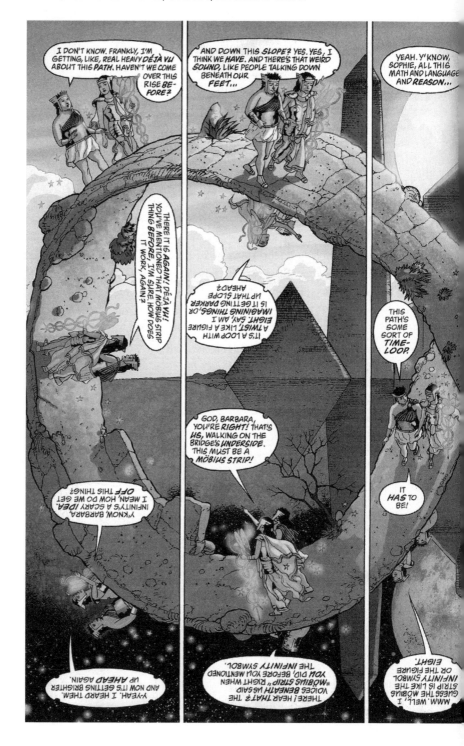

Fig. 2-14. Promethea and Barbara discuss infinity in the sphere of Hod. From *Promethea Book 3*, pages 64–65. © America's Best Comics.

However, the primary object of the novel's metafictional reflection is the language of comics themselves. Let us go back to Barbara and Sophie, who are both traveling as Prometheas in the realm of Mercury. They comment on the hieroglyphics that extensively cover the planet's stone galleries: "Sophie: We're in the Mercurial realm of language, magic and intellect. Its Hebrew name is Hod. That means splendour. Barbara: Why splendour, specifically? Sophie: Well, I suppose communication is how minds reveal themselves. Language gives a shape to the splendours of the intellect. . . . Hmm. You know all these decorations, they're Egyptian hieroglyphics and things. I guess that telling stories with pictures is the first kind of written language. Barbara: Hey, probably that's why Promethea's mostly appeared in comic books this last century. Gods used to be in tapestries, but now they're in strips" (60–61). Moore thus claims a privileged site for the rich and ancient tradition of comics, obviously not without irony, as he ascribes nearly divine qualities to the medium.

The author takes up this concept again in the last chapter of the novel, where he ambitiously summarizes the whole development of his work in a single entity: the chapter (originally issue 32 in the series) is actually one big page depicting the protagonist's face on both sides. Several smaller Prometheas are superimposed on the portrait; they directly address the reader as they go over the novel's plot and theories again. Those who read this chapter as a single issue can turn the pages as they would do with any common booklet, and then remove the staples so as to unfold it and reveal the painted plate in its entirety (also see Fischer, "Charmageddon!"). Of course this is not possible for those who read the collected book edition, therefore the plate has been reproduced as a poster and added in appendix to the book (it must be noted, though, that the smaller size of the poster does not allow the reader to fully appreciate the spread). While revising the principles enunciated throughout the novel, the character of Promethea highlights the ability of comics to involve all the faculties of human intellect: "It's also appropriate that I'm talking to you through the medium of a comic-strip story. . . . Words being the currency of our verbal 'left' brain, and images that of our pre-verbal 'right' brain, perhaps comic strip reading prompts both halves to work in unison?" (*Promethea Book 5*, 188).

If Promethea is a heroine ready to rush to the aid of humankind, then language and narration can save the world; and it is the language of comics that takes this task upon itself, for the characteristics of Promethea, an Egyptian divinity and Wonder Woman at the same time, bring prestigious innovations to a genre (superhero narrative) that has risked losing its effectiveness, as in the case of the useless Five Swell Guys, or that is often confined to sadly aping, trite models, as in the case of "Weeping Gorilla," the most famous comics series in the fictional world of *Promethea*. It is clear that "Weeping Gorilla" is quite self-referential in character, too; perhaps Moore uses the pathetic, perennially depressed and self-pitying giant ape to parody the abundant (and not always brilliant) production of comics featuring "characters in crisis" that was partially triggered by the success of his own *Watchmen*. Through the refashioning of the conventions of the comics medium and experimentation and hybridization with other languages—both verbal and visual—Moore's work becomes exactly what Promethea herself represents: a celebration of the imagination. At the end of the novel, the superheroine initiates the Apocalypse, which takes place in the biblical sense of Revelation. She is shown sitting in a room, by a fireplace; in that same moment her image is revealed to all the characters of the novel, appears in every nation of the world, and even reaches the authors of her own story, who are busy scripting and drawing that very page (see fig. 2-15).

But the actual fulfillment of the revelation takes place in the following pages, where the protagonist "meets" the reader and talks to him or her. The reader is represented as a hand stretching out toward Promethea's. It is not recognizable as male or female, and in the flickering firelight it looks first white and then black. This is a sort of universal reader indeed, thus confirming the universality of the concept of imagination as expressed throughout the text. During Promethea's address to the reader, imagination discloses its deepest essence as the creative force at the core of any human activity:

Yes, Promethea's a fiction. Nobody ever claimed otherwise. . . . I'm an idea. But I'm a real idea. I'm the idea of the human imagination... which, when you think about it, is the only thing we can really be certain isn't imaginary. No, don't say anything. Just hold my hand and listen. Your hand's warm. That's nice. It makes this all sort of girlfriendly. See, I'm imagination. I'm real, and I'm the best friend you ever had. Who do you think got you all this cool stuff? The clothes you're wearing. The room, the house, the city that you're in. . . . All invented. All made up. All the wars, the romances, the masterpieces and the machines. And there's nothing here but a funny little twist of aminoacids, playing a marvelous game of pretend. Nothing here but me and you. Me and you, little lifesnake. By the fire where we've always been since this room was a cave. Do you remember? When you first thought you saw things in the flames, in the dancing shadows... and you need me to tell you a tale. A story grand and glorious. (140–41)

Fig. 2-15. The coming of the Revelation in *Promethea Book 5*, page 131. © America's Best Comics.

Hence, imagination appears as man's best friend: as the creator of clothes, rooms, houses, cities, stories, incidents, and machines. Promethea is suggesting the same conception of imagination that Northrop Frye developed in his 1962 essay "The Imaginative and the Imaginary"—a force that can transform mankind because it can create "everything that we call culture and civilization" (Frye, *Fables* 152).[8] But the "maniac's anxiousness" (167) and the innovative language the artist uses to regenerate culture in Frye's belief correspond, in Moore's view, to the hybrid language of comics. Through *Promethea*, comics reassert not only the central power of imagination, but also their own capacity to become a means for representing contemporary culture, and to create stories "grand and glorious" (Moore, Williams, and Gray, *Promethea Book 5*, 141), the great narrative myths that recur in the literary tradition. Nonetheless, the essential condition for this process to take place is that comics themselves undergo constant formal experimentation, so as to avoid becoming a sterile inventory of repeated conventions. As *Promethea* suggests, in order to change the world, comics stories must first of all change themselves. The study of chronotopes in Moore's texts, then, seems to highlight the ability of the medium to expose its own staging and to question its own narrative assumptions. This process is not an end in itself, nor a mere postmodern pastiche. It is rather—as chapter 1 and the beginning of this chapter have already pointed out—a plurivocal discourse *à la* Bakhtin; and the representation such discourse produces is open to precise historical, social, and cultural issues. The following chapter is meant to confirm and consolidate this analysis.

CHAPTER 3

MOORE AND THE CRISIS OF ENGLISH IDENTITY

This chapter analyzes the relationship between some aspects of Moore's work and the historical and ideological dynamics that have characterized the development of the United Kingdom and its notion of identity, of "Englishness." Many of the works examined in previous chapters clearly show the way in which Moore reworks specifically American comic narrative patterns. Nevertheless, it is important to remember that his graphic novels also retain a very tight bond with distinctively English cultural, social, and aesthetic contexts, which are often exposed through parody or subtle criticism; this bond has become stronger in a few recent developments of his work. In this sense Moore's attitude is close to that of some contemporary English prose writers, an aspect that will be explored in the conclusion to this book.

A short terminological elucidation is needed, at least in order to clarify why, as we talk about Great Britain, we are going to lay emphasis on "Englishness" and not on "Britishness." These terms have been much discussed and often laid out as controversial, especially in the years after World War II, the fall of the British Empire, and its decolonization; the physical and ideological boundaries of the United Kingdom were questioned, and a reflection on what constituted and differentiated the identity of its local and "extended" citizens became urgent. On the political plane, this sometimes resulted in exaggerated nationalism, as in the cases of Enoch Powell in the late sixties (see Baucom 14–15) and Margaret Thatcher in the eighties (see 7, and the following sections in this chapter). The many faces of Englishness are still under discussion, as testified by the diverse results of several recent scholarly studies (see, for instance, Baucom, Colley,

Marzola, Pagetti and Palusci, and Rogers and McLeod). I shall not enter into the tangle of definitions and debates about the subject here, but will confine myself to providing the most useful general distinction for our purposes. Therefore, "'Englishness' . . . will be defined as a sense of cultural (rather than political) identity. 'Britishness', by contrast, will refer to the legal status, the rights and duties, of persons holding British passports. 'England', then, will be treated as a cultural, 'Britain' as a political entity" (Mergenthal 17). It is Englishness that Moore deals with, a set of cultural values connected with social class, gender, ethnicity—identity—and the way these values are embodied in the lived experience of the English. Like many writers and artists born in the fifties, he cannot be free from the need to reassess these coordinates. This chapter will show how he manages significantly to focus on the importance of Englishness, and yet to avoid spilling over into the coarse territory of nationalism. He chooses instead to embrace a critical perspective in which the crisis of English values leads to the acknowledgment of a wider, more vibrant and variegated notion of identity.

FACING IMPERIAL LEGACY

The critical vision of English imperial culture emerges significantly in the parodistic narratives of *The League of Extraordinary Gentlemen* I and II. Moore himself presented such books as essentially ludic works (see Kavanagh), and yet the *League* panels transpire the author's serious critical intention toward Victorian culture as the fullest representative of the imperial mind, its ideals of dominance and oppression, and its systematic repression of otherness. The legacy of imperial culture still lurks in dark corners of contemporary English society, Moore claims. Writer Michael Moorcock commented on the *League* by expressing the same opinion; according to him, Moore's work

inhabits the world of late Victorian and Edwardian imperialism only to examine it, confront it, subvert it and so cast a cold eye on contemporary imperialism, manifested in the deeds and actions of George W. Bush and . . . Tony Blair. Moore has produced a series which at its most popular level calls on our nostalgia for a world in which unselfconscious white men defended and expanded European and U.S. empires, putting down rebellious "natives," whether in the Middle East, India, Africa or the American homeland, giving their lives to preserve the expansionist values of the nation states they served. While he never labours

Fig. 3-1. The Gentlemen as they were sketched by Adam Hughes. Reproduced from *Comic Book Artist 25* (2003), page 36. Art © Adam Hughes. Characters © Alan Moore and Kevin O'Neill.

his metaphors and allegories, they are always present, always speaking to the concerns and sensibilities of the modern reader. (Moorcock, "Homage" 53–54)

From the visual point of view, the nature of the pages of the *League* highlights parody as the core mode of the narration. Kevin O'Neill is different from the majority of the artists Moore chose for his other works. Their styles can be more or less realistic, but are usually rather far from being purely caricatural. O'Neill's most distinguishing feature is the grotesque, hyperbolic trait, which is characterized by "an exaggerated and cartoony quality" (Khoury, *Extraordinary* 183). It is no accident, then, that O'Neill figured as the best choice and was preferred to the other *Gentlemen* candidate Adam Hughes, whose art is definitely less extreme. A comparison between the representation of Mr. Hyde grabbing Mina Murray's hand as portrayed by the two artists (see figs. 3-1 and 3-2) is peculiarly effective, in that it shows how O'Neill tends to simplify the characters' physical features and to exaggerate their proportions at the same time. Apart from his special attitude toward the grotesque, there is another reason why Moore might have chosen O'Neill: his peculiarly British visual influences, which carry "very strong traces of the often brilliant British juvenile comic book artists, like Leo Baxendale, people like Paddy Brennan, Dudley Watkins, and

Fig. 3-2. Mina and Mr. Hyde. From *The League of Extraordinary Gentlemen*, volume I, page 136 (excerpt). © Alan Moore and Kevin O'Neill.

also great British caricaturists . . . like Hogarth and Gillray" (Nevins, *Heroes* 210; for an overview also see Perry and Aldridge, and Gravett and Stanbury). With such prerequisites, O'Neill cannot but be the ideal artist to have the Gentlemen materialize on paper.

Several elements of criticism of British imperial culture appear in this work. The opening page of the first volume reports the message of the fictional editor Scotty Smiles, who presents the book as a special Christmas bumper compendium, thus immediately calling to mind the late-Victorian tradition of children's and young adult literature. In a handful of lines Mr. Smiles's words summarize the faults and contradictions of the Victorian Age: the editor greets all the children of the world and philanthropically states that a peculiar salutation is due to the poorer ones—except that they will only be able to get hold of their copy of the book in the far future, if its current readers, who are surely more respectable and "possibly Eton-educated," decide to be generous enough. He very Victorianly illustrates some "morally instructive points . . . : firstly, women are always going on and making a fuss. Secondly, the Chinese are brilliant, but evil"; and he concludes by wishing a merry Christmas to all those who are not "currently incarcerated, or Mohammedans" (Moore and O'Neill, *League I*,

Fig. 3-3. Victorian paupers and laughing Britannia in *The League of Extraordinary Gentlemen*, volume I, page 5. © Alan Moore and Kevin O'Neill.

5). This short introduction comes with an illustration that represents a street crowded with several characters, in which one can make out the caricatures of Moore and O'Neill— depicted as two paupers with drawings under their arms—but most of all a young opium smoker and a curvaceous, bespectacled Britannia who laughs heartily and holds a pint of beer in her hand, uncaring and oblivious to the destitution of the people around her (see fig. 3-3). Thus, from the very first page of the story text and image both work parodistically to expose the Victorians' willing blindness to the paradoxes of their own society.

The protagonists of both *League* graphic novels, whose identities and literary backgrounds were enumerated in chapter 1, have a significant critical function toward Victorian culture and toward the representation of that culture provided by nineteenth-century authors, even though most of the aspects Moore develops and elaborates on are already present in the works he used as sources. For example, H. G. Wells hinted at the Invisible Man's malevolent nature in his 1897 novel, thereby inspiring our author to turn Hawley Griffin into an assassin and a pervert, as shown by his raids into Mrs. Coote's correctional house (see 44–51),[1] his heinous and groundless crimes (see 118–20), his alliance with the aliens (see Moore and O'Neill, *League II*, 52–54), and his assault on Mina Murray (70–71). Allan Quatermain, "the empire's favorite son" (Moore and O'Neill, *League I*, 20), is actually an old man and an addict weakened by laudanum and opiates. Captain Nemo is equipped with a particularly clear eye when it comes to singling out the inconsistencies of the British imperial system, but often behaves like a lunatic; and he looks inhuman in his total lack of pity toward the English population, who in his eyes is just an emanation of the much-loathed empire. What he says as he converses with Mr. Hyde when London is devastated by the aliens can serve as an example: "HYDE: Huh. Goodbye South London, then. NEMO: Possibly. If we are fortunate, there are no more canisters to come. Those creatures already here can only destroy so much. As for the population, hopefully they can escape in time. If not, it is hardly a major strategic loss. They are only… HYDE: Human? NEMO: English" (Moore and O'Neill, *League II*, 95).

A positively emblematic character is Dr. Jekyll, who as the novel progresses takes on the personality of Mr. Hyde more and more often, just like in R. L. Stevenson's original work. According to Moore, Stevenson's *The Strange Case of Dr. Jekyll and Mr. Hyde* aptly represents the quintessence of the Victorian Age: "The plight of Henry Jekyll is resonant as a metaphor for the whole of a Victorian society where virtue was never lauded so loudly in public nor vice practised so excessively in private. You can almost see in that novel the exact point where the mass Victorian mind became uneasily aware of its own shadow: Hyde as Jekyll's shadow" (Sim, "Correspondence Part I" 315–16). Moore's interpretation of Stevenson's most popular character corresponds with the theories of gothic literature scholars Martin Tropp and Fred Botting, who lay stress on Jekyll/Hyde as a symbol of his age, for he emblematizes and problematizes its fundamental conflict. The Victorian will to preserve public steadiness and decency clashed with the fears brought about by a complex historical and cultural moment where new scientific discoveries and industrial progress were developing, and where the old system was starting to show its incapability of restraining phenomena such as social change or the expression of female sexuality (see Botting 135–54 and Tropp 110–32).[2] In Moore's rewriting, Mr. Hyde is as violent and savage as the wild creature conceived by Stevenson's imagination. Or perhaps he is even more terrifying: his brutality is made more visually manifest by the gigantic proportions of his apelike body and by the bare nerves and muscles that stick out of his face, whereas in Stevenson's description his character is a humpbacked, malformed small man. Nevertheless, Moore's Hyde reveals an unexpected sensitivity toward Mina (see Moore and O'Neill, *League II* 49–51), and is eventually ennobled by his sacrifice in the attempt to save the nation from the alien invasion (see 142–48). As the following discussion shows, the scary Other might actually hide (or maybe, uncoincidentally, "hyde") more positive aspects than the commonly accepted, more ordinary members of society.

To sum up, the Gentlemen effectively embody the maxim by Campion Bond—their self-styled boss and principal—that appears as an epigraph to volume I: "The British Empire has always encountered difficulty in distinguishing between its heroes and its monsters" (*League I* 6). Heroes and monsters at the same time, engaged in fighting wars at the side of the empire against any kind of otherness that may threaten it from the outside—the Chinese "yellow peril" in the first book, the horrid Martians in the second—and yet representative of that very otherness themselves, Moore and O'Neill's protagonists incarnate Victorian ambivalence and its ironic modernity. Their condition as outsiders allows them to cast an embittered, disenchanted glance on the society and culture that surround them, as when Nemo and Quatermain comment on the British people's attitude toward the Martian invasion and on the way the British government managed the Sudanese Mahdi colonial trouble in 1885: "NEMO: I must confess I admire the British people's bravery. With horror at their doorstep, they seem unconcerned. QUATERMAIN: Huh. Hardly unconcerned. More blinkered, I'd have said. Pretending everything's tickety-boo, Nemo. It's the great British pastime. . . . Holmes said Samson is a Mahdi veteran, and that we should remain optimistic, as we did then. Actually, the Mahdi revolt's a perfect example of England's complacency. We warred on a culture we didn't understand... and we were massacred" (*League II* 64).

The character who probably emerges as the most significant in both novels is that of Mina Murray. Originally Jonathan Harker's fiancée in Bram Stoker's *Dracula* (1897), Mina is less manifestly "monstrous" than her fellows but, as a woman, embodies otherness all the same. Moore declares that while he was ransacking nineteenth-century literature in order to create the *Gentlemen*, he had trouble finding a female character he could define as really "round": most Victorian literature, in his opinion, tends to limit the role of women or to reduce them to the trite image of the "angel in the house."[3] As he believed that having at least one female protagonist was crucial for the story, he was compelled to rehabilitate the figure of a Victorian woman by modifying some of her characteristics, namely by making her tougher and more independent (Kavanagh). In Moore's version, Mina married Jonathan but divorced him shortly after the wedding to become a suffragette. Her choice is despised by most of her fellow characters, who do not refrain in labeling her irritatingly "waspish tongue" as "but one of the many unattractive features of the modern suffragette" (Moore and O'Neill, *League I* 41). The reasons for her divorce from Jonathan become known only in the second volume of the saga, when Quatermain removes the red scarf Mina usually wraps herself up in, thus revealing the woman's neck and the burn-like scars that cover it (see *League II* 110–11). In Moore's rewriting, the mark left by Mina's meeting with Count Dracula was too deep for her husband to bear. Her character is definitely engaging from this point of view, and also considering the now well-established interpretation of literary representations of vampire encounters as a disclosure of the darkest sides of the characters' identities and, in particular, as a confrontation with the sexual drives that Victorian society took so much trouble to contain, at least in public.

In his 1999 study *Images of Fear*, gothic literature scholar Martin Tropp dedicates two chapters to *Dracula*. The theory he puts forward from his analysis of Stoker's text is not dissimilar from Moore's understanding of the potentialities of Mina's character: he equates Lucy with the "angel in the house" who, after being corrupted by contact with the vampire, turns into her frightening opposite, the fallen woman. Unlike her, Mina's main features are her practical sense and strong temperament, which make her a precursor of the New Woman of the twentieth century (see Tropp 133–69). Similarly, Moore and O'Neill outline Mina as the bravest and most clever character in the ranks of the Gentlemen. Mina—"the heart of our book" in O'Neill's words (Moore, *League I: Scripts* II)—is the main tool Moore uses to expose the insubstantiality of the Victorian ideals of strength and respectability, of imperial rule and especially of male authority. She is usually in charge of coordinating expeditions and of organizing her colleagues, whom she reprimands without a moment's hesitation when she realizes that their patriarchal attitude can only partially conceal their weakness: "Are you men, or little boys?" she scolds them angrily (Moore and O'Neill, *League I* 123), actually pronouncing a sentence taken straight from Stoker's text (qtd. in Tropp 164). Then she goes on; "You play your little games with your elephant guns and your submersible boats, but one raised voice and you hide like little children! . . . I'm supposed to be the person organizing this... this menagerie! But that will never do, will it? Because I'm a woman! They constantly undermine my authority, him [Nemo] and Quatermain" (Moore and O'Neill, *League I* 124). Mina is the only person capable of respecting Mr. Hyde and of obtaining his respect in return. Moreover, when she establishes her affair with Allan Quatermain, she demonstrates she has overcome the typical Victorian prudery to become a modern, independent woman, for their relationship begins and ends because of her decision, and the legendary explorer can only come into line with it (see *League II* 96–102 and 151–52). These features make Mina the exact opposite of the traitor Griffin, a.k.a. the Invisible Man, who immediately reveals his hostility toward her and who always appears as a racist and a male chauvinist, thus embodying the meanest aspects of the mindset of the late nineteenth century. The contrast between Mina and Griffin resembles the opposition between the sheer madness of Dr. William Gull and the humanity of the prostitutes of London's East End in *From Hell*.

Mina Murray and the East End women are not the only female characters Moore has created, and most of all they are not his only positive female characters. Women very often hold an important position in his graphic novels, to the extent that this issue requires a short digression. *The Ballad of Halo Jones*, for example, is entirely suffused in the feminine: the interstellar worlds where Halo travels are populated by several male characters, but most are either negative— such as the killer dog Toby and the callous, grotesque general Luiz Cannibal— or ridiculous because of their excessive self-assurance, like Mix Ninegold (see Moore and Gibson 86–87). The only figure who stands out from this pattern is planetary mogul Lux Roth Chop, who approaches Halo with modesty and politeness. Nevertheless, Lux is still a kid, so his kindness might well be bound to the fact that he has not entirely grown into an adult. Despite their undeniable human imperfections, in *Halo Jones* it is women who represent the ideals of compassion and strength of mind that the story calls for.[4] In *Skizz*, young Roxy decides to welcome the alien (see below); in *Lost Girls* sex drives reach their apex in the experience of the three women protagonists (see chapter 1 and especially chapter 4 of this book). Then, of course, *Promethea* has a female focus too, because the mystic and Kabbalistic discourse that underpins the entire work is closely connected to the femininity of its main character. As a woman, Sophie/Promethea is more naturally prone to welcome knowledge, compassion, and understanding (see Moore, Williams, and O'Neill, *Promethea Book 4* 69–79) that are key elements of the final apocalyptic revelation at the end of the story. Moore's women are the bearers of a fruitful, dynamic vision of existence, whereas the traditional male world often appears as dispersed and self-destructive, if not parodistic or ridiculous. Victorian-age women like Mina and the *From Hell* prostitutes thus appear as the ideal ancestors of many characters who turn out to be very significant in Moore's works, even when the setting is in a different epoch like the recent past of *Lost Girls*, the writer's present of *Skizz*, or the future of *The Ballad of Halo Jones* and *Promethea*. They provide his narrative with the female connotation that scholar Nicoletta Vallorani recognizes as a common denominator of much contemporary fiction, especially by English writers such as Angela Carter, Martin Amis, Fay Weldon, Iain Sinclair, and Will Self (see 30).[5] The attention Moore dedicates to the Victorian Age in significant works such as *From Hell* and *The League of Extraordinary Gentlemen* confirms his vision of that time as a pivotal moment in the development of English identity. For it is in the marginalization of otherness caused by the Anglocentric, patriarchal vision of the Victorians that the contemporary author ironically locates the proliferation of the most fruitful, vibrant aspects of Victorian culture itself. Marginal figures and outsiders, then—monsters, lunatics, and especially women—become Moore's favorite instrument to examine the past and its effects on the present time.

ALAN MOORE VS. MARGARET THATCHER

The second element that places Moore's work and aesthetics in the specific context of the reflection on Englishness is his attention to social problems that emerged during the years of the ascent and consolidation of Margaret Thatcher's power. With Thatcher as Britain's Prime Minister from 1979 to 1990, the political scene went through a process of radicalization. The fictional works in which Moore most effectively explores this issue are *V for Vendetta*, *The Ballad of Halo Jones*, *Skizz*, and his unfinished series *Big Numbers*. However, the most direct of Moore's political contributions against Thatcher is not in the form of comics; it is represented by the long poem "The Mirror of Love," released in 1988 in a self-financed booklet produced by the author together with his wife Phyllis and with their mutual partner Debbie Delano. The three had just created the independent label Mad Love Publishing, which would collapse shortly afterwards. The booklet came out with the title *AARGH! (Artists Against Rampant Government Homophobia)* and collected Moore's text, which was illustrated by Rick Veitch and Steve Bissette for the occasion (and reprinted in 2004 featuring photographs by José Villarrubia; this is the edition I use), plus contributions

Fig. 3-4. Pretense and performance in *V for Vendetta*, page 10 (excerpt). © DC Comics.

by other comic artists such as Dave McKean and Robert Crumb. The 550-line free verse poem sums up the history of homosexuality through the lives of some of its best-known representatives in the field of the arts, mentioning—among others—Sappho, Michelangelo Buonarroti, Oscar Wilde, Pyotr Tchaikovsky, Colette, Joe Orton, and David Hockney. It exposes the acts of discrimination that homosexuals had to endure over the centuries, but Moore created it as a specific protest against Section 28 (also known as Clause 28), a provision of the British Local Government Act that was approved by the British Parliament in 1986 and only repealed in 2003. Passed as a consequence of the fears raised by the discovery of AIDS (which the British popular press defined as a "gay plague," Moore, *Mirror* 72), Section 28 directed local authorities not to encourage homosexual behavior, especially in schools; it defined homosexual relations as "a pretended family relationship" (see "Clause 28" and, for an unabridged text of the clause, Moore, *Mirror* 111). Moore's words harshly condemn the choices of the British government: "Policemen claimed / To speak for God, / Describing persons / Having AIDS / As swilling in / A self-made cesspit, / While Councillor Brownhill, / A conservative, / Recalled an earlier / Final solution, / Offering to 'gas the queers.' / And Margaret Thatcher praised their forthrightness. / She let a clause / Pass into law / That her chief minister / For local government / Described as / Being aimed / At banishing / All trace / Of homosexuality: / The act itself, / All gay relationships, / Even the abstract concept / Would be gone, / A word torn / From the dictionary" (74–76).

Nineteen eighty-eight is also the year when *V for Vendetta* was published as a single volume. The ideological tension and political dissidence that take an explicit form in "The Mirror of Love" are the same elements that emerge from the dystopian fictional transposition of the graphic novel—which, by the way, Moore and Lloyd started creating in 1981, only two years after Thatcher had risen to power. The science-fiction setting of *V* describes the United Kingdom of 1997 as devastated by a nuclear war and controlled by an Orwellian totalitarian regime. The introductions by Moore and Lloyd that open the book are very outspoken in asserting the connection between the novel and the historical moment that saw its creation. According to David Lloyd, "*V for Vendetta* . . . is for people who don't switch off the News" (Moore and Lloyd 5), while Moore's statement is more structured and definitely more accusing:

Naiveté can . . . be detected in my supposition that it would take something as melodramatic as a near-miss nuclear conflict to nudge England towards fascism. . . . It's 1988 now. Margaret Thatcher is entering her third term of office and talking confidently of an unbroken Conservative leadership well into the next century. My youngest daughter is seven and the tabloid press are circulating the idea of concentration camps for persons with AIDS. The new riot police wear black visors, as do their horses, and their vans have rotating video cameras mounted on top. The government has expressed a desire to eradicate homosexuality, even as an abstract concept, and one can only speculate as to which minority will be the next legislated against. I'm thinking of taking my family out of this country soon, sometime over the next couple of years. It's cold and it's mean spirited and I don't like it here anymore. (6)

In the opening pages of the graphic novel, the characters of Evey and V get ready to go out of their homes. The panel captions report the statements of the "Voice of Fate" (9), the national radio program that broadcasts the bulletins approved by the regime (see fig. 3-4). One piece of news is about the fabulous attire worn by sixteen-year-old Queen Zara during a public event, and appears in a panel where Evey, her contemporary, is putting on the minidress she has chosen to launch her new career as a prostitute. The radio goes on in the following panel: "Britain's industrial prospects are brighter than any time since the last war" (10). We are now in V's room and see a detail of his wig and gloved hand. The juxtaposition of words and pictures highlights a common element of pretence. The two sixteen-year-olds, sadly, have dressed up for very different reasons: the Queen to display the wealth and happiness of her country, and Evey to adjust to her new role. The British government is staging a nonexistent, deceitful prosperity, and V thus prepares his disguise, because he, too, will start off a spectacular performance.

As stated above, the first chapter of *V for Vendetta* was written in 1981, also the year in which, according to historian Martin D. Pugh, "the British economy suffered its worst slump since the 1930s. During 1981 alone the gross national product diminished by 3.2 per cent and unemployment rose to 2.7 million, a level not experienced previously by any but the oldest British people. Eventually a quarter of all British manufacturing capacity was destroyed during the first depression of the Thatcher years" (Pugh 237). In Moore's novel, 1981 is the year when young Evey, who will eventually succeed V, is born. In the fictional 1997 of *V*, the eighties are remembered as a time of heavy recession, followed by a nuclear war that has obliterated Africa and continental Europe from Earth in 1988, and by the rise of the Fascist Party in 1992. As soon as it takes control of the country, the Party does away with "all the black people and the Pakistanis... White people, too. All the radicals, . . . the homosexuals" (Moore and Lloyd 27), as well as with the Jews, as confirmed by the song "This vicious cabaret" that V plays on the piano at the beginning of Book II: "There's mischiefs and malarkies / but no queers / or Yids / or darkies / within this bastard's carnival" (92–93). The Party tries to toughen nationalist fanaticism by celebrating racial and spiritual purity—the official governmental motto is "Strength through purity, purity through faith" (105)—and by creating specially dedicated TV programs, such as the aptly named science fiction soap opera *Storm Saxon*. This serial-within-the-fiction recounts the heroic deeds of a rigorously Wasp champion who defends the world of the future, especially when it comes to helpless white females, from the "black butchers" who "rape our women, . . . burn our houses, our possessions" (107). The reactionary superhero addresses his black enemies calling them "mongrel trash" (107) and "black cannibal filth" (108), and the enemies themselves are depicted as ridiculous savages who are unable to speak proper English. The few words they pronounce before the hero wipes them out are: "So! Dis am the famous Storm Saxon! ...And my oh my! Who dis pretty white lady?" (107). The insertion of this grotesque soap opera into the story allows Moore and Lloyd to detach themselves for a few panels from the apocalyptic atmosphere of *V*; moreover, they thus use the powerful weapons of parody to criticize the exaggeration of nationalism that constituted another typical feature of Thatcher's politics, and that reached its apex in the military recapture of the Falkland Islands, confirming the status of 1980s Britain as a country "profoundly and viscerally nationalist and distrustful of the outside world" (Hobsbawm 412).

The issue of homosexuality is also given special attention in *V*. It is often repeated that the victims of state persecution are, among others, "the nancy boys and the beatniks" (Moore and Lloyd 33); the actress Rita Bond is placed in a concentration camp to be subjected to genetic experimentation because she is lesbian (see 80). All of this happens in a society where power is in the hands of violent, reactionary individuals who, uncoincidentally, are unable to communicate with women. They eventually turn out to be impotent, like party official Derek Almond, who rejects his wife's emotional and sexual demands because he would rather spend his time polishing his gun (see 65–66), thus raising rather obvious psychoanalytic implications (also see Mills, "V for Verbal Violence"). Or like the crazy Leader, who falls in love with the governmental computer Fate (see Moore and Lloyd 184). Before Evey officiates at V's funeral, she is tempted to take his mask off for a second. The two-page sequence (see fig. 3-5) is made very intense by the peculiar breakdown of the panels. As Evey approaches V's dead body, she tries to imagine what she might find under his mask. The panels containing the captions with the girl's voiceover alternate with silent ones, which show what V's face could look like if it were revealed: it might be black, or it might be white. It might belong to an old man, or it could be the face of Evey's long-lost father. In a nutshell, V's face might belong to any of the people the dystopian system has marginalized. In the last silent panel of the sequence, Evey imagines that the mask might disclose her own face as it looked when V first rescued her from the police. But in the next image we see that she is still standing far from the hero's corpse: "... and at last I know. I know who V must be" (250). Evey has understood that there is no need to unmask V. Instead, she is now going to *become* V, and as his spiritual heir she will perpetuate his role as a rebel and an avenger. Once again, it is a woman who takes control of the situation; Evey makes it clear for the reader that V must remain an idea, an emblem of otherness that becomes victorious when it defies those who try to annihilate it, because "ideas are bulletproof" (236).

The aspect of the Thatcher years that Moore most vigorously emphasizes in *Halo Jones* and even more prominently in *Skizz* is the issue of unemployment and of young people's social discomfort in the British urban environments of the time. As noted in chapter 2, Halo is a jobless eighteen-year-old who lives

Fig. 3-5. Evey muses about V's identity. From *V for Vendetta*, pages 249–50. © DC Comics.

Fig. 3-6. Interpreter Zhcchz is on his way to Birmingham. From *Skizz*, page 12 (excerpt). © Rebellion.

in a degraded future society populated by punks and misfits, which in fact resembles the vision of the future of England offered by Derek Jarman in his 1977 film *Jubilee*, thus confirming Moore's penchant for erudite quotation while also paying tribute to another great homosexual artist. The society of *Halo Jones* proves unable to provide for its members: the young woman ends up roaming the galaxies, because the lack of a steady job compels her to move constantly. Unemployment is also among the central motifs of *Skizz*, which Moore published in 1983 in collaboration with artist Jim Baikie. In this work, the jobs issue powerfully stands out thanks to the setting: the story takes place in the industrial city of Birmingham in the 1980s. An alien from a faraway planet lands in the outskirts of town after an accident with his spaceship. Before managing to leave the Earth, he makes friends with a young student called Roxy despite the merciless persecutions of the British intelligence. The plot of the graphic novel develops a motif well known in science-fiction narrative, and besides, *Skizz* was serialized shortly after Steven Spielberg's film *E.T.* was released. Its most striking elements, then, reside in the abundance of references to English culture. As Brent Keane stated in an article on *NinthArt*, "*Skizz* is very much a product of its time and place: the early days of England under Thatcher. A time of high unemployment, of miners' strikes and white riots, of another music in a different kitchen—the dying strains of punk, dub and reggae infecting the mainstream. . . . Far from being jarring, though, the cultural details serve to anchor the story, rather than to pull focus from it" (Keane "*Skizz*"). Moore is right when he ironically defines his comic book as "an ultra-realistic saga" (Moore, "Skizz" 5) in his introduction to the collected edition. The science fiction story,

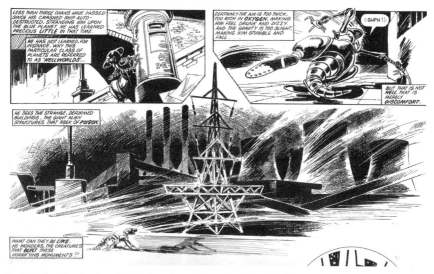

Fig. 3-7. The little alien is terrified by the ugliness of Britain's industrial landscape. From *Skizz*, page 13 (excerpt). © Rebellion.

in fact, tells a lot about the very earthly context it encroaches upon, and realism is the key on which Moore and Baikie tune the narrative and graphic structure of the text: in spite of the fantastic elements of the plot and of the digressions that show us the alien's dreams and memories, *Skizz* is above all the picture of a metropolitan microcosm caught in a precise historical moment.

The first impact of Tau-Cetian interpreter Zhcchz (later renamed 'Skizz' by young Roxy, who cannot otherwise pronounce his name) with planet Earth is traumatic. After he has survived the accident, the alien ends up on a motorway junction toward Birmingham (see fig. 3-6) and then reaches the industrial suburbs of the metropolis, which loom on him in all their incomprehensible monstrosity (see fig. 3-7). The third-person captions describe the mood and sensations of the bewildered creature: "He is interpreter Zhcchz of the Tau-Ceti Imperium and he is terrified. . . . He has not learned, for instance, why this particular class of planets are referred to as 'Hellworlds'... He sees the strange, deformed buildings, the giant alien structures that reek of poison. What can they be like, he wonders, the creatures that built these horrifying monuments?" (Moore and Baikie 13).

The representation of Skizz's first encounter with the human species is endowed with a good amount of irony, and again aptly epitomizes the anxieties of young people in the 1980s. The alien runs into two rioting gangs of punks

Fig. 3-8. The incommunicability between Skizz and some British youngsters. From *Skizz*, page 15 (excerpt). © Rebellion.

and skinheads. He feels dismayed by the apelike appearance of the inhabitants of the new planet and, incapable of understanding their ignorance and brutish behavior, he starts wondering whether humans might be seriously ill or maybe just busy in performing some unknown ritual dance. Disgusted by the violence he is compelled to witness, Skizz then moans in horror and attracts the attention of the drunken youngsters, who start to chase him and thus put him to flight (see 15). The wall of incommunicability that separates Skizz from the gruesome English youth is highlighted by Moore and Baikie's use of visuals instead of common language: the small alien's frightened scream is perceived as a prolonged "ü" sound, whereas the clamor of the angry human voices fills the balloons with a series of strange symbols that neither Skizz nor the reader can understand (see fig. 3-8).

However, the most significant signal of the social unease that affects many of the characters of the novel is the apathetic, estranged attitude of Cornelius Cardew, a thirty-seven-year-old plumber who has "not been a working bloke for eight months. Eight months!" (53) and who lost both his job and his unemployment benefit because of the government's industrial politics: "They took his job. Then they took his supplementary benefit. After that, they just took the mickey. They hadn't left him very much at all" (89). Unemployment made an outcast of Cornelius, and this characteristic enables him to feel a peculiar empathy toward Skizz. When he meets the alien, he immediately recognizes him as someone who, like him, is marginalized by society: "'Ello. You're from outer space. I wish I was from outer space. Sometimes I feel like I'm from outer space. Any jobs going out there? I'm a pipefitter. Do they have pipefitters in outer space?" (59). The only person Cornelius associates with is his friend Loz, who uselessly calls at the jobcenter with him every day and who accompanies him to the local pub and pool hall, where they meet other unemployed people together with students and vagabonds. The attention Moore dedicates to these characters is surely reminiscent of the disillusioned and yet sympathetic and somehow affectionate portrait of the British working class that emerges from films such as Mike Leigh's *Life Is Sweet* (1990) or Ken Loach's *Raining Stones* (1993) and *My Name Is Joe* (1998). It will be the unemployed, the students, and the "dossers" (47) that, together with Cornelius, Loz and Roxy, will fight to free Skizz, whom they acknowledge as an emblem for their own social and cultural otherness.

The social and economic crisis of the Thatcher years also comes forward in *Big Numbers*, an unfinished graphic novel of which only the first two installments were published in 1990. The reasons for the incomplete state of the work have been quickly mentioned above and will now be explained more in detail. Mad Love Publishing entered a moment of serious crisis after the release of *AARGH!*: its proceeds were given almost entirely to associations for the defense of homosexual rights, and the money left over was not enough to support such an ambitious project as *Big Numbers*. Its first two issues sold well (65,000 copies for the first issue, and 40,000 for the second, according to data reported by Khoury, *Extraordinary* 151); nevertheless, Bill Sienkiewicz's excellent artwork took a long time, and the episodes were published on high-quality paper in an unusual square format; production costs were high. The deterioration of the relationship between Moore, his wife Phyllis, and Debbie Delano only made things worse. The enterprise was abandoned, even though it had been projected in its entirety; had it been finished, it would have amounted to twelve episodes, or chapters, for a total of about 500 pages. Rumor has it that *Big Numbers* had been optioned to become a television serial, but there has been no trace of it so far, and Moore has already declared he has no intention of resuming the project for a book (see De Abaitua).

However, let us focus on what makes *Big Numbers* such an interesting chapter in the long story of our author's artistic creation, in spite of its incompleteness. The author started working on it after the great achievement of *Watchmen*, because he started to feel the need to break with his past success and to experiment with a different kind of narrative. As a consequence, *Big Numbers* does not follow the pattern of any genre or kind of formula fiction: "It had no genre; it was about shopping and mathematics. Not a big section down at anybody's local bookshop" (Khoury, *Extraordinary* 151). The unfinished novel depicts the microcosm of an English small town—the imaginary Hampton, a rather transparent figuration of the author's own Northampton[6]—through chiefly realistic narrative modalities. The results are remarkable, also thanks to the artwork by

Bill Sienkiewicz, whose peculiar style combines photographic objectivism with a strongly pictorial quality (see fig. 3-9).

Big Numbers represents and examines the impact of the first symptoms of globalization and of the socioeconomic changes of the 1980s on a circumscribed community that fears them and perceives them as the harbingers of a time of confusion and insecurity: hence Moore's particular attention to numbers, and his intention to use the mathematical theory of chaos to organize some parts of the narration. Even though the work has not been completed, these elements are rather easily identifiable in the two existing episodes, especially in the light of Moore's own indications:

> I wanted a world where there wasn't that simplicity of vision. I wanted to explore a world that was much more complex to the point of being chaotic, which is exactly where I got the central idea for *Big Numbers*, which was the then relatively new concept of fractal mathematics and what was chaos maths. And I wanted to see if in this relatively new mathematical idea, there were possibilities for new ways to see the world. . . . This was certainly the case in the late '80s when I was starting to work on *Big Numbers*. The world was growing increasingly chaotic. Of course then we didn't know how much further it had to slip into chaos. But really the signs were certainly very evident. It struck me that it might actually be helpful to people if we kind of explain that the chaos they could see around them . . . was purely a matter of perception. . . . Chaos maps offer us new ways in which to understand the world and . . . those ways were perhaps more useful, more optimistic, less doomed. (Khoury, *Extraordinary* 149–50)

One of the core narrative elements of this would-be graphic novel, as they are anticipated in the first two issues, is the creation of a massive shopping mall that an American company is planning to build in Hampton, the heart of a now declining "nation of shopkeepers" (Moore and Sienkiewicz, *Big Numbers #1* 21). The mall is bound to spark off the mechanism that will cause the small world of the community to be swallowed by chaos: "Completion of the mall would completely wreck things and disfigure the community that had previously been there—completely alter it forever. As an example, the chaos that we were talking about—that things change, economics change, history changes—the shopping mall that's built—the community that had been there for hundreds of years suddenly starts to fall apart under new and unfamiliar strains. New alliances are formed; some people are ground under by the experience, some people emerge renewed" (Khoury, *Extraordinary* 153). However, the threat to the life

Fig. 3-9. A sample of Bill Sienkiewicz's unique style. From *Big Numbers #1*, page 26 (excerpt). © Alan Moore and Bill Sienkiewicz. All Rights Reserved.

of Hampton's community comes not only from commercial globalization. The social changes under way also involve jobs and the welfare state. For instance, Moore exposes the cuts in expenditures for the National Health Service that occurred when the Thatcher government decided first to reduce the number of hospital beds, and then to shut down many of the hospitals themselves, thus depriving many patients of the assistance they needed, and of course also eliminating many jobs (also see Pugh 238–39). This happens, for instance, to Mrs. Gathercole, the mother of Christine (one of the main characters) and her sister Janice. The situation is effectively summed up by this dialogue between two former mental hospital patients, an acquaintance they meet on the bus, and Mrs. Gathercole herself, whose strong dialectal accent betrays her working-class background.

MR. KILLINGBACK: I'm not really a smoker, I just come upstairs for the view. Shan't be coming this way much more, though, with 'em shuttin' down occupational therapy. It's our last day, isn't it, Mr. World? Going back into the care of the old community.

MR. WORLD: That's right. Excuse me, is this seat taken? I'm Mr. World. It's my last day.

Fig. 3-10. The conversation between figurines in *Big Numbers #2*, page 30 (excerpt). © Alan Moore and Bill Sienkiewicz. All Rights Reserved.

HILARY: Sit where you like. I'm not prejudiced.

MRS. GATHERCOLE: Hilary? Hilary Glasscock! . . .

HILARY: Oh, that's right. Janice's mum. . . . Janice alright, is she? . . . Still at the D.H.S.S., is she?

MRS. GATHERCOLE: Yiss. So shall I be soon: lost me canteen job at Jude's. These two are from Jude's. Goin' into community care, ent yer? Not that they do, mind.

HILARY: Do what?

MRS. GATHERCOLE: Care. The community couldn't give a bugger, most of 'em. (Moore and Sienkiewicz, *Big Numbers #1* 23)

Mr. World and Mr. Killingback appear again at the D.H.S.S. (Department of Health and Social Security) counter where young Janice works (see Moore and Sienkiewicz, *Big Numbers #2* 12–13), to collect their welfare services forms. These two characters, both suffering from mental trouble and in need of medical assistance, will be left to their own devices until their files are processed. The problems that came from the cuts in state benefits and pensions also become apparent in the words of the unemployed youngster Kevin Sorry (see 11) and in Christine's father's miserable living conditions (see 8–10). In short, the portrait of England in the 1980s that *Big Numbers* presents is that of a nation in the grip of estrangement, recession, and identity crisis. The utopia of the efficiency and prosperity of the former heart of the empire can only find a niche in the imagination of an Indian immigrant that manages a small shop: among the altercations with his wife and the running of his little store, he sets aside some time to pursue his hobby, building a plastic model of a miniature city equipped with little houses and figurines. The Indian shopkeeper places two spruce white Englishmen beside the railway track at the station and has them perform an unlikely dialogue (see fig. 3-10):

MR. BROWN: Hello, Mr. Green.

MR. GREEN: Hello, Mr. Brown. I did not see you arrive. Is your business doing well?

MR. BROWN: Oh, yes! That is what I like about England. If a man works hard he can get ahead.

MR. GREEN: Yes, that is what I like too. Thank goodness we have a strong government. Is this your train?

MR. BROWN: No, I will catch the next one. This one is leaving now. See: there it goes.

MR. GREEN: Yes. British Rail is very good, now there are no more strikes. I am sure our train will arrive soon.

MR. BROWN: Oh yes, Mr. Green. Our train will arrive soon. I am sure of it. (Moore and Sienkiewicz, *Big Numbers #2* 30)

The two puppets converse in such simplified, unproblematic English that they sound downright unnatural—also considering that their exchange is staged by the Indian shopkeeper who, on other occasions, only speaks his mother tongue—thus revealing Moore's mordant intention: the Thatcherist society in which the protagonists of *Big Numbers* live gives them very few opportunities to achieve their ambitions. Even though they might not be entirely conscious of it, they are stuck waiting for a train that probably will not appear soon.

THE SENSE OF (AN ENGLISH) PLACE

The wealth of references in *Big Numbers* to the socioeconomic context of its time must not let us disregard the other important feature of this work: its

Fig. 3-11. Mr. Slow's history lesson in *Big Numbers #1*, page 28 (excerpt). © Alan Moore and Bill Sienkiewicz. All Rights Reserved.

geographical specificity. *Big Numbers* is the site of the first manifestation of the quasi-archaeological investigation of English spaces that has frequently appeared in Moore's work, especially from the nineties onwards. In the first issue of the unfinished graphic novel, history teacher Mr. Slow helps his students become aware of their need to feel they belong to a place by showing them maps and photographs. The professor's speech is long and dense; Mr. Slow's balloons are spread across two pages, thanks to Bill Sienkiewicz's free arrangement of elements in grids that actually break big, single images into smaller fragments (see fig. 3-11).

It is clear that the author's own voice is concealed behind Mr. Slow's. Through the teacher's two-page lesson, Moore provides his readers with a declaration of intent and with a key to interpretation of the story:

> Okay. So there it is. It's Hamptonshire. It's where we live, right? The place we're dealing with this term... that some of us will be dealing with all our lives. Where was Mary Tudor beheaded and Richard III born? Here. Where was Beckett persecuted and Boadicea reputedly buried? Here. Where was it produced gunpowder plotters and George Washington's great-great grandfather? Here. Hamptonshire. Where were the civil war and the War of the Roses decided?

Where were England's last witches burned? Here. Who was it took their country's greatest poet and stuck him in a madhouse? It was us. Two world wars full of young men with their boots on, and who got rich making those boots? We did. It's important to have a sense of where we're living... of when we're living... of time's passing... I mean, that's the important thing, isn't it? To understand our context; the community surrounding us? If we don't... I say, if we don't pay any attention to the place where we are, well... then we might as well not be here. (Moore and Sienkiewicz, *Big Numbers #1* 28–29)

The essential recognition of the context where the characters—and the readers—live, the importance of which is so openly expressed by the fictional history teacher, heralds Moore's formulation of the concept of psychogeography, which he borrows from the British author who has used it most extensively—his friend and collaborator Iain Sinclair, whose writing will also be considered in the conclusion. The practice of psychogeographical writing is a process that consists of putting down on the page the results of a series of journeys and researches that are physically carried out in a selected location—not by randomly walking as in the well-established tradition of *flânerie*, but "walking with a thesis" (Sinclair, *Lights* 75) in order to look for historical, anthropological, cultural impressions and memories, and to let them come to the surface (also see Dameson and Vallorani 14–49). Psychogeography becomes "a means of divining the meaning of the streets in which we live and pass our lives, and thus our own meaning, as inhabitants of those streets" (Babcock). The geographical experience—be it urban or not—becomes a palimpsest where a fictional map, both subjective and universal, is traced for the reader to confront and to recognize his/her own cultural references and identity. This leads to the awareness of the necessarily fictional nature of the human perception of the world: man constantly interprets history, geography, and culture in order to steer his knowledge of what surrounds him.

The geographical significance of fiction as expressed by Moore reaches its apogee in the final chapter of his novel *Voice of the Fire* (1996), where historical narrative is equated with the map of a fictional territory to move on: "This was always the intention, this erasing of a line dividing the incontrovertible from the invented. History, unendingly revised and reinterpreted, is seen upon examination as merely a different class of fiction; becomes hazardous if viewed as having any innate truth beyond this. Still, it is a fiction that we must inhabit. Lacking any territory that is not subjective, we can only live upon the map"

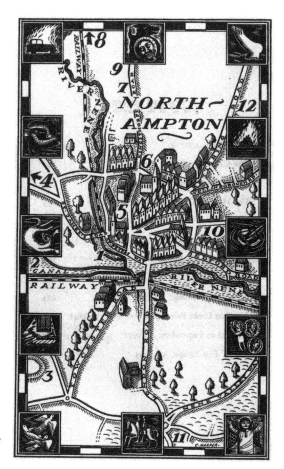

Fig. 3-12. Cliff Harper's map of Northampton in *Voice of the Fire*, page 8. © Alan Moore.

(Moore, *Voice* 310). *Voice of the Fire*, Moore's only prose novel so far, develops and examines the issues raised by *Big Numbers* more in depth and deserves to be considered even if it is not in comic-book form, because its motifs are relevant to Moore's production in its entirety. In the twelve chapters of the novel, the author gives voice to as many characters who lived within a ten-mile radius from Northampton between 4000 BC and AD 1995, sometimes elaborating on figures whose existence has been historically documented, such as Sir Francis Tresham, the poet John Clare, or the alleged serial killer Alfie Rouse, each of whom is devoted a chapter. Although the protagonists all live in different epochs, the narration acts as an intermediary for them to become connected; the primary element in that connection is the city of Northampton, its buildings, and its territory. Even though the book is wholly in prose, it opens with an illustration, a stylized map of Northampton and of the surrounding area equipped with numbers that indicate the locations of the events described in the novel and framed by twelve images (see fig. 3-12). Each chapter of the novel corresponds to one of these images, which is reproduced on its first page.[7]

One of the most successful representations of the link between place and storytelling that constitutes the core narrative motif of the novel can be found in the second chapter, "The Cremation Fields—2500 BC." Olun, a shaman whose body is entirely covered in tattoos,[8] experiences a state of total symbiosis with the place in which he lives. The problems of the village and of its inhabitants become wounds and scars that plague his body:

> "This willage is too much a part of me. Its sicknesses are mine. If there are beetles in the grain down at the southfields, then it gnaws my vitals here." His hand, a brittle crab, moves low across his belly. "And if the old rounds up on Beasthill, fall to ruin and neglect, then in my back the bones grow weak as yellow stone and crumble where one scrapes upon the other." Now he lifts his fingers, gestures to the useless clotted eye, like curdled milk. "This happens when the dye-well in the meadows west of here runs dry. Or else a tunnel in the under-willage floods, a cave subsides and leaves me pissing blood from one moon to the next. They burned the trees from off the great east ridge to level it atop, and now my will no longer stands. The hairs fall out and make it like a babe's." (73–74)

At the end of the chapter, the reader realizes that Olun's tattoos, which he calls "crow designs" (86) and which initially seem impossible to decode, are actually nothing but a bird's eye view of the village, and the reason why he identifies with it in such radical manner. The shaman—guardian of knowledge and of his people's traditions—*is* the village, because he carries its map written on his body: "That is the means by which the old man knows each track and by-way. There's the reason Olun feels the willage is too much a part of him: the all of it is etched upon his hide" (119). Olun's character is strongly connected to Moore's narrative voice. The writer appears as the shaman of modern times, for he masters the practice of writing and is thus enabled to channel knowledge and ideas, to evoke entire worlds through the magical process of combining words to create fiction. Moore has explained his beliefs about the connection between shamanism, magic, and literature in several interviews. He referred to Aleister Crowley by describing magic as an essentially linguistic phenomenon (see Campbell, "Alan Moore" 4) and declared: "I am primarily a writer. That is what I'm best at. I love to manipulate words, and to manipulate consciousness by manipulating language" (Khoury, *Extraordinary* 195). Shamanic and literary practices overlap; the writer is capable of evoking the voices of the past as they emanate from places.

In the last chapter of the novel, the narrator manifests his presence with postmodern awareness and materializes in the fabric of narration: "The final act: no more impersonations. No sleight-of-voice or period costume. The abandoned wigs and furs and frocks are swept away. Discarded masks and death-husk faces are returned to Property and hanging on their pegs. . . . Pull back now from the screen, the text, the cursor and its mesmerizing trancebeat pulse. Become aware of sore eyes, overflowing desk. . . . The author types the words 'the author types the words'" (Moore, *Voice* 292–93). Here Moore's own voice claims to be speaking, listing the characters he has mentioned throughout the narrative, quoting the books he has referred to while writing his manuscript, declaring he has stepped into the novel. The text opens out to a metafictional reflection on the nature of narrative and thus is far from any assertion of realism. Even though the protagonist of the chapter is Moore himself, he becomes a part of the set of fictions and impersonations that constitute the very essence of the art of telling stories; he abandons his material identity as the author of the book and turns into a character. Moreover, the author chooses never to use the words *I*, *me*, or *mine* in this part of the novel with the precise intention of erasing his own presence and universalizing his narrative persona, in order to help the reader start his/her own psychogeographical experience: "If you remove the letter 'I' it becomes a universal I. Everybody is the author walking down those streets while they are in the prose" (De Abaitua). The shaman-writer moves along the streets of the city, going over its collective history and placing it side by side with his own memories, because if Northampton as a place has triggered the mechanism of narration, then "that tends to place the burden of responsibility for finishing the novel on the town itself. If all its themes, motifs and speculations are to be resolved, then they will be resolved in actual brick and flesh" (Moore, *Voice* 296). Brick and flesh, then: in both the case of Olun the shaman and that of Moore the contemporary writer, space is a body covered in signs that must be interpreted. The same process occurs in the space of the city of London, where Gull and Netley perform their hallucinatory journey, another psychogeographical expedition that ends with self-reflexive considerations about the impossibility of separating alleged historical truth from fiction (see Moore and Campbell, *From Hell* Appendix II 1–24).

Moore goes on to enumerate the glories and illustrious inhabitants of Northampton, and then to explain the development of the town from a small, lively working-class center to the current state of poverty and degradation, marked by the decline of its traditional shoe production and of the trading businesses that disappeared to be replaced by "Barclaycard and Carlsberg, perfect icons of the Thatcher years reflecting our new export lines: the lager lout, the credit card casualty" (Moore, *Voice* 301–2). He then recalls his own family story through the figures of his grandmother, brother, daughters, relatives, and acquaintances. The identity of the narrator is constructed through the connection of events and people whose lives are inextricably woven into the fabric of the town. Past and present Northampton, already described as a body made of brick and flesh, now melts with the storyteller's own body and becomes a part of it; or, vice versa, the storyteller becomes an integrant part of the town, once again recalling Olun's symbiosis between man and place: "Town as a hereditary virus. Cancelled streets and ancient courtyards have become implicit in the blood" (306).

Besides highlighting Moore's attention to geographical specificity—a topic that emerges, as we have seen, in other comics and also in the performances that are briefly dealt with later in this book—*Voice of the Fire* has the merit of creating a connection with the work of an extremely significant figure in English culture, Raymond Williams (1921–1988). Both academic and well-known popular commentator (see Eagleton), Williams is the author of several works of criticism in cultural historiography, social studies, and media studies. In addition, he wrote a few novels; one of them—left unfinished and published shortly after his death—*People of the Black Mountains* (vol. I 1989, vol. II 1990), has many aspects in common with *Voice of the Fire*. First of all, place and body are associated. The introducing paragraph of the novel is told by an omniscient narrator who directly addresses the reader and invites him/her to equate the territory of the Welsh Black Mountains, where the story is set, with a part of the human body:

See this layered sandstone in the short mountain grass. Place your right hand on it, palm downward. See where the summer sun rises and where it stands at noon. Direct your index finger midway between them. Spread your fingers, not widely. You now hold this place in your hand. . . . This is the hand of the Black Mountains, the shape first learned. . . . Press your fingers close on this lichened sandstone. With this stone and this grass, with this red earth, this place was received and made and remade. Its generations are distinct but all suddenly present. (Williams, *People* I 1–2)

After this introducing section, the novel follows a young man, Glyn, as he marches on the moors in search of Elis, his grandfather and a great connoisseur of the region, who has not yet come back from a walk. Glyn paces along the path and starts to hear strange voices that seem to rise from the land: each voice tells him the story of someone who used to live in the region in the past. First is the story of "Marod, Gan and the Horse Hunt" (13–28), set in the year 23000 BC, in the Stone Age; the last, in volume II, takes place in AD 1415, but a postscript added by Williams's widow Joy in 1990 informs us that the author's original plan included getting as far as the twentieth century, telling the story of Elis's great-grandmother and then of Elis's youth (see *People* II 322). All of the tales are fictitious, but Williams often drew inspiration from historical facts, archaeological findings of the area or, in the case of the most recent stories, from his own personal memories. The scanty notes he left about the conclusion of the project speak of "'the connection of memory through remembered generations,' and also of 'memory across a place.' Another note just says 'Learning'" (323). What is more, Williams makes clear at the end of the first volume that "His [Glyn's] search for Elis on the high moors was part of a quest for himself, for a history and a landscape that had shaped his being. His search must go on and he knew now that this long history, too, would continue to unfold . . . told through the long-vanished voices of the people of the Black Mountains" (*People* I 358).

Moore's novel clearly shares both its topic and its narrative structure with *People of the Black Mountains*. Although Moore does not overtly mention drawing inspiration from it for his book, he may easily know and appreciate Williams's work. In many of his essays (such as *Culture and Society*, 1958; *The Country and the City*, 1973; or *Culture*, 1981) Williams, a Gramscian and a Marxist thinker, highlighted the importance of lived experience as a basis for cultural analysis and came to consider all cultural forms and media not as the mere result of aesthetic experience, but as a complex process that involves society, ideology, and the individual awareness of class and gender. Viewed from this perspective, *Voice of the Fire* appears an indirect tribute to an intellectual who, from the fifties onwards, acutely anticipated the outlook Moore would take up in the course of his career as an artist. Williams's interest in seeing the dynamics of society as a composite intertwining of public and private, of global and local identities, anticipates the analysis of Englishness—and of its crisis—carried out by Moore in the development of his work.

In their focus on the individual experience of place as a means to reach more universalizing perspectives on society as a whole, another element the two authors share is that both manage to avoid slipping into boorish nationalism disguised as regionalism or localism. Regional consciousness has always been a part of the English identity and has been consolidated from the beginning of the eighteenth century, with the coming of the Industrial Revolution and the first fears of what we now call globalization. The highest risk regionalism implies when it is made explicit, as R. D. Draper correctly observes in *The Literature of Region and Nation*, is the overflow into dogmatisms or into inappropriate tendencies toward Celtic revival. But the best regional literature does not embrace ideological extremism, because its localism is no end in itself, but a stimulus to remain "open to indeterminacy, variety, vision and revision" (8). In this view, Moore's geographical specificity and emphasis on sense of place becomes a means to enrich his perspective on Englishness. The author surely retains a strong consciousness of his identity as an Englishman—an identity that is urban, local, regional, and national—but in the very process of exposing its crisis and looking for its weak spots, he manages to unearth its most vital forces. Moore's concern about place and identity, together with his study of shamanism, the Kabbalah, and the occult practices that saw their outcome in comics in the creation of *Promethea*, also led him to conceive performances he staged between 1995 and 2003. These performances will not be dealt with in detail here, but as they are relevant to some recent developments in Moore's aesthetics they will briefly be considered in the conclusion. However, we need to dwell for a while on the latest evolution in Moore's output, the publishing of *Lost Girls*. While not concentrating on an English location, this graphic novel is focused on the issue of identity (especially in terms of gender and sex), its crisis, and the possibility of reversal and self-empowerment. The flaws and accomplishments of Moore's latest ambitious and provocative enterprise are investigated in the next chapter.

CHAPTER 4

FINDING A WAY INTO
LOST GIRLS

THE CONTROVERSIES OF PORN

This chapter is devoted to examining how the three key aspects that were developed over the previous pages—structure and intertextuality, the chronotope, and the issue of identity—are addressed in *Lost Girls*. As mentioned above, this graphic novel was published in summer 2006 after a long period of gestation. Moore and Gebbie started outlining the idea shortly after they met in the late eighties, and the first six chapters of the comic book were serialized in *Taboo* magazine (issue 5 through issue 7); reprinted by Tundra publishing; and later collected in two booklets printed by Kitchen Sink Press (see Shindler). But the book was financially demanding, publishing house support not steadfast, and creating such an ambitious and problematic work taking so massive an amount of the authors' time that they decided to wait and publish it as a single product once it had been completed. Moore's readers, then, had to wait until 2006 to see the release of the three-book-slipcase published by Chris Staros's Top Shelf Comix.

As briefly noted in the preceding chapters, the *Lost Girls* are three women who meet in a luxury hotel in Austria in 1914. The First World War is at the gates, but in the time they spend together before violence explodes, they share each other's stories of sexual awakening, thus recollecting their childhood selves. Their stories actually reinterpret in a pornographic vein the works the characters are extrapolated from: Carroll's *Alice's Adventures in Wonderland* and *Through the Looking Glass*, Barrie's *Peter Pan*, and L. Frank Baum's *The Wonderful Wizard of Oz* all become tales of sex, which is here imagined, practiced, and in a few instances forced. As they tell their stories, the protagonists have sex with each other and with other characters, and so do most of the people who live and work in the hotel. An orgiastic climax takes place right before everyone leaves, as the hotel is being taken over by the military. Moore and Gebbie's intent in creating *Lost Girls*, as they stated in several interviews, was to highlight how sex can be a powerful, imaginative, healing experience, and to break the cultural taboo that makes the idea of childhood as an already sexualized age unacceptable to most societies. The authors' means to this end are a reworking of pornography as a genre via aesthetic ennobling, and a praise of the imagination—any kind of imagination, obviously including sexual fantasy, no matter how extreme it may become—as a beneficial force.

The graphic novel started off selling reasonably well (see Weiland) and, at least according to online information, is currently in its third printing and still selling well, despite a few difficulties in distribution. Due to its supposedly outrageous content, the book was rejected by some U.S. stores, which refused to market it for fear of suffering legal consequences (see Johnston); after the initial controversy, most stores agreed to sell it provided the slipcase was wrapped in plastic, or to limit its sales to special orders. The European context has been more problematic. For example, the French translation of the book has been indefinitely suspended by Delcourt Publishing, and publication was banned in the U.K. by the official holder of the copyright to Barrie's *Peter Pan*, London's Great Ormond Street Hospital for Children. Moore claimed that the copyright to Barrie's book had not been infringed, for it concerned performance of the original work and not the creative refashioning of its characters (see Malvern). His complaints were indeed legitimate, for Peter Pan's figure has been endlessly rewritten and reused in art without the need to request formal permission from the copyright holder. It is clear that here, too, the controversy originated from the thorniness of the subject matter of *Lost Girls*. The diatribe continued for a while, but eventually Top Shelf managed to come to an agreement with the hospital, also considering that copyright would lapse at the end of 2007 (see Brady). The U.K. release of the book finally occurred in early 2008.

As regards critical response, it must be noted that so far it has been more negative than not. Yet, the main reason for criticism is not what one might have predicted. *Lost Girls* has inspired contrasting opinions less for its pornographic, supposedly offensive content than for its formal and narrative flaws. Of course there have been positive reviews: Neil Gaiman manifests his appreciation by describing it as "a bitter-sweet, beautiful, problematic, exhaustive, occasionally exhausting work. It succeeded for me wonderfully as a true graphic novel. . . . Whatever you call it, there has never been anything quite like this in the world before, and I find myself extraordinarily pleased that someone of Moore's ability actually has written that sort of comics for adults" ("*Lost Girls*"). Douglas Wolk from Salon.com judges the book a bit far-fetched in terms of formalism, but he does not hesitate to define it "a victory as art"; Richard Gehr from the *Village Voice* states: "*Lost Girls* is to erotic literature what Moore's now classic 1987 *Watchmen* (with Dave Gibbons) was to the superhero scene. Each busts the frames of its respective genre with formal precision; each reflects upon its own ways and means through books within the book; and, most importantly, each kicks great writing into hyperdrive with dense and resonant imagery." Finally, Michel Faber defines the novel as "a sophisticated, cunningly conceived narrative that builds with Tantric sureness towards its finale. . . . Despite its sometimes over-explicit philosophizing, [it] is ultimately a humane and seductive defence of the inviolable right to dream" (Faber). Nevertheless, in the arenas where a more exhaustive approach to the book was attempted, the debate became more heated, and opinions more severe.

Two magazines, the *Comics Journal* and the online periodical *ImageTexT*, have been particularly significant sites for the controversy. Most of the reviews that appeared in the *Journal* in issue 278 (October 2006) border on devastating critique. While admitting that the novel is the result of years of painstaking work and that it features most of the peculiar traits of Moore's style—excellent word and image interplay, intertextuality, metafiction, stories-within-the-story, political commitment, and so on—these reviews claim that there is nothing new in comparison to what we already knew about the author, or to what we might expect from him. The structure of *Lost Girls* is deemed too schematic and the content too didactic, thus resulting in "a kind of wrong turn" (Crippen 139) and in "crushing boredom" (Fischer, "The Straw Man" 137); moreover, Moore's penchant for form and meticulous narrative construction is seen here as a mania (138). Silliness is spotted in his approach to pornography, for "he is willing to be as stupid as pornography requires, to pretend that writing about sex means writing about people engaged in great chain-fucks, and to pretend that these chain-fucks don't violate laws of common sense and probability" (Crippen 140). According to Noah Berlatsky, Moore and Gebbie's emphasis on female figures as opposed to negative male characters who are ultimately involved in war "is pregnant with gynocentric political meaning" that results in a far too simplistic representation of the Eros-versus-Thanatos conflict (the power of love and sex versus the deathly violence of war), because "to suggest that the first is some sort of meaningful resistance to the second seems ridiculous" (143). Berlatsky is the only critic who attacks Gebbie's otherwise appreciated art to define it as "sometimes garish and even ugly" (141). Inflamed by these pieces of harsh criticism, *Comics Journal* contributor Michael Dean spoke in defense of the book in issue 281 and later again in issue 284 (thus reaching July 2007), as a response to a letter from fellow contributor and *Lost Girls* detractor Craig Fischer. Dean ultimately claims that for all its flaws, the novel is still valuable, because its re-elaboration of well-known children's books can challenge the canon and thus result in a necessary and productive cultural process. In his view, *Lost Girls* is a winner in this confrontation, because it embraces the canon without overlooking its own nature as a comic book: "[it] is prepared to confront the canon on the canon's terms, while remaining true to its own aesthetic roots in comics and pornography" (Dean 22).

The online debate on *ImageTexT* is surely characterized by less bitter tones, but its contributors have readily pointed out defects and imperfections as well. The discussion was published in issue 3:3 (2007) in the shape of a roundtable that involved several scholars. In his introduction, moderator Philip Sandifer (who was one of the few critics to define the book as "very good, very hot" in the review he published in the same magazine in 2006) immediately remarks that the novel is open to much criticism and that practically all the participants in the roundtable have found it unconvincing. Kenneth Kidd notes that the book will certainly accomplish academic appreciation, and that the friction between the pornographic and the highly literary can be productive; yet, he states that he feels "more bored than titillated." Charles Hatfield is even more critical: after correctly emphasizing the considerable, albeit sometimes overlooked, importance of sex in Moore's pre–*Lost Girls* work, he defines the book "exhausting," "a lofty example of meta-porn," and "a boondoggle" (Hatfield, "A Review and a Response"). Meredith Collins and Tof Eklund are fault-finding, too, even though less bellicose: Collins argues that despite somewhat naively exaggerating the healing power of sex to the extent that it seems miraculous—thus leading toward what she calls a "pandering sexual utopia"—Moore and Gebbie do a good job in modernizing the Victorian and Edwardian pornographic imagination, because the protagonists are shown as aware of the consequences of sexual intercourse (for instance, Dorothy takes precautions in order not to become pregnant when she has sex with Rolf Bauer: see Moore and Gebbie, *Lost Girls*

Book 1 ch. 2, 5–6). Eklund focuses on the theme of imagination—in this case, sexual imagination—as the core element in Moore's conception of magic, and observes that the novel is probably excessively didactic in its ritual-like structure, but that it nevertheless succeeds in creating "a magical realism of the fuck."

As one can easily understand, *Lost Girls* has indeed created some commotion. My own feelings toward it have been conflicting: I must admit that when I first read it I felt the same sense of exhaustion that both Hatfield and Kidd lament. I immediately perceived this previously unexperienced fatigue in reading Moore's work as a sign that there are indeed narrative flaws in *Lost Girls*, but perhaps, as often happens, truth lies somewhere between the extremes. I started appreciating the book more during subsequent readings, doling it out into small portions. While I would not say that this novel is an indisputable masterpiece, neither would I claim it is unacceptable or entirely useless. In an attempt to point out what does work and what does not, I will now review some of its aspects in relation with the themes examined in this book.

FORMAL ASPECTS AND INTERTEXTUALITY

Extreme emphasis on structure and formal devices has always played a considerable part in Moore's aesthetics, and *Lost Girls* is no exception; the author's customary penchant for verbal and visual intertextuality, circularity, and formal subtlety becomes manifest here, too. Of course the first citations Moore and Gebbie barrage their readers with are the ones from the source works mentioned above, which provide them with practically universal protagonists. Alice, Dorothy, and Wendy come from English-language children's tales but are widely known, and thus immediately recognizable, outside the English-speaking context. This element is significant in itself, because these characters have been the object of endless rewrites and reassessments—from intertextual references in other books to adaptations into films, TV series, videogames and so forth. Most of these refashionings are replete with allusions to the more adult and often uncanny potential hidden in each of their stories.

In particular, the character of Alice—some darker symbolic aspects of which are clearly discernible in Carroll's book—has been made the most of in order to tell tales of growth and development that feature sex, fear, and the unknown as main ingredients. A significant instance in the considerable number of works produced in this field is the outstanding *Neco z Alenky/Alice* (1988), a movie by Czech master of stop-motion Jan Svankmajer. A horror movie inspired by *American McGee's Alice* videogame is to be released soon, and rumor has it that visionary gothic director Tim Burton is in pre-production with a film version of Carroll's book as well. As regards literary rewrites, Angela Carter, who has been mentioned on the pages of this book for the aesthetic and ideological features she shares with Moore, included in her 1979 short story collection *The Bloody Chamber* a tale about a weird young girl, raised by wolves, who discovers her body and identity through her reflection in a mirror; it is no accident that the story is called "Wolf-Alice" (see Carter, *Bloody Chamber* 119–26). Last but not least, independent director Terry Gilliam's latest movie *Tideland* (2005) is a sort of lysergic mind trip where the protagonist, an abused and abandoned child named Jeliza Rose, explores a distorted wonderland populated with freaks and talking squirrels. Gilliam's young girl actually conflates the characters of Alice and Dorothy: the prairie landscape she explores is strongly reminiscent of the wide expanses of Kansas, and the madwoman embalmer she meets might well be seen as a version of Baum's Wicked Witch.

The story of Peter Pan, of course, has been rewritten too, both on the screen (including Steven Spielberg's 1991 *Hook* and Marc Foster's 2002 *Finding Neverland*) and on the page, in the latter case finding one of its freshest and most subversive reinterpretations in the recent novel *Kensington Gardens* (2006) by Latin American writer Rodrigo Fresán.

In light of these considerations, then, it must be remarked that *Lost Girls* is underpinned not only by a trio of noteworthy source works, but also by the complex stratification of subtexts and already "adult" by-meanings that arise from the massive amount of rewrites their protagonists have been subjected to, and which to great degree have become rooted in the collective imagination.

Going back to the original works, the main characters' derivation is made clear both by overt quotations and through less direct allusions. First of all, while anticipating the theme of rediscovery of the women's once lost or hidden tales of sexual initiation, the title of the book also hints at Peter Pan's follow-ers, the so-called "lost boys." Moreover, the quotes appearing on the jacket flap of each book of the trilogy—the first words the reader sees as he or she opens the volume—are taken from the source works and, of course, are recontextual-ized in their new environment. Book 1 opens with a short extract from Lewis Carroll's prelude to *Through the Looking Glass*: "We are but older children, dear, who fret to find our bedtime near." These words both evoke *Alice* and suggest that the protagonists are now adult at the same time: after reading the book, the idea of fretting to find bedtime near will resonate with new meaning as an allusion to the characters' sexual drives. The jacket flap of Book 2 derives from one of the first pages of *Peter Pan*: "Of course the Neverlands vary a good deal." In this volume the Lost Girls become acquainted and devote themselves to exploring the different lands of their memories and sexual fantasies. Book 3's epigraph is a quotation from the third source author, L. Frank Baum: "I am Oz, the great and terrible. Who are you, and why do you seek me?" This sentence is slightly more cryptic than the others and could be read in at least three ways. First, sex itself could be seen as great and terrible, for in this book it reaches its most extreme manifestations and thus results as an unstoppable, awe-inspiring force. Two further interpretations become clearer if we consider the context the sentence was extrapolated from. In Baum's book Oz pronounces these words when Dorothy and her companions finally reach him. To their dismay, they realize that the great wizard they have been expecting to meet is actually a dull little man who implores them in a trembling voice: "Don't strike me—please don't—and I'll do anything you want me to. . . . I have been making believe" (Baum 111). The great and terrible power, then, might be regarded as the force of fiction and imagination: they are able to conjure majestic visions and even scary fantasies of violence and abuse, and yet they remain safe and harmless because of their fictional nature. Such reading of the quotation sounds particularly appropriate with regard to the final part of Book 3 (see Moore and Gebbie, *Lost Girls Book 3* ch. 22, 4–7), when the hotel manager, monsieur Rougeur, gives a speech in defense of pornography (which will be examined in the final section of this chapter). However, the final and perhaps most fitting explanation identifies the "great and terrible" entity as war. At the end of the book, war storms into the sexual idyll of the Himmelgarten in all its nonsensical ferocity. The force of war is indeed scary, and yet, as the authors make clear throughout their work, it comes from mankind's meanness and narrow-mindedness. Wars produce great terror to conceal human weakness, just like a pathetic little man hides behind the mirage of Oz the Terrible—except that, unlike fiction, wars do cause harm, as the last page of *Lost Girls* unmistakably demonstrates.

In addition to the three original works and their implications, Moore and Gebbie weave an intricate fabric of other subtexts into their graphic novel. Moore describes their work as admittedly a sort of female *Decameron* (see Tantimedh, "Finding the *Lost Girls* Part 2"). The book by late-fourteenth-century Italian author Giovanni Boccaccio inaugurated the successful genre of narratives set in a single place where characters take turns telling tales, and was indeed focused on sex. It can thus be considered a proper forerunner to *Lost Girls*: not only was it used by Geoffrey Chaucer as a basis for his fifteenth-century *Canterbury Tales*, but it also provided the framework for a contemporary rewrite that the authors, as Gebbie recalls in an interview, read before starting to work on their own book. In Russian writer Julia Voznesenskaya's novel *The Women's Decameron* (1985, translated into English in 1987; see Valenti), ten Leningrad women are trapped in a hospital as war rages on the outside; they decide to kill time by telling stories about life, food, love, sex, and rape. Among further references for the book, Moore has mentioned Jean Genet's play *Le Balcon* (*The Balcony*, 1956) and Michael Moorcock's 1982 *The Brothel in Rosenstrasse* (see Tantimedh, "Finding the *Lost Girls* Part 1"). Thomas Mann's *Der Zauberberg* (*The Magic Mountain*, 1924) is certainly alluded to, at least as an inspiration for the setting of the Himmelgarten hotel and the oncoming war; moreover, the character of officer Rolf Bauer, who resides in the hotel as he convalesces from war injuries, is obviously reminiscent of the protagonist of the German novel, who spends seven years in the hotel-sanatorium on the mountain. Then, of course, the influence of many works of erotica and pornography is suggested, especially as regards Pierre Louÿs, Franz von Bayros (see Amacker, "The Virtues of Vice Part 2"), and the inevitable Marquis De Sade.

As usual, intertextuality is not limited to texts but embraces the visual plane as well, making the most of Gebbie's special ability for imitating other artists' technique. Among the most notable examples are her pastiches reproducing the unmistakable style of British Decadent illustrator Aubrey Beardsley's *Venus and Tannhäuser* (see *Lost Girls Book 1* ch. 3, 3–4), and that of German Expressionist painter Egon Schiele's watercolors (see *Lost Girls Book 2* ch. 13, 1–8). In both cases the illustrations are inserted into the narration in the form of pages from the pornographic books the hotel manager—lascivious Monsieur Rougeur—leaves at his customers' disposal, thus reviving another of Moore's most beloved tricks, that of the *mise en abyme*—the story within the story. The music of Stravinsky's *Rite of Spring* is also referred to: in the book the three women attend its first staging as a ballet in Paris, which Gebbie depicts after carefully researching the original choreography and costumes. However, the artist's most evident visual influences here are probably Art Nouveau and Impressionism, for both artistic currents rely on curved contours and on a "sort of musicality" (Vylenz, "Interview with Melinda Gebbie") that mingle well with the soft, rounded shapes that already characterize Gebbie's style. Art Nouveau, in particular, is important to the author because its lines are delicate and its patterns

Fig. 4-1. Art Nouveau patterns in *Lost Girls Book 1*, chapter 5, page 1 (excerpt). © Alan Moore and Melinda Gebbie. All Rights Reserved. Image reprinted here with permission.

often floral (see fig. 4-1), thus providing the viewer with a direct connection to the sensuousness of nature, in tune with the act of giving in to the sexual drive as the most natural of human impulses.

While working on the book Gebbie also visited Catalan modernist architect Antoni Gaudí's buildings in Barcelona, and later says that "we naturally go towards rounded and asymmetrical shapes because they are reiterative of nature's generous impulses, and the undulant way things grow" (Vylenz, "Interview with Melinda Gebbie"). Her sweet lines are complemented by the influence of Impressionist painting, which of course emerges from her peculiar use of color. In the interview with Dez Vylenz quoted above, the artist also claims she remembers telling Moore right when they started work on *Lost Girls* that she "want[ed] color to be an actual part of the storytelling device." Color is a storyteller here indeed: Gebbie's pastels are carefully applied in layers on the page and often spread in little dots *à la* Seurat, thus providing the texture of the characters' skins with consistency and participating in their carnality.[1] Moreover, Gebbie's palette changes according to the subject matter of the narrative: colors are thus colder in Lady Alice Fairchild's memories of violation; warmer when Dorothy recalls having sex in farm barns or in the hot flat stretches of land of her native Kansas; and alternate with rigid black-and-white silhouettes as Wendy evokes the days of her repressed and puritan young age. Nuances darken considerably when war is involved: when the Archduke is shot, the women wake up after a merry afternoon of storytelling and sexual entertainment on the shores of the Bodensee, feeling that something has changed. As they go back by boat, their dark, now isolated profiles stand out against a gloomily tinted sky (see fig. 4-2).

Fig. 4-2. Alice, Dorothy, and Wendy leave the island. From *Lost Girls Book 2*, chapter 20, page 8 (excerpt). © Alan Moore and Melinda Gebbie. All Rights Reserved. Image reprinted here with permission.

In the same way, the last page of the book, which portrays the horror of war by showing a soldier whose body has been slashed open, is entirely dominated by nuances of red and black (see *Lost Girls Book 3* chapter 30, 8).

Last but not least, Gebbie's pastel coloring and delicate lines are also evocative of the rich tradition of the so-called golden age of children's book illustration, which saw its most notable representatives in George Cruikshank (1792–1878), Sir John Tenniel (1820–1914), and Arthur Rackham (1867–1939) in Britain, and Maxwell Parrish (1870–1966) in the United States. The legacy of these artists, some of whom were in charge of illustrating the *Alice* and *Peter Pan* books,[2] is constantly embraced by Gebbie's drawings, which pay tribute to this tradition while ironically reutilizing it in the context of erotic narrative.

Of course, references are not limited to painting and illustration but, as happens in practically all the works examined in this study, also comprise the world of comic books, in this case pornographic and erotic comics. Moore acknowledges the influence of Howard Chaykin's *Black Kiss*, Gilbert Hernandez's *Birdland* (see Groth, "Pornographer Laureate" 121), and the work of Robert Crumb in general, where sexuality is always a central issue (see Moore, "Bog Venus"). But most of all, *Lost Girls* pays its respects to the subversive tradition of Tijuana Bibles, whose anonymous authors often toyed with well-known literary characters. Moore and Gebbie retain the eight-page format of classic Tijuana Bibles by creating eight-page chapters;[3] but far from being the size of a cigarette pack like its predecessors, the bulky slipcase of *Lost Girls* becomes one big, blatant Tijuana Bible itself and brings to light a long-hidden experience in comics culture with tongue-in-cheek barefacedness.

As usual, then, intertextuality is pervasive, and it combines with the typical regularity of Moore's narrative structures. Each volume is circular: it begins and ends in the present, while devoting its central part to the past moments when the protagonists recount each other's stories of sexual awakening. Just like sex, each volume strives to reach a climax: the frenzy accompanying the premiere of the *Rite of Spring* in Book 1; the women's sexual intercourse while Archduke Franz Ferdinand is shot in Book 2; and their last threesome after the collective orgy—and before the escape from the Himmelgarten Hotel—in Book 3. Sections dedicated to the Lost Girls' pasts are graphically differentiated: in addition to the coloring mentioned above, each woman's story features its own graphic layout. As a result, the Dorothy chapters systematically include horizontal, rectangular panels that suggest the idea of the boundless flat landscapes of Kansas; the Alice chapters are all told in oval shapes that remind the reader of a mirror, or of the pool where she used to look at her reflection as a child; finally, Wendy's story of her meetings with Peter in Kensington Gardens is told in elongated, claustrophobic vertical panels that hint at her repressed sexuality and at the shape of park railings (see Santala) or of the stained-glass windows of late Victorian houses (see Vylenz, "Interview with Melinda Gebbie"). When the protagonists' present or the events taking place in the hotel are shown, layout varies, but images usually share a common fluency and smoothness. When sex is depicted, shapes and bodies are often not contained within panel borders and tend to cross them (e.g. Moore and Gebbie, *Lost Girls Book 1* ch. 2, 5); other times there are fixed frames where characters are progressively zoomed in on, thus enhancing the voyeuristic quality of the reader's gaze (see for instance the homosexual encounter between Harold and Rolf, *Lost Girls Book 2* ch. 13, 1–7). The circularity of the whole novel is also emphasized by its first and last chapter, for in both instances the events are observed only through their reflection in

Lady Fairchild's mirror. Chapter 1 thus shows us Alice as she masturbates and later announces her departure from her home in Pretoria, South Africa, and then the voyage to the Himmelgarten; later, in Chapter 30, we see the protagonists' last lovemaking, their departure, and the arrival of the German soldiers who eventually shatter the glass to burn its wooden frame.

Word and image puns that create mischievous double entendres, in the tradition of erotica, are not missing from the book; for example, in an episode where Wendy and her husband Harold have the most tedious of conversation, their shadows mimic multiple sex positions (see fig. 4-3), thus exposing what might be the thoughts and secret desires hidden in their otherwise inhibited married life.

In another instance (*Book 2*, ch. 11) the pun is extended over an entire chapter. The only text in these pages, a letter from supercilious Harold to his boss, comments on the dullness of life in the hotel and of his own wife's company; but as we read the letter the pictures show us what is really going on within the walls of the Himmelgarten, clearly clashing with his pretense of omniscience and producing an ironic sequence of double meanings. So, while he supposes that odd Lady Fairchild seems to be obsessed with cleanliness and that she "must spend half her time in the bathroom" (*Lost Girls Book 2* ch. 11, 3) we do see Alice's legs approach the bathroom door, but Dorothy is waiting for her on the floor, stark naked and ready for sex. Then Harold praises officer Rolf Bauer's attention for clothing as we see the soldier masturbate with one of Dorothy's shoes (4). And so on: each panel comments ironically on the words in the captions. But the bawdiest sexual pun at Harold's expense occurs in Book 3 when Wendy, now a sexually liberated woman, waves him goodbye from her window. He mistakes her moans for signs of wifely despair, whereas she is actually having sex with two bellboys and Dorothy, who is equipped with a strap-on. Harold says, "If I didn't have to go I'd be right behind you, you need have no fear," and Wendy answers, "I... I think I'm sufficiently covered in that... oowh... in that department," as the triple sodomy is represented (*Lost Girls Book 3* ch. 21, 7).

All these elements considered, it is easy to see *Lost Girls* as a refined, triumphant catalog of all the skills Moore has exhibited over the development of his work. However, there is not really anything new save for the sensitive subject matter these skills are applied to, and this sort of formal fetishism (see Wolk) results in a rather stiff narrative construct, for there is such an excess of perfectly organized items that the story tends to spill over into schematism. Once it is clear that every feature of the original tales is going to be turned into sex—Dor-

Fig. 4-3. Word-and-image puns as Wendy talks to her husband in *Lost Girls Book 1*, chapter 3, page 8. © Alan Moore and Melinda Gebbie. All Rights Reserved. Image reprinted here with permission.

othy's meeting with the Straw Man becomes her having sex with a simple and not too clever guy; the Cowardly Lion is a big but meek farmhand she makes love to later; and so on—and that any action the characters take is going to lead to further sex, the plot begins to suffer from predictability and from an excess in mechanicalness. Thus I cannot agree with Richard Gehr's observation that *Lost Girls*, in its own genre, repeats the achievement of *Watchmen*: in comparison with the latter, the former tends to lack in narrative substance and to list less to the side of Bakhtinian *heteroglossia* than to the one of playful but ultimately unsatisfactory pastiche.

As briefly mentioned in chapter 1, *Lost Girls* is the first among Moore's major graphic novels where he did not write his scripts by producing massive texts for the artist to work on. He instead provided Gebbie with thumbnails with rough indications about the wording that he would expand and add later (see Vylenz). It is possible that this detachment from the author's usual writing habit led to a partial loss of control on the organicity and balance of the text, but Moore is far too expert a writer to end up having trouble just because of a change in technique. Moreover, usually hardly anything in his works is left to chance or shows not to have been carefully and deliberately made to appear the way it does. Therefore, it is more likely that the exceedingly schematic (and sometimes inevitably repetitive) quality of *Lost Girls* is absolutely intentional, that it is a premeditated risk the authors decided to run. Moore and Gebbie's intention was precisely to expose the clichés of pornographic fiction for political reasons that will be better examined in the last section of this chapter, and which basically consist in debunking the common social taboo against the enjoyment of porn. So, a pornographic work must depict sex mechanically, for one of the main rules of the genre is that the sexual act is to be exaggerated, exalted, magnified, and endlessly reiterated (what Guilbert calls the "accumulation principle"). Should *Lost Girls* not obsessively reiterate sexual intercourse, then it would not be pornography anymore; it would be mildly erotic, or would belong to some other genre. This does not justify the narrative monotony that often flaws this work, but perhaps it explains the underlying dynamics; the authors' main focus is probably less narrative than formal, political, and theoretical. Richness of narrative is thus sacrificed for the sake of purpose: to emphasize that porn can be made ethically and aesthetically viable. The resulting schematism permeates the whole work and also influences the way the authors manage the space and time of narrative, which is examined in detail in the following section.

THE CHRONOTOPE OF SEX

The way the connection between space and time is established in *Lost Girls* is bound to the main theme of the book—sex as connected to the power of the imagination. Imagination and storytelling are what allows the protagonists to heal from the past traumas they recall, for those events are not only remembered, but also re-elaborated and shared. This outbreak of imagination—mainly in the form of sexual fantasy—ultimately reconciles the women with the different repressed contents of their sexual selves and leads them to dare taking the next step, that of uninhibitedly putting their fantasies into practice. The lack of imagination, in the authors' view, conversely generates war and destruction, for the incapability of envisioning alternative ways of dealing with the world around us leads inexorably to radicalization and violence.

Indeed, sex has always been an important topic in Moore's work. The sexuality of characters is considered in *Swamp Thing, From Hell*, and *Watchmen* (also see Hatfield, "A Review and a Response"). It is found in *The League of Extraordinary Gentlemen* and in *Top Ten*; it is the main topic of the short comics story "Act of Faith," which the author created with Steve Bissette and Michael Zulli in 1988 (see Alaniz, "Rutting in Free-Fall").

Most importantly, sex is a pivotal issue in *Promethea*, where it is directly linked to imagination, and consequently to magical practice. Promethea's esoteric enlightenment begins when she is introduced to magic by having intercourse with Jack Faust (see Moore, Williams, and Gray, *Promethea Book 2* 81–106), and during her journey in the Immateria she witnesses the act of eternal "Godsex" (*Promethea Book 4* 96–97) that brings about all creation and existence. The beginning of her apocalyptic revelation is later aided by the sexual encounter between the New York mayor, porn star Uvula Cascade, and the multiple personalities of her predecessor Sonny Baskerville (see *Promethea Book 5* 121–23). Sexuality in *Promethea* is deeply connected to the all-embracing, illuminating power of imagination, and is thus based on the same notion that underpins *Lost Girls*. Like Sophie, whom fantasy enables to travel in the Immateria as Promethea while in the real world she is not actually moving, the three protagonists of *Lost Girls* develop a special relationship with space and time while chiefly remaining in the enclosed area of the Himmelgarten—save their occasional sorties to the theater for the *Rite of Spring* (see Moore and Gebbie, *Lost Girls Book 1* ch. 10, 1–8) or to the Bodensee (see *Lost Girls Book 2* ch. 18, 1). Yet, while the supremacy of the chronotope of the imagination in *Promethea* results

in a grand narrative where magical concerns give rise to significant formal experimentation and ultimately merge with epic adventures, in *Lost Girls* Moore
and Gebbie create what we might call a chronotope of sex, leading to a different
outcome that will be now taken into consideration.

Alice, Wendy and Dorothy travel into the moments and locations of their
memories through the power of storytelling. As, set in a realistic context, they
recount their stories throughout the book, the space and time of narrative are
dislocated into the fantastic, for their recollections are eroticized re-readings of
their original tales. Each of these stories reaches a climax in conjunction with a
moment of revelation (for example, the first time Dorothy masturbates in *Book
1* ch. 1, 6; Wendy's first dream of flying in ch. 8, 7; or the vision of Alice's "en-
chanted garden" of schoolgirls in *Book 2* ch. 16, 6) or, more often, with a sexual
encounter. This peak is usually represented by a wordless splash page (a page
entirely occupied by a panel or an image) that fuses the protagonists' supposedly
"real" life with its fantastic projection, thus laying bare the connections with the
sources of *Lost Girls*. For example, when recounting her sexually gratifying but
emotionally disappointing relationship with the farm laborer she lost her virgin-
ity to, Dorothy comments: "Truth is, he looked good but he weren't real bright.
. . . See what it is, I wanted to be doin' it with somebody who had real thoughts
an' feelins just like I did, but sometimes I'd hold him an' there wasn't nothin'
there. I might as well have humped a ragdoll, or somethin' you stick out in a
field to scare the birds" (ch. 14, 5). These observations are followed by a splash
page where Dorothy, her back naked, clings to a scarecrow in a corn field (see
fig.4-4), thus providing a sexual interpretation of her meeting with the Straw
Man in Baum's book.

The same happens with Wendy and Alice; relevant moments in their stories—the fights between Peter Pan and Captain Hook, the hallucinations, the
meeting with the Red Queen and with the amazing creatures of Wonderland—
are highlighted by splash pages that regularly appear in the book to punctuate
episodes where reality, fantasy, and memory blend. The considerable size of the
single panels provides a significant break with the narration that precedes them,
while their fantastic content, together with their wordless nature and with the
frozen, often statuelike attitude of the depicted characters (for example, the
image featuring Wendy, Peter, and Captain Hook in *Book 3* ch. 25, 6) endows
these moments with a timeless quality, thus suggesting both the eternal power
of imagination and the suspension of time perceived in the intense moment of
the orgasm. A climax is thus reached where narrative seems to halt for a while,

Fig. 4-4. Dorothy and the Straw Man. From *Lost Girls Book 2*, chapter 14, page 6. © Alan Moore and Melinda Gebbie. All Rights Reserved. Image reprinted here with permission.

in order to leave the reader time to take in the current stage in the protagonist's sexual development—and to recontextualize the children's books he or she supposedly knows so well, but which must now be contemplated in a new light. A sense of timelessness is also attained in Book 3, as seven entire chapters (22 through 29) are entirely devoted to the unremitting practice of sex, first in a collective orgy featuring the staff of the hotel, and then in a prolonged threesome in which the women conclude their tales and finally fall asleep, exhausted from storytelling and from repeated orgasms (see *Book 3* ch. 29, 8).

However, the connection between sex, space-time, and the imagination is best illustrated in Book 2, chapter 20: Alice, Wendy, and Dorothy go on a trip to an island in the Bodensee known for its lush vegetation and surprisingly warm climate on June 28, 1914, the same day when the Austrian Archduke Franz Ferdinand is parading through Sarajevo with his wife. Both sequences of actions are represented throughout the eight pages of the chapter, commented on by the words from Lady Fairchild's journal. The upper panels, which fill roughly two thirds of each page, depict the women, while the lower panels show the aristocratic couple's parade. The size of the panels already speaks for itself: bigger panels are needed to portray the wild, irrepressible force of the sexual instinct, while smaller ones are used to embody the meanness of violence and war. The women undress, smoke opium, and have sex with each other in the luxuriant, flowery landscape of the island. They gradually attain a state of blissful symbiosis with their own bodies and the surrounding nature, where time, once again, is frozen in the eternal present of the sexual act: "We were beyond the looking-glass, engulfed by our own satin-fingered fantasies, caught up entirely in the legendary game" (*Book 2* ch. 20, 3). Sex is a "legendary," almost mythic activity, a ritual that transports its practitioners "beyond the looking-glass," beyond the limits of everyday life into a dimension where all its primeval power is revealed. In the two following pages, the women's faces turn into multicolored masks and are surrounded by wild animals and black men as their fantasies converge on Africa, the timeless cradle of humankind: "We writhed and kicked as creatures caught within a luscious amber, swallowed in a dream of cunt and jungle... We lived a thousand years . . . When we came, our spend was Africa, was cannibals, was zebra panic thundering down the pubic veldt." In the subsequent panel, the protagonists' bodies become a snake-like shape, their skins covered in scales, as they lick each other forming a circle: "We became one great coiled thing that licked its own vagina, lazy and contented. An ecstatic loop of squirming spit-slick muscle. An Ourobouros."[4] As we know, the snake has great importance in Moore's esoteric beliefs. A universal icon of the unending cycle of life, a symbol for the sexual drive, and a reminder of the coiled spires of the DNA, the snake appears on Promethea's caduceus and in the author's considerations on the universal dance of creation in works such as *Snakes and Ladders* (see Moore and Campbell, *Snakes,* especially 16–22).

If these images show the overwhelming power of sex as it reaches its peak and becomes the very symbol for eternity, the parallel narrative that flows beneath them acts as anticlimax, for it depicts the Archduke's parade and shooting at the hands of the Bosnian revolutionary Gavrilo Princip. The bullet explodes right when the women descend into their imaginary Africa and feel "stark white lightning in dry tinder trees" (*Book 2* ch. 20, 5); the dead bodies of the nobleman and his wife are placed under the image where the women coil into the reptilian shape. Alice writes, "Didn't I read somewhere that this Archduke fellow has a serpent tattooed on his breast, above the heart? Why should I think of that? I'm sure it doesn't matter" (6). But it does matter to the reader, because it tells us that the snake, so heavily loaded with vital symbolic meaning in the utopian moment of collective sex, makes no sense on a corpse: it looks ominous but is deprived of deeper significance because of the very uselessness of war. In pairing these two sequences Moore and Gebbie show the eternal quality of the sexual encounter and the gloomy small-mindedness of human violence simultaneously, on parallel tracks. Even though the women are not spectators to the tragic act, after the shooting they wake up feeling cold and clumsy, aware that "the spell [is] broken" because "something quite glorious [is] finished with for good" (7). Something has changed in their perception and they travel back to the hotel feeling sad and dazed.

This sequence anticipates the failure of the chronotope of sex that will be sanctioned by the coming of war at the end of the story. Following the pattern of the events that took place on the island, after the bliss of the last prolonged orgy the women will wake up finding they have to leave the hotel in a hurry, so as to avoid running into the soldiers (*Book 3* ch. 30, 1–3). Ordinary time has been restored; it cannot be stopped, and likewise place cannot be preserved. Compulsively seeking to freeze space and time in the rapturous, empowering moment of the orgasm through extensive sexual activity has not been enough. World War I comes and Moore and Gebbie themselves acknowledge the ultimate failure of the chronotope of sex, for the transient delight of orgasm cannot last.

While *Promethea* is more strongly grounded in an all-inclusive idea of imagination (as an entity that embraces all kinds of fantasies, not only sexual ones) and can thus indulge in imagining the utopia of a world that welcomes the Revelation and turns into a beautiful place where doves fly and even shop signs celebrate love and understanding (see Moore, Williams, and Gray, *Promethea Book 6* 150–58), the world of *Lost Girls* ends with war, and with a picture of a disemboweled soldier whose mutilated penis lies a few feet from his body (Moore and Gebbie, *Lost Girls Book 3* ch. 30, 8). Even though the role of imagination is obviously judged as fundamental—for the protagonists have now been healed, as the next section will show more in detail—its transposition into unremitting sexual practice ultimately appears insufficient to really affect the human race.

When referring to the metanarrative aspects of *Promethea* in chapter 2, it was claimed that in order to change the world, comics must first of all change themselves and not be reduced to the repetition of conventions. The idealistic chronotope of sex of *Lost Girls*, then, malfunctions in its attempt to stop the foolishness that drives men towards war, just as the adherence by the book to the iterative patterns of pornography outlined in the previous pages ultimately damages its own narrative substance. On a metanarrative level, the novel thus unavoidably ends by showing the breakdown of the very principle the authors wanted to celebrate throughout its development. A praise of the imagination stemming from the charming idea of intertextually joining some of the most beloved characters in literature, *Lost Girls* curiously ends with a triumph of the lack in imagination itself.

Once again a work by Angela Carter comes to mind. Her novel *The Infernal Desire Machines of Doctor Hoffman* (1972) tells the story of a Faust-like scientist who tries to accomplish a "project of ecstatic annihilation" (Carter, *Infernal Desire* 202) that, through the release of massive amounts of "eroto-energy" (206), will unleash the power of imagination and desire, thus making fantasies true and ideally freeing the whole world by clearing from it the limiting notions of common space and time. The means of production of this energy, according to the doctor, is a room filled with eternally copulating couples, who constitute "a pictorial lexicon of all the things a man and a woman might do together" (214) and who "do not die . . . [because] they have transcended mortality" (215). Nevertheless, when the protagonist Desiderio (whose name means "desire") sees them, he decides not to join them together with his beloved Albertina, the doctor's beautiful daughter, whose touch he has craved throughout the long journey described in the novel. He ends up killing both the doctor and Albertina, and goes back to his city as space and time become ordinary again, for they are no longer filled with the hallucinations generated by Hoffman's sexual machinery.

Itself built on a thick fabric of intertextual references to several other books—among them much of De Sade's work, Deleuze and Guattari's theories, and *The Wonderful Wizard of Oz*—*Doctor Hoffman* shares many of its concerns and assumptions with *Lost Girls*, including the failure of the chronotope of sex. However, there is an important difference in the endings of the two novels. Carter's Desiderio renounces blissful annihilation with Albertina because he realizes that he has never really known her, for her looks and personality change according to his desire every time they meet. He is disappointed by the doctor's totalitarian wishes and by the lovers' eternal sexual imprisonment; as for his beloved, he feels that to crave perfection is better than to hold it in your hands.[5] After killing everyone, he goes home to become a disenchanted politician. There are issues common to *Lost Girls* here—the nature of desire, the power of fantasy, and a critique of patriarchal assumptions about women—but Moore and Gebbie's work ends on a far less hopeless note if compared to Carter's. True, war has come, and the image of a horridly butchered man dominates the last page.

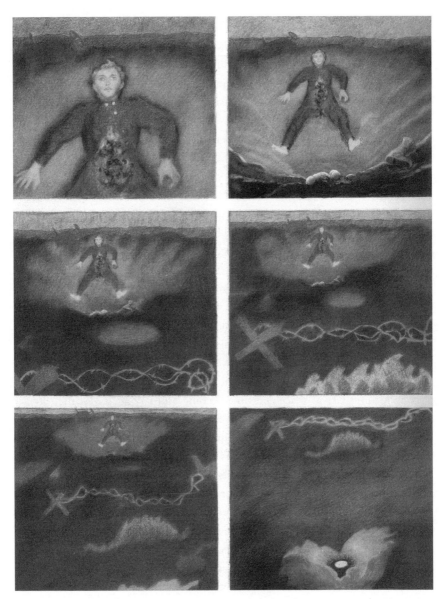

Fig. 4-5. Death and life in the last page of the novel. *Lost Girls Book 3*, chapter 30, page 8. © Alan Moore and Melinda Gebbie. All Rights Reserved. Image reprinted here with permission.

But the protagonists have now turned into stronger women, and a red flower blooms in the very last panel of the novel (see fig. 4-5), a widely recognized metaphor for the female sexual organ that of course more broadly epitomizes women (who are often referred to as flowers by Lady Fairchild throughout the book: e.g. see *Book 2* ch. 16, 5–8) and life in general. This leads us to consider another important aspect in this work: the way Moore and Gebbie handle the issue of identity.

THE POLITICS OF SEX AND PORNOGRAPHY

Lost Girls was born largely from a reflection on matters of individual identity as connected to the social perception of sex. In Moore and Gebbie's perspective, re-pressing sexual drives and fantasies damages the self and dooms society to repeat its mistakes, as the coming of war shows. But, as briefly noted in the preceding discussion, a slight note of optimism is given by the appearance of the flower on the last page of the book, and especially by the fact that Alice, Dorothy, and Wendy come out of the Himmelgarten as three new, happier women. The fulfillment of a total sexual utopia may not be possible, but the restoration of an organic identity through personal healing and self-empowerment is. To un-derstand this means to become aware of a crucial point in the political content of *Lost Girls*—or, in terms that resonate more with Moore's language, of its relevance to contemporaneity. As happened in the case of previous works—such as *V for Vendetta* or *Skizz*, both of which came with introductions that hinted at the trouble with Thatcher—Moore has not been secretive about his political agenda. In several interviews (see, for example, Amacker, Santala, Tantimedh, and Baker, especially 35) he explains that the intention behind his and Gebbie's effort to have pornography publicly recognized as a form of art stems from a critique of current Western society, which is excessively sexualized on its surface and hypocritically repressive in its essence.

He expresses these concepts even more straightforwardly in an essay en-titled "Bog Venus Versus Nazi Cock Ring," published in Jay Babcock's *Arthur* magazine in 2006. Moore reviews the manifestations of erotic imagery—in all its forms, including what is now considered pornography—through history, starting from antiquity and going through centuries of illustration and art, get-ting as far as the hypersexualized attitude of famous pop stars and the frequent coarseness of much contemporary advertising. He goes through the history of ancient Greece and Rome; signals the rise of Christianity as a watershed in the consideration of sex as something that must be concealed or repressed; and considers the sexual imagination and the trouble it caused from William Blake to D. H. Lawrence, from Oscar Wilde to the movie industry of the 1970s and '80s. He compares Great Britain and the United States to countries such as Denmark, Germany, and the Netherlands, where the representation of sex is not judged as shameful, and where sexual crime rates are statistically lower than in other parts of the world. As a consequence, he concludes, the English-speaking countries are dominated by a bigot society that prefers to suppress the vital urges of sex rather than recognize their wholesome, cathartic power. Such a society actually encourages the production of bad pornography, because that plays into its own hands: to support a morbid conception of sex is to disempower people by stifling one of the basic aspects of human nature. It is because of this ideology, Moore claims, that pornography as the term is meant today is a "grubby, under-the-counter genre in which there are absolutely no standards" (Amacker, "The Virtues of Vice Part 1"). If it were possible to raise those standards and create good pornography, people would be able to talk, think, and act more freely. By accepting their own previously untold fantasies and possible dark sides, they would not feel the urge to dominate and oppress the Other, with a consequent improvement for contemporary civilization.

Such is the idea that buttresses *Lost Girls*: Moore and Gebbie tackle an issue anticipated by Angela Carter and take on the task of the "moral pornographer" Carter had called for in her 1979 essay *The Sadeian Woman* (19). Moore himself mentions "wonderful and greatly-missed" Carter together with Simone de Beauvoir, Kathy Acker, and Andrea Dworkin (Moore, "Bog Venus") as he lists a series of intellectuals who, each in a different way, invoked a more intelligent use of pornography, especially one that would not espouse violence and the humiliation of women. Carter's voice, which has been important as a tool for reading our author's work throughout this book, reverberates most powerfully in "Bog Venus."

In her unconventional essay about Sade's influence on the conception of womanliness, the English writer mentions several figures of women, including Hollywood actresses from Mae West to Marilyn Monroe, but above all examines two key figures in the writing of the Marquis: the characters of Justine and Juliette. The former epitomizes the model of the submissive, suffering woman who is constantly abused by her virile partners, whereas the latter is exactly her opposite: she is cruel and tyrannical, and willingly exploits sex in exchange for power. While constructing "a diabolical lyricism of fuckery" (Carter, *Sadeian Woman* 26), by juxtaposing these characters Sade also envisages the possibility for women to let loose their otherwise repressed sexuality, because "if he invented women who suffered, he also invented women who caused suffering. . . . Sade remains a monstrous and daunting cultural edifice; yet I would like to think that he put pornography in the service of women, or, perhaps, allowed it to be invaded by an ideology not inimical to women" (36–37). Carter, then, acknowledged the considerable subversive potential inherent in pornography, and saw the possibility to make moral use of it in order to subvert the very assumptions of patriarchal power on which the genre is grounded. He who tries to provide pornography with such moral value will discover that this reversal process is of a deeply political nature, because "he will begin to find himself describing the real conditions of the world in terms of sexual encounters, or even find that the real nature of these encounters illuminates the world itself; the world turns into a gigantic brothel. . . . The pornographer has it in his power to become a terrorist of the imagination" (21).

Seeing the world as a gigantic brothel is exactly what Moore and Gebbie attempt with *Lost Girls*, because, in tune with Carter's stance, "sex is a metaphor for everything else, and everything is a metaphor for sex" (Vylenz, "Interview with Melinda Gebbie"). Their perspective actually reaches even farther than Carter's, for their agenda—like hers—clearly originates from a feminist background, but widens to embrace a comprehensive reflection on pornography and the social implications of sex in general, thus including not only the issue of female identity and awareness but also representations of taboos such as incest and the sexualization of childhood. They indeed become two terrorists of the imagination, in a clear act of protest against a patriarchal world that ascribes obscenity to sex but not (to mention the most shameful example) to war.

The authors' provocative choice to raise sensitive issues such as sex in childhood and incest is one of the most delicate points about this book. While Dorothy is about sixteen when she first has sex, Alice's initiation occurs at a far younger age; she is abused by one of her father's friends, who causes her first moment of disassociation from herself (see Moore and Gebbie, *Lost Girls Book 1* ch. 9, 2–7). As for Wendy, her first meetings with Peter also involve her younger brothers, who are shown as they masturbate each other; the sexual games they play with Peter (who is a young prostitute) and his friends from the spinney include Peter's sister Annabel (the equivalent of Tinkerbell), who is later raped and killed by an old pedophile with a deformed hand, of course the sexualized version of Captain Hook. Sex with children also occurs on the pages of one of Monsieur Rougeur's pornographic books, which the hotel owner promotes as a reproduction of a work by Pierre Louÿs and Franz von Bayros (see Moore and Gebbie, *Lost Girls Book 3* ch. 22, 2–8), and again in Rougeur's recollections of raping kids when he used to live in Paris as a counterfeiter (his memories, however, are declared fake by Lady Fairchild; see *Book 3* ch. 23, 3–6).

Through these representations the authors try to make two points. The first is that the presence of sexual instincts in each of us since a very early age need not be repressed or considered shameful. They assert:

> back in Victorian times . . . we came up with this fabrication of what childhood is supposed to mean, which is contrary to any real experience. . . . Childhood is a frightening, savage time that is awash with emotions that are probably more powerful than any that we will ever have for the rest of our lives. . . . It has got everything in it. It has got terror, it has got sex, it has got everything that, as adults, we try to protect children from. And we know from our own experience that you can't protect them from it, and that is the world in which they live. (Tantimedh, "Finding the *Lost Girls* Part 1")

As a consequence, Moore and Gebbie expose the hypocrisy of a society that claims to preserve innocence—for instance by pretending that children are asexual—while actually accepting worse forms of violence and constantly abusing that very innocence both through overt aggression, as occurs in the case of wars or of juvenile exploitation (see Amacker, "The Virtues of Vice Part 2"), and through the covert, and thus even more dangerous, sexualization of infancy that often appears in pop culture (see Tantimedh, "Finding the *Lost Girls* Part 1").

The second point the authors make is even more strictly connected to Moore's theory of imagination, which, in his view, must be considered as such, and which holds the right to be completely free. Therefore, child sex in *Lost Girls* should not be regarded as troubling, provided we bear in mind that it is just fantasy. This notion is thoroughly explained in the most didactic part of the book—chapter 22, where the tale by Bayros and Louÿs displays drawings of children having sex with each other and with their parents as they are pleasantly watched by a dog and a small, domestic monkey. As in other instances, a parallel narrative is offered, for the lower parts of the pages show the progression of the final collective orgy that is taking place in the hotel. Rougeur is reading the story aloud for the pleasure of his sexual partners, but Wendy brings forward the issue of incest. The hotel manager then seizes the opportunity to deliver a lecture on the pornographic imagination:

> WENDY: It's an... unngh... exciting story, but the children, doing things with... ungh... with their own Mother! I mean, I have... unngh... a son myself, and I'd never dream... unngh... never... dream of...
>
> MR. ROUGEUR: But of course you would not, dear Madam. Your child is real. These, however, are only real in this delightful book, *mais non*?
>
> ALICE: I quite agree. Do tell us more, Monsieur Rougeur. What happens next in this entrancing idyll?
>
> MR. ROUGEUR: You see? Incest, *c'est vrai*, it is a crime, but this? This is the idea of incest, no? And then these children: how outrageous! How old can they be? Eleven? Twelve? It is quite monstrous... except that they are fictions, as old as the page they appear upon, no less, no more. Fiction and fact: only madmen and magistrates cannot discriminate between them. Ah well. Let us read on... You see, if this were real, it would be horrible. Children raped by their trusted parents. Horrible. But they are fictions. They are uncontaminated by effect and consequence. Why, they are almost innocent. I, of course, am real, and since Helena, who I just fucked, is only thirteen, I am very guilty. Ah well, it cannot be helped. Let us read on, and see events come to a head... (Moore and Gebbie, *Lost Girls Book 3* ch. 22, 3–8)

The authors clearly are aware of the problematic nature of pornographic representations of children, for they have Rougeur admit he is guilty of having sex with a minor. Of course the sentence is ironic, because the man himself is fictional, but its presence nevertheless signals Moore and Gebbie's consciousness that the issue can indeed be ethically thorny. In the same way, the authors do not pretend that sex is a perfect utopia for everyone; they concede that there can be instances where it is performed nonconsensually, which obviously involves serious consequences, such as Alice's estrangement and mental trouble, and Annabel/Tinkerbell's death. But it must be remarked that this aspect is not explored in further detail, for Moore and Gebbie prefer to focus on the positive outcomes of sex in general. As objected by Noah Berlatsky, this political agenda can appear unsophisticated or even naive in its insistence on love and sex as a sort of panacea. Moore also admitted to this himself when he stated:

> Looking back . . . we realized what I suppose should have been glaringly obvious from the beginning: that this is a profoundly hippie piece of work betraying how both myself and Melinda were formed in the 1960s. It's got a bold make-love-not-war message, it's pro-erotica, it's pro-sexuality, it's pro–art nouveau, and there are lots of psychedelic and drug sequences. It's not got rock and roll, but it's got Stravinsky. And it revolves around children's fantasy characters, which were also very popular then. (Gehr)

However, it is rather clear that, for all its political naivety and narrative flaws, *Lost Girls* does not fail in calling attention to the experience of sex and to how we feel about it. It brings up issues—sexuality and childhood, women's sexuality, the gendered nature of reading and storytelling, and the incorporation of formerly subversive cultural forms into the mainstream—that might stimulate cultural debate, or spark further exploration in other works of art. Perhaps Moore is not too idealistic when he affirms that "if pornography was used correctly, it could give a kind of forum for discussing sexual ideas" (Amacker, "The Virtues of Vice Part 2"). I doubt that most consumers of porn as it is commonly known and marketed nowadays will have the chance or the interest to get hold of a copy of *Lost Girls*, and I hardly believe in porn as a cure-all for the evils of the world; but if there is one goal the book achieves, it is that of raising questions and making people talk about how sex is experienced and represented.

Let us now come to a conclusion: what does *Lost Girls* ultimately say about Alan Moore? These considerations have pointed out that this highly controversial, beautifully drawn novel includes heavy intertextuality and genre re-elaboration, word and image play, a strictly structured narrative, and circularity; it manipulates space and time, and in so doing reflects on gender and sexuality, society, literature, and the power of imagination. As suggested in these pages, it constitutes a sort of overcrowded list of what Alan Moore can do in a comic book. Despite the strong opinions expressed by some of the critics mentioned above, I would not dismiss the novel too harshly, even though it is not entirely successful: too little of what it has to offer is really new, which inevitably leads to the feeling of boredom that so many critics—including myself—have reported. But as the previous pages have hopefully demonstrated, *Lost Girls* does feature a few well-accomplished aspects or at least stimulating cues for discussion. Moore, then, must at least take credit for provoking his readers into thinking, and for not fearing the possibility of a fiasco. Indeed, he is still true to the writing principles he imparted in *On Writing for Comics*, which he first published in the now distant 1988. In its Afterword (added in 2003) he reasserted what a writer should do: "Take risks. Fear nothing, especially failure. As a living and progressive process, your writing should constantly be looking for the next high windswept precipice to throw itself over. . . . Don't worry about going too far. There isn't a Too Far" (Moore, *Writing* 46–47). I would add that regardless of Berlatsky's view, Gebbie's artistic achievement is winning, because the rigidness and the often repetitive, mannerist quality of the book are mitigated by the softness and delicacy of her crayon layers. Where narrative fails by becoming too schematic or else too thick with intertextual tricks, Gebbie's visuals make the novel a simply beautiful artistic object in itself, perhaps finally accomplishing what Monsieur Rougeur, the authors' didactic alter ego, means when he recalls how sexual and pornographic pleasure is located in an ecstatic wordless—and so perhaps more purely visual—dimension: "Pornographies are . . . our secret gardens, where seductive paths of words and imagery lead us to the wet, blinding gateway of our pleasure... beyond which, things may only be expressed in language that is beyond literature... beyond all words" (Moore and Gebbie, *Lost Girls Book 3* ch. 22, 8).

CONCLUSION

This book has tried to build a route into the dense work of one of the most prolific comic book authors of our age. As noted at the very beginning, this study is by no means exhaustive; on the contrary, it has many gaps, for it has considered only *some* aspects in *some* of Moore's works. There is so much in his production that could provide material for further analysis. So, there are a lot of things about Alan Moore's work that this book has not said. But of course there are also things it *has* said, and it is these that we review now, because there are still remarks to be made, and conclusions to be drawn.

We began with an overview on the dispute about the validity of the term *graphic novel* and noted how the most recent criticism seems to have managed to get past the debate, especially thanks to the contribution of scholars like Charles Hatfield who, in his 2005 study *Alternative Comics: An Emerging Literature*, pointed out both the advantages and the limitations of this term with admirable clearness. However, as remarked in the introduction, there are a few reasons why the much-loved and -hated term comes in handy, in particular when examining our author's work.

We then moved on to examine Moore's declarations of intent about comics scriptwriting, and the narrative strategy he makes most conspicuous use of, that of building a robust intertextual structure to buttress his fiction. As highlighted in chapter 1, his intertextuality is broad-based, encompassing literature, cinema, music, the figurative arts and, last but obviously not least, the comics tradition itself. However, the accumulation of references that in varying degrees characterizes Moore's works does not usually fall off into postmodern pastiche. Fiction, for him, is never created for its own sake and indeed becomes a scalpel, a dissecting instrument ready to work both on itself, thus self-reflexively opening out to metafictional considerations on the possibilities of narrative, and on the world that surrounds us, thus examining precise historical, social, and cultural issues.

The latter two points were examined in chapters 2 and 3, first through an analysis of chronotopes in some relevant graphic novels—*The Ballad of Halo Jones*, *From Hell*, and *Promethea*—and then through an investigation of the crisis of Englishness as it is exposed in works such as *The League of Extraordinary Gentlemen*, *The Mirror of Love*, *V for Vendetta*, *Skizz*, *Big Numbers* and, finally, Moore's prose novel *Voice of the Fire*. The stress on the perception of a sense of place and the interest in geographical specificity that emerge from the latter novel create a connection with the work of Raymond Williams, whose views on cultural theory are unmistakably ingrained in our author's vision, and also provide us with a starting point for some of the concluding observations presented in the following pages.

Chapter 4 slightly detaches itself from the previous ones in that it is dedicated to one single work, Moore's 2006 *Lost Girls*, created in collaboration with his partner Melinda Gebbie. A pornographic novel, the book raised considerable controversy for its outrageous content and ultimately diverges from most of Moore's graphic novels because, albeit acting as a compendium of the authors' technical ability, it is only partially successful in terms of narrative substance. Nevertheless, far from being a useless piece of work, *Lost Girls* still tells us something about the path Moore is currently following—an issue that will be tackled again before this final section is over.

A TRULY PERFORMING WRITER

Moore's interest in place, merged with his studies on the Kabbalah and on the practice of shamanism, has found a remarkable outlet in his performances, which we will now briefly deal with. Such pieces were usually one-off events based on reading performed by the author, sometimes accompanied by music, video screenings, and dance. All of these elements followed the outline of a draft, but there was room for improvisation. The shows were recorded on CD and in some cases (*The Birth Caul*, 1995, and *Snakes and Ladders*, 1999) they were adapted into comic-book format by Eddie Campbell, but they were never repeated. The performances stemmed from Moore's will to craft an artistic experience bound to a precise place and historical moment, in order to guide the audience's awareness toward a consideration of their own identity, with an incessant interplay of cross-references to both universal and personal history.

> I've attempted to construct a process and a context for performance art and poetry that builds on and makes use of the shamanic worldview to direct the audience through a structured mental landscape to a predetermined level of awareness. Each performance that emerges from this process is considered a unique event to be performed on one occasion only, at a specified location that is felt to be appropriate to the intention of the work, on a specific date considered to be equally significant. (Moore, "Birth Caul [essay]")

Thus the performances *The Birth Caul: A Shamanism of Childhood* (1995), created in memory of the death of Moore's mother; *Snakes and Ladders* (1999), which recollects the figure of Arthur Machen from London's Red Lion Square; *The Highbury Working* (2000), dedicated to the London area that bears the same name; and *Angel Passage* (2000), which evokes the poet William Blake from the streets of the British capital, are all indissolubly connected to the places where they were staged. They replicate the process Moore carries out in the final chapter of *Voice of the Fire*—a process they also expand by directly involving the audience not only through words, but also through other media (see Singer and my own paper from 2005). The reflection on identity that is so central in the author's view and so strictly bound to the individuality of certain locations, then, seems to reach its climax by way of performance.

Moore's fondness of performativity can be traced back to a deep-rooted tradition connected both to the world of comics and to the author's specifically English cultural heritage. There is quite a substantial list of comics artists who also tried their hand at performing. The first one to be remembered is Winsor McCay (1869–1934), the prolific comic artist who was also the precursor of the birth of the animated film in the early twentieth century and a well-known vaudeville recitalist. Many others have followed his footsteps, experimenting in several ways: for example, Ben Katchor performs solo readings that become little acts of sardonic theatre, while cartoonist, actress, and musician Dame Darcy prefers mixed media; Eric Drooker used to organize comics readings featuring musical accompaniment (see Lanier); Art Spiegelman, together with avant-jazz musician Philip Johnston, created a proper experimental project that mixed comics, music and multimedia (see Spiegelman, *Drawn to Death* and "The Ephemeral Page"); finally, the Chicago-based group called Live Action

Fig. 5-1. *Dan Leno's Comic Journal.* Reproduced from the *Penguin Book of Comics,* page 60. © George Perry and Alan Aldridge.

Fig. 5-2. *The Firefly*. Reproduced from the *Penguin Book of Comics,* page 73. © George Perry and Alan Aldridge.

Cartoonists has tried to renovate the practice of chalk talks (see Live Action Cartoonists).

But as suggested above, our author's fascination with theater derives also from his local cultural background; the magnitude of theatrical tradition in Great Britain is a known fact, and Moore cut his artistic teeth in the theatrical groups that originated from the Arts Labs, which were a genuinely English phenomenon. The first Arts Lab in the U.K. appeared in Drury Lane, London, in 1967, as a countercultural institution devoted especially to independent cinema. Following its example, several other laboratories were founded around the country; they allowed people to try and experiment with whatever form of artistic expression they felt inspired by. In Moore's recollections, the Arts Labs represented a unique experience, based on the idea that "in any town, anywhere, there was nothing to stop like-minded people who were interested in any form of art from getting together and forming completely anarchic and experimental art workshops—magazines, live events, whatever they could imagine doing" (De Abaitua). Regular attendance at the Northampton Arts Lab proved crucial for seventeen-year-old Moore, who got the chance to meet other aspiring artists and to first approach live poetry reading and theatrical performing, thus laying solid foundations for an experience that, as we have seen, he would develop later in his career (also see Campbell, "Alan Moore" 9).

There is a special connection between the tradition of English theater and comics. Unlike other countries, where theater as an institution mostly tended to address an essentially highbrow audience, in the U.K. it has always been considered popular entertainment, at least since the Middle Ages. For this reason, English theater has often manifested a distinct disposition to merge with other artistic forms, eventually including comic books. As George Perry and Alan Aldridge recall in their *Penguin Book of Comics* (1971), actors and characters coming from music-hall, popular theater, and radio comedy were a constant presence in British comics, especially in the time span from the late nineteenth century to the aftermath of World War II. Their adventures were scripted into comics, or they very often appeared as the alleged editors of comic magazines themselves: this happened in the case of Dan Leno, his *Dan Leno's Comic Journal* being published from circa 1898 to 1900 (see fig. 5-1), or that of T. E. Dunville, who appeared in the front pages of *The Firefly* (see fig. 5-2) between the 1910s and the twenties; in the forties the celebrated Yiddish comedian Issy Bonn, known for his stand-up shows and BBC radio broadcasts, became the protagonist of *Radio Fun* comics. Of course, comics also hosted characters who moved from music-halls to the movie industry, such as Laurel and Hardy or Charlie Chaplin (in this regard see Perry and Aldridge 45–91, and Gravett and Stanbury 42–57). The fruitful exchange between comics and popular theater actually dried up a bit after the fifties, but it stayed firmly rooted in the collective memory of English popular culture, and it is from this repository that Moore has so deliberately recovered it.

The emphasis on theatricality, which finds its maximum expression in Moore's performances of the period 1995–2000, casts a new light on his comics production too: in this perspective, his performances only articulate in a more explicit manner what is already present in his comics. As we have often noted in the preceding chapters, most of his works are characterized by a more or less evident performative aspect: *V for Vendetta*, of course, probably features the most persistent theatricality, with its masked hero, vaudeville-like intermissions, and constant reminder that "all the world's a stage" (Moore and Lloyd 41). But performativity is inherent in all costumed hero narrative, hence also in *Marvelman*, *Watchmen*, *Promethea*, and so on. It is present in Doctor Gull's staging of the ritual murders in the streets of London in *From Hell*. It pervades *Lost Girls* in the continuous sexual role-playing of the characters, who stage erotic situations as they recount their stories, and who indulge in a cross-dressing frenzy during their final threesome (see Moore and Gebbie, *Lost Girls Book 3* ch. 25–28, always 1 and 8; ch. 29, 1).

On a further level, performativity is present in every work where Moore turns self-reflexive and plays with metafiction, in every page where he reminds his readers of the ephemeral line that separates what we call reality from narrative, history from tale—therefore, in *Swamp Thing*, *Big Numbers*, *From Hell*, *Promethea*, and *Lost Girls* to name but a few. In this sense, Alan Moore can be defined as a truly performing writer: a writer who not only crosses over into performance in practical terms, but who also consciously performs the act of narrating; a writer whose characters become aware of playing a part on the huge stage of society, like V, or proudly declare they know they are a story (which, in the author's view, means they are real all the same, because they are real *as* stories), like Promethea, or even launch themselves in an ardent defense of their own fictional status, like Monsieur Rougeur from *Lost Girls*; and above all, a writer who has devoted most of his artistic activity to an intrinsically performative medium like comics, where the illusion of mimesis is incessantly broken by the blatant antirealism of the lines that intertwine on the page.

MOORE AND CONTEMPORARY BRITISH WRITERS

Performativity and metafictional awareness, intertextuality, a sense of place, and identity in its different and yet closely connected components of gender, class, and ethnicity, be they represented in direct form or in the recurrent metaphor of otherness: these are the major stops we have taken in this journey into the vast territory of Moore's creation. In fact, he is not alone in raising these issues: some British authors who belong to his generation share his concerns. At least three of them—all of them principally prose writers, albeit of an unusual quality—are worth mentioning here.

The first is Angela Carter (1940–1992), whose name has often come into play in this book. Besides being quoted by Moore himself as one of the writers he appreciates most, Carter is known for her subversive writing practice and incessant experimenting with genres, spanning from science fiction to erotic narrative (most notably in works like the already mentioned *The Infernal Desire Machines of Doctor Hoffman*, or her 1977 *The Passion of New Eve*), from realism to fairy tale (for instance in *Love*, 1971, and *The Bloody Chamber*, 1979), from fascination with the gothic to the bildungsroman (such as her first novel *Shadow Dance*, published in 1966, and *The Magic Toyshop*, that came out the following year).[1] The crisis of English identity and the possibility of reversing class and gender roles through performance are at the core of *Nights at the Circus* (1984), where priggish Victorian England is shattered by the bursting, hilarious monstrosity of the winged woman Fevvers, the "cockney Venus" (Carter, *Nights* 7) who likes to baffle her audiences with her daring shows. Gender is obviously also at the center of *Doctor Hoffman* and the essay *The Sadeian Woman*, both of which, as suggested in chapter 4, provide many interesting perspectives when read against *Lost Girls*. Both unconventional and uninhibited works, her novel and essay act as fictional and theoretical counterpoints to Moore and Gebbie's book, thus dialoguing with its discourse about the representation of sexuality and the subversion of the patriarchal ideology of porn. Again manifesting a meeting of cultural interests with Moore, Carter's last novel *Wise Children* (1991), which we mentioned in chapter 1, is an appreciation of the tradition of popular theater and of the space of London: its protagonists are the old twin sisters and music-hall dancers Dora and Nora Chance, who have specialized in Shakespearean remakes and parodies. Their bawdy working-class personalities and their defiant attitudes toward gender constraints and social conventions make them appear as the proper standard bearers of Carter's ethics, and the fore-

runners of Moore's. Finally, in her essay writing Carter shows a deep preoccupa-
tion with English identity too: some of the articles she wrote for *New Society* and
for other magazines between the seventies and the early nineties are an exploration of Englishness and its symbols (like the English flag, or the city of Bath;
see *Shaking*, especially 150–202) and advocate for a flexible, disruptive notion of
identity. As John McLeod puts it, she "envisions replacing 'uniform Englishness'
with something more heteroglot and untidy, embracing Englishness in terms
of historical flux rather than in terms of the stasis and petrification of English
'heritage' . . . an Englishness best conveyed for her by the image and spirit of the
Notting Hill Carnival" (McLeod 9).

As regards Iain Sinclair, his connection with Moore is just as tight. Place,
performativity, and intertextuality are of primary interest for this artist, who
critic Roz Kaveney has defined as one of the main practitioners, with Peter
Ackroyd, of the so-called "London novel" (39), a genre that has numbered
the most disparate writers among its representatives, from Charles Dickens to
Derek Raymond, from Arthur Machen to Clive Barker. As noted in the preceding chapters, Sinclair's *White Chappell, Scarlet Tracings* (1987) was one of the key
reference books Moore consulted when creating *From Hell*, which, among other
things, is our author's own tribute to London. Britain's capital rises to the status
of proper obsession for Sinclair, who almost compulsively makes it the focus
of his narrative. As Kaveney, again, observes, in the attempt to convey all the
symbolic, mythic, and imaginative layers that have created the image of London
over the centuries, he cannot help being "intertextual, because collage is the only
way to represent all the Londons that Sinclair maps, and polyphonic because he
tries to do justice to all the London voices he can hear" (39). Intertextual practice and the concept of polyphony easily remind us of the Bakhtinian notion of
heteroglossia that was applied to Moore's writing in chapter 1.

What Sinclair is best known for, however, is his notion of psychogeography, on which Moore has directly drawn, as mentioned in chapter 3 (also see
Campbell, "Alan Moore" 7). Psychogeographical writing is a performative act
in itself, in that it involves the practice of walking in order to dig out what lies
beneath the surface of the streets; but Sinclair's psychogeographical experience
goes far beyond this. Like Moore, he has experimented with the use of other
media, especially with the aid of director Chris Petit. Together this pair created two videos: the recent *London Orbital* (2002), where a loop drive on the
M25 (the beltway that surrounds London) is accompanied by footage shot on
closed-circuit cameras, and a series of site-specific interviews; and, most nota-

bly, the previous *The Cardinal and the Corpse* (1992). The latter was filmed for British Channel 4, and featured both Sinclair and Moore, whose task was walking through the streets of London, supposedly looking for a lost book of magic (a plot that was re-elaborated by Sinclair in his 1994 novel *Radon's Daughters*, which features a man looking for a lost horror novel in the darkest corners of the British capital). The two authors' common interests resulted in a concrete achievement in this collaboration.

Unlike Sinclair, there is no evident or known personal acquaintance between Moore and Peter Ackroyd (1949–), but again the concerns and motifs that characterize their work appear coterminous. For instance, Ackroyd's many novelistic biographies of major British figures constitute an essential substratum for those who, like our author, systematically revisit literary and artistic tradition through narrative: among them we find *Hawksmoor* (1985), *Dickens* (1990), *Blake* (1996), and *Shakespeare* (2005). Moore himself acknowledges consulting *Blake* while writing *From Hell* (Moore and Campbell, *From Hell* App. I, 41),[2] but it is likely that he is familiar with the first two books as well, considering how relevant both Dickens and Hawksmoor are in the creation of our author's London-set novel. The representation of the British capital in the collective imagination as a whole is a topic Ackroyd delved deeper into by writing a biography of the city itself, *The Illustrated London* (2003), even though it was published after *From Hell* had been completed; therefore, Moore had had to be content with Christopher Hibbert's 1969 *London: The Biography of a City* (see Moore and Campbell, *From Hell* App. I, 15). Ackroyd's interest in place is not restricted to London; *Albion: The Origins of the English Imagination* (2002), which lies halfway between narrative and essayistic writing, traces the English artistic tradition back to the physical and geographical aspects of the British Isles.

However, the work that seems to encompass the entire assortment of Ackroyd's agenda, and to most effectively demonstrate its similarities with Moore's, is perhaps his novel *Dan Leno and the Limehouse Golem* (1994). This book is intricate and therefore difficult to sum up in a few lines; it includes serial killings in the gloomy alleys of Victorian London, music-hall stars (the fictional Elizabeth Cree, who eventually turns out to be the serial killer, plus the really-existed Dan Leno, who is among the suspects before the murderess is discovered, and Charlie Chaplin), a self-reflexive mixture of fiction and nonfiction (as embodied by the "real" characters of Leno, Chaplin, George Gissing, and Karl Marx), class matters (as represented by Elizabeth and Gissing), ethnic issues (in the depiction of the Jewish otherness of some figures, Marx for example), and uncertain genders (there are cross-dressers and gay characters). In short, *Dan Leno and the Limehouse Golem* offers a hybrid, often metafictional narrative, the ultimate concern of which is that "'Englishness' . . . must acknowledge its dark shadows, and must accommodate diversity, including differences of class, sexual orientation, psychological makeup, and ethnicity" (Mergenthal 65).

As these short considerations show, the commonality of narrative motifs and stylistic patterns between Moore and the above-mentioned writers is substantial. Our list could go on to include other same-generation authors who focused on location, such as Michael Moorcock (e.g., *Mother London*, 1988), or on intertextuality and performativity, like Kathy Acker (e.g., *Don Quixote: Which Was a Dream*, 1986), but the cases of Carter, Sinclair, and Ackroyd are the most striking. Like Moore these authors are difficult to include in a single artistic movement or tendency and can only be generically grouped under the label "postmodern"—the definition of which, of course, is problematic. The necessity to bring it in is open to discussion, for the aim of this book is not to create a niche in the canon where Moore—or anyone else—can be comfortably placed. In an age of hybrid cultures, the cumbersome notion of "canon" has almost entirely lost its prescriptive power. The intention of this study is to bring relevant concerns in Moore's work to the surface, and to see how, through the fictionalization of these concerns, he voices some of the great issues of contemporaneity. In this perspective, it will suffice to maintain that Moore's work can be plausibly located in a significantly shared artistic terrain, the main focus of which ultimately is reflection on the idea of identity: hence the recovery of tradition through new codes and modalities of representation; the focus on gender, ethnic, and class trouble; the consideration of otherness and its contribution to the evolution of the U.K.; and the examination and reassessment of the locations of Englishness, from the space of London to the emblematic microcosm of a town in the heart of the nation, such as Northampton. The latter aspects—especially the nearly obsessive attention to location—reveal a strong impulse toward localism, which probably comes from the need to define one's cultural distinctiveness in the face of globalization of goods and dissipation of the contemporary sociopolitical context. Nevertheless, this impulse does not turn into mere, superficial nationalism, something Moore himself explicitly condemns;[3] as we have seen, his comics, prose, and performances always move from the local to the universal, and vice versa. This is true for the above-mentioned authors as well, for they (just like Raymond Williams, who was mentioned in the same regard in chapter 3) all resolutely keep away from localist—or nationalist—pitfalls. Carter, Sinclair, Ackroyd, and Moore's production, then, clearly expresses both a local and a global vocation.

But there is an element of difference that provides Moore with an edge over these fellow writers: the medium of comics. Comics make the local/global dynamics all the more powerful and sweeping: Moore's work is local in that it is always place-, time-, and culture-specific, and global not only in its themes but in the immediate, all-pervasive power of the image as a means of expression. Through the "inherent plurality of comic art" (Hatfield, *Alternative* XVI), whose very nature encompasses stratification and polysemy together with universalizing immediacy, the author articulates an effective reworking of the relationship between identity, history, culture, and a comprehensive representation of reality.

WHICH DIRECTION FOR THE FUTURE?

At the present moment, at least in the French- and English-speaking world, comics have gained the position they deserved in the spectrum of culture and have won considerable attention in terms of readership, market, and academic recognition. And yet, right when the medium Moore so keenly developed and tended to is finally free of the reductive labels that used to accompany it in the past—right at the moment when the potentialities hinted at by its first supporters seem to be confirmed—he seems to want to go beyond it, to get far from it in order to devote himself to other things, as exemplified by an interview he gave in 2003.

> I am primarily a writer. That is what I'm best at. I love to manipulate words, and to manipulate consciousness by manipulating language. That's what I've always been interested in. And I should imagine that a lot of what I do in the future will be writing. Some of it will be comics, but probably not the majority. . . . I feel that I've made my primary impact on comics 20 years ago. Near enough. Obviously, there are still things that I can add to that and develop and all the rest with regard to comics, but I think that in the field of magic I've got a lot more to offer, because it's fresher. . . . The field of magic is pretty much the same kind of state that the field of comics was back in 1980. It's ripe for plunder. (Khoury, *Extraordinary* 195)

If the above statement is true, Moore is orienting his aesthetics more and more toward the written and spoken word, thus achieving the twofold result of prose and performance. Be they in the "pure" form of prose (*Voice of the Fire*) or the hybrid, mystical idiom of performance and ritual, words attain a deeply evocative power that epitomizes the nature of magic as Moore means it, as "a disease of the language" (Campbell, "Alan Moore" 4). It is surely an extreme choice, which well suits the characteristics of our author, who has always proved curious toward new forms of communication and challenging his own creative skills through experimental forms. He recently published a short story in Iain Sinclair's collection *London: City of Disappearances* (2006); moreover, recent rumor has it that he is writing a new novel called *Jerusalem*, which is supposed to deal once again with Northampton and with personal and collective history by blending realist and fantastic fiction. In the author's own words, "there are angels and demons and God turns up in the prologue, but yet it's gritty, almost painful social realism" (Santala). The following project will be an elaboration of the concept of *grimoire* (book of magic)—which, in its turn, will go back to visual language: "I would like to make it a very visual experience because magic to me is a very visual and a very colorful experience. . . . And also to be playful, and amusing, which I also find magic to be" (Santala).

Nevertheless, Moore is still creating comics or collaborating in their creation, despite his statements about concluding his career as a comic artist. Two *Top Ten* spinoffs, *Smax* and *Top Ten: The Forty-Niners*, came out in 2004 and 2005. In 2006 he collaborated on the series *Albion* (another refashioning of English superheroes), created by his daughter Leah together with John Reppion and illustrated by Shane Oakley and George Freeman; and, most importantly, he finally published the long-awaited and much-debated *Lost Girls*. The volume *The League of Extraordinary Gentlemen: The Black Dossier* was published in early 2008, and it sounds like there are other volumes of the *League* to come (see Santala and also the interviews in Nevins, *Heroes* 207–39, and *Blazing World* 243–86). Moore explained fairly recently that "it feels really good getting back to writing comics. . . . By the time I was finished doing the *America's Best Comics* work I was absolutely sick of writing comics. . . . But now that I'm getting back into the saddle with my comics work, I'm finding that the break from it has replenished my enthusiasm" (Santala).

At this point, it is difficult to say which direction Moore is going to take in his future artistic production. He probably still has much to say, and to elaborate on, in the field of performance. And yet, for all its charm and richness in cues for reflection, performance as our author has approached it is probably limited in terms of practical realization and of audience-reaching. Of course there are Campbell's comic book adaptations, at least for two of the shows, but it is clear that they are something different from the live act and cannot entirely make up for its absence. The field of prose, perhaps, can yield further possibilities for experimentation, but Moore's output so far has been too scanty for us to assess it properly; moreover, what we have for now—*Voice of the Fire*—is definitely remarkable, but it can still be seen more as a continuation of the discourse he previously developed in comics than as a fresh start in something new and entirely original.

In short, it still seems that comics are what Moore is best at. Granted, his latest enterprise *Lost Girls* has its limitations; its formal crystallization and narrative flaws can be regarded as symptoms of the partial fatigue in comics writing the author lamented not long ago. But despite its imperfections, this ambitious graphic novel shows that Moore still has excellent knowledge of the tricks of the trade, and that he still feels like arousing comment. Besides, the news about future publications suggests that some interesting new output can be expected from him (see Santala). *The Black Dossier* by Moore and O'Neill features a 3-D section, and from what we know so far, its forthcoming "absolute" edition will include a 7" vinyl single. As for its structure, Moore claims that some parts of it are so experimental that "it feels like a new form—like it [the comics medium] has mutated into something else" (Amacker, "Opening the *Black Dossier* Part I").

In my view, the suppleness and indeterminacy of the comics medium—which cultivates the coexistence between the immediacy of visuality and the instability of the possible "continual rewriting of its grammar" (Hatfield, *Alternative* XIV)—can still be excellent vehicles for the flexible mind of an author in constant search of both formal experimentation and intellectual challenge about identity and creation, two of the great issues that haunt late-twentieth-century and early-twenty-first-century culture. This same indeterminacy must be borne in the mind of the critic of Moore's work, for a hybrid medium allows for a multiplicity of critical approaches, even more so on the work of such a thought-provoking artist. This book represents only one approach, and I hope it will provide ideas for continuation and improvement. For more than twenty years Moore has demonstrated that he is a challenging, inventive, and inspired author; what he might have in store for the future cannot but stir up our curiosity and liveliest expectations.

NOTES

INTRODUCTION

1. Comics were considered deprecable examples of lowbrow culture for a long time before being recognized as art. A key moment in the United States was the publication of psychiatrist Fredric Wertham's *Seduction of the Innocent* (1954), which led to cultural ostracism and extended prejudice toward what consequently came to be considered a cause of juvenile delinquency (see Nyberg and Wright for further reference), even though comics already had their appreciators (see, for example, Abel and Manning White, or Geipel). Wertham's theories had consequences in Europe, too, especially in Britain. However, it must be noted that other intellectuals started moving toward recognition of the validity of popular culture—including comics—right from the fifties. Among the fundamental contributions, it is important to remember French critic Roland Barthes with his *Mythologies* (1957), Italian semiotics expert Umberto Eco (*Apocalittici e integrati*, 1964; *Il superuomo di massa*, 1970), and the constitution of the Birmingham Centre for Cultural Studies in the U.K. in the 1960s. For an overview on the ups and downs of comics in social consideration, see Inge and again Wright.
2. Eisner, who was also actively engaged as a comics teacher and scholar (see *Comics and Sequential Art*, 1985), offers further considerations on the graphic novel in his book *Graphic Storytelling* (1996).
3. Chris Ware's work is extremely complex and his comics, which often border on graphic design, constitute an appropriate example of visually constructed narrative. For an overview on his production, I recommend Daniel Raeburn's concise but fairly complete monograph *Chris Ware* (2004).

CHAPTER 1. FORMAL CONSIDERATIONS ON ALAN MOORE'S WRITING

1. It is also interesting to remark that Burroughs scripted a short comics story, "The Unspeakable Mr. Hart" (artwork by Malcolm McNeal), that was published in *Cyclops* magazine in 1964.
2. Moore certainly knows Raymond Williams's work, as testified by the profound influence that his *People of the Black Mountains* had on Moore's *Voice of the Fire*, which will be dealt with in chapter 3.
3. In the *Sandman* series McKean only worked as a cover artist (see McKean). However,

he has long collaborated with Gaiman on a regular basis, in the fields both of comics, producing such works as *Violent Cases* (1987) and *Signal to Noise* (1992), and of children's narrative (*The Day I Swapped My Dad for Two Goldfish*, 1997; *Coraline*, 2002; *The Wolves in the Walls*, 2003). One of their latest creations is the animated movie *Mirrormask* (2006).

4. In this regard, see the declarations provided by Dave Gibbons in Salisbury's *Artists on Comic Art*, especially 74–97, and by Eddie Campbell in his interview with Moore on the pages of his own magazine *Egomania*. Geoff Klock (15) also explains that, when writing comics criticism, one must take into account that it is a collective narrative, but that everyone usually tends to refer more to scriptwriters than to artists for reasons of clarity and synthesis.

5. Among the many authors Moore mentions, Harlan Ellison (1934–) is particularly important, for he edited *Dangerous Visions* in 1967. The short stories he collected in this anthology were an attempt to break with the formulaic sci-fi conventions that constituted a trend in the sixties and seventies. He thus focused on stylistic experimentation and, in some cases, on representation of the characters' inner world. Therefore, *Dangerous Visions* anticipated somewhat the revisiting of science-fiction formulas Moore carried out later. Moreover, Ellison himself manifested an interest in word and image interaction: he published an adaptation of his short story *A Boy and His Dog* (1969) as a comic book titled *Vic & Blood* (1989, art by Richard Corben), and later wrote *Mind Fields* (1994), thirty-three short stories that draw inspiration from as many paintings by Polish neo-surrealist artist Jacek Yerka (see Ellison and Yerka).

6. The last name Moore and Gebbie have chosen for the character of Alice constitutes another intertextual reference, to *The History of the Fairchild Family* (1818) by Mary Martha Sherwood, a famous Calvinist book for children. The authors are being ironic, for their Alice is a sophisticated, opium-addicted, middle-aged lesbian who has always contravened the rigid customs of her wealthy family.

7. As for "misprision," we must remember that in Bloom's terminology this term indicates the act of "misreading," which implies a creative, emotionally deceptive interpretation of the literary tradition (see Bloom 94–95).

8. The character of Gargunza is actually a bit comic, starting with his funny name that could remind us of the Italian-sounding last names of typical villains in gothic fiction (see Botting and Punter). It is clear that if the superhero character is revised—thus losing his essential heroic feature—his antagonist is revised too, in this case by assuming a parodic quality, as often happens in Moore's narrative.

9. Similarities with the Charlton superhero team were quite evident, but on a suggestion from publisher Dick Giordano, Moore and Gibbons decided to change them considerably, especially in order to avoid the common copyright trouble. In this regard see Stewart, "Alan Moore" 95.

10. For a few general considerations on the musical quotations in *Watchmen* and other works by Moore—especially *V for Vendetta*, but also *Promethea*—and on the author's relationship with music (which has been remarkable in his education as an artist, and which has recently become more prominent in his productions) see Shirley, in particular the chapter "Alan Moore Knows the Score," 137–45.

CHAPTER 2. CHRONOTOPES: OUTER SPACE, THE CITYSCAPE, AND THE SPACE OF COMICS

1. To my knowledge, there are no specific critical essays or articles devoted to *Halo Jones*, except some references in interviews with Moore or in essays actually dedicated to other topics. The character of Halo has been mentioned as a possible feminist icon (see "Shazam! The Hero Breaks Down") but, as this chapter maintains, the remarkable features of this work are not restricted to gender-related issues. A more recent note was made by Brent Keane in his review on *NinthArt* (see "*Complete Ballad*").

2. It is interesting to notice that the idea of the lecture is common to Canadian writer Margaret Atwood's novel *The Handmaid's Tale*, published in 1985, a year before the last episodes of *Halo Jones*. Atwood's novel shares more than one aspect with Moore's—the futuristic setting, the centrality of the female character, and the open conclusion—and ends with an appendix titled "Historical Notes on the Handmaid's Tale" (Atwood 379–95) reporting the proceedings of a historical studies conference held in 2195 and which is partially dedicated to the discovery of the tapes on which the main character, the handmaid Offred, recorded her testimony. It is hard to conjecture a possible contact between the two writers, and Moore's "Brunhauer Lecture" takes place far too early in the novel to have been devised after Atwood's book was published; this could actually work perfectly as a proof of the communality of Moore's Ideaspace, but for us it will remain an unsolved mystery, or a curious coincidence.

3. For critical analysis of the conception of cities as bodies, see Sennett, especially the section "Arteries and Veins" (317–47), which is devoted to London.

4. Ian Brady (1938–), the so-called Moors murderer, killed five young people in Manchester and its environs between 1962 and 1965 with the help of his accomplice Myra Hindley. Peter Sutcliffe (1946–) murdered thirteen women between 1975 and 1980. Moore provides some information about the two serial killers in the notes at the end of the volume (see Moore and Campbell, *From Hell* Appendix I, 42).

5. See especially chapter 4, "Re-imagining London" (96–119), where Brooker comments on some recent works of art set in Whitechapel, such as the audio-installation *The Missing Voice* (1999) by Canadian artist Janet Cardiff, works by Patrick Keiller and Rachel Lichtenstein, and of course by Iain Sinclair, probably the best-known name in this field, along with that of his collaborator Chris Petit. Sinclair's own *White Chappell, Scarlet Tracings* (1987) is in fact among the sources Moore used when drafting *From Hell*. To this respect, see Vallorani and Maffi for several helpful insights. Although he makes no reference to Moore, Maffi defines the city as "una rara concrezione spazio-temporale" ("an uncommon spatio-temporal agglomerate," 76, my translation) that expands in concentric circles, thus presenting a series of thought-provoking considerations we might also apply to the circular aesthetics of Moore's fiction.

6. In spite of the scarce availability of publications by Charles Hoy Fort (1874–1932), Moore certainly knows of the U.S. scholar in paranormal phenomena, who is today considered a predecessor of modern ufologists and—according to some—also of so-called psychogeography, which this book will deal with later. Fort was especially known for his *Book of the Damned*. In *Lo!* he recounted a series of inexplicable aerial sightings. For further information, see the *Fortean Times* online review, www.forteantimes.com.

7. This is not the first time such a technique was experimented with. Although through far more rudimentary technology, Gilbert Shelton had his *Fabulous Furry Freak Brothers* turn "real" in a 1982 story (co-authored by Dave Sheridan and Paul Mavrides) where the brothers try to start the day without dope. The result is that the characters begin looking more photographic and talking about everyday chores; however, after barely four pages they get so bored with real life that they promptly resume their smoking and sniffing, thus immediately going back to their happier cartoon selves (see Shelton 331–36). Moore is possibly playing with quotations as usual, and taking the opportunity to honor a renowned underground comix artist.

8. This is not the only concept Moore shares with Frye; for instance, they have a mutual interest in the forms of myth and the view of the moment of apocalypse as "reality in its highest form. It is what the human imagination can conceive at the extreme limits of desire" (Denham 49). Frye's thought and Moore's aesthetics can actually be traced back— at least in part—to a common origin: both authors were deeply affected by the writings and the figure of William Blake, to whom Moore paid tribute with *Promethea*, *From Hell*, and with his 2000 performance *Angel Passage*. With regard to Frye, the above-mentioned considerations from Denham's introduction to *Fables of Identity* were particularly helpful, as well as Carlo Pagetti's observations (see Pagetti, *Astolfo*, especially 29–39).

CHAPTER 3. MOORE AND THE CRISIS OF ENGLISH IDENTITY

1. In *The League of Extraordinary Gentlemen* Moore and O'Neill often unearth the plentiful world of the Victorian pornographic imagination (as happens with the fake adverts mentioned in chapter 1). In particular, here they refer to the character of Rosa Coote, created by William Dugdale (1800–1868) as the protagonist of the novel *The Convent School, or Early Experiences of a Young Flagellant* (1876) and of the anonymous *The Yellow Room* (1891; see Nevins, *Heroes* 45).

2. Martin Tropp's argument is peculiar, in that it associates the popularity of *The Strange Case of Dr. Jekyll and Mr. Hyde* with the Jack the Ripper mythology that became popular in the same time, for both stories share the figure of a possibly mad doctor and the emerging awareness of the fragility of Victorian decorum. Again, Moore's choice of subject matter matches the focus of much literary and cultural criticism.

3. Such a vision of Victorian literature can of course be judged as reductive, as an abundance of remarkably "round" female characters can be actually found among its pages. However, Moore's generalization is not wholly incorrect, for the "angel in the house" was the most commonly appreciated and promoted image of woman in everyday Victorian culture.

4. Women's capacity for empathy in *Halo Jones* is equaled only by certain aliens such as the space cetacea, who are considered far wiser than the whole human race (see Moore and Gibson 63, 101, and 104–5). Even among the space cetacea, females hold an important position and stand out for their compassionate nature. The Minister of Peace sends a female dolphin as an ambassador to Moab in order to inspect the planet after the war has ended. The dolphin is horrified when she finds how the local population is suffering after the devastation of their land. Halo comments: "If you could give conscience a shape, it would look like a dolphin" (178).

5. In her 2003 study on London in the current literary imagination, Vallorani claims that many contemporary writers, including Carter, Amis, Weldon, Sinclair, and Self, favor women figures and assign them the role of "guides," who accompany other characters along the intricate maze of the city and who conduct the reader into the fabric of narrative. Such female connotation is not limited to metropolitan settings and shows how "the crisis of male identity that emerged in the early twentieth century . . . evolves . . . by designating the feminine as its favored location" (30, my translation). Moreover, Vallorani herself recalls Moore's mention of Boudicca, Queen of the Iceni, in *From Hell*, and appoints her the predecessor of the female protagonists of contemporary narrative, who seem to follow the trace she left in London: "She left a stripe of ash, a cold black vein in London's geological strata" (Moore and Campbell, *From Hell* ch. 4, 8).

6. Also see page 40 in Moore and Sienkiewicz, *Big Numbers* #1: the panel shows a drawn hand indicating Hampton/Northampton on a road map of England that is actually reproduced as a photograph, so as to highlight the superimposition of the fictional town with the materially existing one.

7. I refer to the first edition of the novel, which was published in 1996 with illustrations by Cliff Harper. *Voice of the Fire* was reprinted by U.S. publisher Top Shelf in 2004, and in this newer edition Harper's drawings were replaced with digital photographs by José Villarrubia.

8. The magical function of the tattooed body can be traced back to ancient tribal practices in several parts of the world, and it is a recurring element in many of the texts Moore may have used as references for his own writing, thus confirming the ever-present intertextual dimension of his work. For instance, the author is very probably familiar with the relevant tattooed characters from Ray Bradbury's *The Illustrated Man* (1951) and from Angela Carter's *The Infernal Desire Machines of Dr Hoffman* (1972), but most of all he must be cognizant of Herman Melville's *Moby-Dick* (1851). Like Queequeg, Olun is tattooed and becomes ill. *Moby-Dick* becomes a part of Moore's thick web of intertextual references in *The League of Extraordinary Gentlemen,* too. The crew of Nemo's Nautilus features penny dreadful protagonist Broad Arrow Jack and a sailor who states: "Call me Ishmael, Captain. You've known me long enough" (Moore and O'Neill, *League I* 83), and in the submarine there is a mysterious box labeled "Pequod" (128).

CHAPTER 4. FINDING A WAY INTO *LOST GIRLS*

1. The amount of work performed by Gebbie to illustrate *Lost Girls* is indeed impressive. She used watercolor, gauche, and mixed media, but most of all she used colored pencils, which she spread in six to eight layers, on average dedicating three days to each panel (see Tantimedh, "Finding the *Lost Girls* Part 2").

2. Rackham illustrated Barrie's *Peter Pan*, while Sir John Tenniel provided both *Alice in Wonderland* and *Through the Looking Glass* with his drawings. For a good overview on the golden age of children's literature and illustration, see Dalby.

3. In his review of *Lost Girls*, Xavier Guilbert remarks that eight-page chapters also recur in Carroll's *Through the Looking Glass* to recall the eight squares on each side of a chess board, thus providing another intertextual prop for Moore and Gebbie's novel.

4. The word "Ourobouros" indicates the magical circle formed by a snake that bites its own tail. A universal symbol for the cyclic nature of existence, deemed especially precious by seventeenth-century alchemists, this figuration is present, under different names, in practically every culture in the world, from Aztec and Native Indian beliefs to Norse mythology, from African folklore to Christian culture, from ancient Chinese legends to Hindu religion.

5. These are the words Desiderio uses to explain how he feels about the possibility of finally reaching the object of his desire: "While I did not know her, I thought she was sublime; when I knew her, I loved her. But . . . I was already wondering whether the fleshly possession of Albertina would not be the greatest disillusionment of all" (Carter, *Infernal Desire* 201).

CONCLUSION

1. Carter's discourse and narrative are characterized by stratification and intricacy (in this, too, she and Moore are similar), but it is neither possible nor appropriate to offer a close examination of her work here. For an overview on the most recurrent themes and structures in her fiction, I recommend Bristow and Broughton, Day, and Tucker.

2. However, Ackroyd is not Moore's only source for the figure of William Blake. In the same appendix (Moore and Campbell, *From Hell* Appendix I, 11) he mentions the other disparate works he used for reference with regard to the visionary poet, such as Alexander Gilchrist's renowned *The Life of William Blake* (1942), Kathleen Raine's *William Blake,* and the interesting paper by Bernard Nessfield-Cookson, "William Blake's Spiritual Four-Fold City" from *The Aquarian Guide to Legendary London* (1990).

3. This is how Moore comments on the widespread phenomenon of nationalism: "In terms of almost everything, things are getting more vaporous, more fluid. National boundaries are being eroded by technology and economics. . . . The physical and material world gives way to this infosphere. . . . The nationalists then go into a kind of death spasm, where they realise where the map is evaporating, and their only response to that is to dig their hooves in. To stick with nationalism at its most primitive, brutal form" (De Abaitua).

BIBLIOGRAPHY

"A Portal to Another Dimension." *Comics Journal* 116 (1987): 80–87.

Abel, Robert W., and David Manning White. *The Funnies: An American Idiom.* New York: Free Press of Glencoe, 1963.

Abruzzese, Alberto. *Arte e pubblico nell'età del capitalismo: forme estetiche e società di massa.* Venezia, Italy: Marsilio, 1976.

———. *Eroi del nostro tempo.* Roma and Bari, Italy: Laterza, 1986.

Acker, Kathy. *Don Quixote: Which Was a Dream.* New York: Grove Press, 1986.

Ackroyd, Peter. *Albion: The Origins of the English Imagination.* London: Chatto & Windus, 2002.

———. *Blake.* London: Chatto & Windus, 1996.

———. *Dan Leno and the Limehouse Golem.* London: Sinclair and Stevenson, 1994.

———. *Dickens.* London: Minerva, 1990.

———. *Hawksmoor.* London: Minerva, 1985.

———. *The Illustrated London.* London: Chatto & Windus, 2003.

———. *Shakespeare.* London: Chatto & Windus, 2005.

Aicardi, Gianluca. *M for Moore.* Napoli, Italy: Tunué, 2006.

"Alan Moore on (Just About) Everything!" *Comics Journal* 106 (1986): 38–45.

"Alan Moore." *The BBC Culture Show* [TV series]. BBC2. London: 9 March 2006.

Alaniz, José. "Into Her Dead Body: Moore & Campbell's *From Hell.*" In Millidge and smoky man, ed. *Alan Moore: Portrait of an Extraordinary Gentleman.* 145–49.

———. "Rutting in Free-Fall: Moore and Bissette/Zulli's Act of Faith." In Millidge and smoky man, ed. *Alan Moore: Portrait of an Extraordinary Gentleman.* 129–134.

Alessandrini, Giancarlo. *La testa nel fumetto.* Torino, Italy: Lo Scarabeo, 1999.

Allen, Graham. *Intertextuality.* London and New York: Routledge, 2000.

Amacker, Kurt. "The Virtues of Vice. The Alan Moore Interview, Part 1." *Mania.com,* Comicscape Section 12 April 2006. http://www.mania.com/50999.html. Accessed 10 January 2007.

———. "The Virtues of Vice. The Alan Moore Interview, Part 2." *Mania.com,* Comicscape Section 19 April 2006. http://www.mania.com/51044.html. Accessed 10 January 2007.

———. "Opening the *Black Dossier.* The Alan Moore Interview, Part 1." *Mania.com,* Comicscape Section 7 November 2007. http://www.mania.com/56564.html. Accessed 15 November 2007.

———. "Opening the *Black Dossier*: The Alan Moore Interview, Part 2." *Mania.com*, Comicscape Section 14 November 2007. http://www.mania.com/56632.html. Accessed 15 November 2007.

Amico, Federico. *Le nuvole britanniche: tendenze del fumetto inglese contemporaneo*. Bologna, Italy: Granata Press, 1992.

"An Interview with Alan Moore." http://www.fortunecity.com/victorian/durer/229/alan .html. Accessed 12 December 2005.

Ardizzone, Paolo, et al., ed. *Fumetto, cinema, televisione, internet*. Torino, Italy: Loescher, 2002.

Armitt, Lucie. *Where No Man Has Gone Before: Women and Science-Fiction*. London: Routledge, 1991.

Artoon: l'influenza del fumetto nelle arti visive del ventesimo secolo. Napoli, Italy: Electa, 1989.

Atwood, Margaret. *The Handmaid's Tale* (1985). New York: Fawcett Crest, 1986.

Babcock, Jay. "The Rational Shaman." *LA Weekly* 2 January 2002. http://www.laweekly .com/general/features/the-rational-shaman/4268/. Accessed 30 March 2003.

Baetens, Jan, ed. *Formes et politique de la Bande Dessinée*. Leuven, Belgium: Uitgeverij Peeters, 1998.

———, ed. *The Graphic Novel*. Leuven, Belgium: Leuven University Press, 2001.

Baetens, Jan, and Pascal Lefèvre. *Pour une lecture moderne de la bande dessinée*. Bruxelles, Belgium: Stitching Sherpa-CBBD, 1993.

Baker, Bill. *Alan Moore Spells It Out: On Comics, Creativity, Magic and Much, Much More*. Hong Kong: Airwave, 2005.

Balshaw, Maria, and Liam Kennedy, ed. *Urban Space and Representation*. London and Sterling: Pluto, 2000.

Bakhtin, Mikhail. *The Dialogic Imagination: Four Essays*. Ed. Michael Holquist. Trans. Caryl Emerson and Michael Holquist. Austin: University of Texas Press, 1994.

Balzaretti, Erik, et al., ed. *Come in uno specchio: immagini narrate tra fumetto e cinema*. Torino, Italy: Multimedia, 1998.

Barbieri, Daniele. *I linguaggi del fumetto*. Milan: Bompiani, 1991.

Barker, Martin. *A Haunt of Fears: The Strange History of the British Horror Comics Campaign*. London: Pluto, 1984.

———. *Comics, Ideology, Power and the Critics*. Manchester: Manchester University Press, 1989.

Barr, Marleen S. *Genre Fission. A New Discourse in Culture Studies*. Iowa City: University of Iowa Press, 2000.

Barron, Neil, ed. *Fantasy and Horror. A Critical and Historical Guide to Literature, Illustration, Film, TV, Radio, and the Internet*. Lanham and London: Scarecrow Press, 1999.

Baucom, Ian. *Out of Place: Englishness, Empire, and the Locations of Identity*. Princeton: Princeton University Press, 1999.

Baum, L. Frank. *The Wonderful Wizard of Oz*. London: Penguin, 1995.

Beaton, Frank. "Practical Magic: An Interview with J. H. Williams III." *NinthArt* 13 January 2003. http://www.ninthart.com/display.php?article=473. Accessed 8 April 2004.

———. "Snake Charmer: An Interview with Alan Moore, Part 1." *NinthArt* 31 March 2003. http://www.ninthart.com/display.php?article=532/. Accessed 15 April 2003.

———. "Snake Charmer: An Interview with Alan Moore, Part 2." *NinthArt* 7 April 2003. http://www.ninthart.com/display.php?article=536/. Accessed 15 April 2003.

Beaty, Bart. *Unpopular Culture: Transforming the European Comic Book in the 1990s.* Toronto, Buffalo, and London: The University of Toronto Press, 2007.

Becciu, Leonardo. *Il fumetto in Italia.* Firenze, Italy: Sansoni, 1971.

Benkemoun, Lise. "Alan Moore @ Comic Box." *Comic World News* 2 January 2004. http://www.comicworldnews.com/cgi-bin/index.cgi?column=interviews&page=72. Accessed 30 March 2004.

———. "Alan Moore @ Comic Box II." *Comic World News* 9 January 2004. http://www.comicworldnews.com/cgi-bin/index.cgi?column=interviews&page=73. Accessed 30 March 2004.

Benton, Mike. *The Comic Book in America: An Illustrated History.* Dallas: Taylor, 1989.

———. *Superhero Comics: The Illustrated History.* Dallas: Taylor, 1991.

Berger, Arthur Asa. *Popular Culture Genres: Theories and Texts.* Newbury Park, London, and New Delhi: Sage, 1992.

Berlatsky, Noah. "Accepting Porn as Your Personal Saviour: A Review of *Lost Girls.*" *Comics Journal* 278 (2006): 141–43.

Bernard, Mark, and James Bucky Carter. "Alan Moore and the Graphic Novel: Confronting the Fourth Dimension." *ImageTexT* 1:2 (2004). http://www.english.ufl.edu//imagetext/archives/vi_2/carter. Accessed 2 October 2004.

Bernardelli, Andrea. *Intertestualità.* Firenze, Italy: La Nuova Italia, 2000.

Bertens, Hans. *The Idea of the Postmodern: A History.* London and New York: Routledge, 1995.

Beseghi, Emy, and Antonio Faeti, ed. *La scala a chiocciola. Paura, horror, finzioni dal romanzo gotico a Dylan Dog.* Scandicci, Italy: La Nuova Italia, 1993.

Bettley, James, ed. *The Art of the Book: From Medieval Manuscript to Graphic Novel.* London: V&A Publications, 2001.

Bissette, Stephen R. "Afterword: A Snowball's Chance in Hell." In Moore, *From Hell: The Compleat Scripts.* 329–40.

Blackton, Stuart, dir. *Animation Legend: Winsor McCay* [DVD]. Lumivision, 1997.

Bloom, Clive, and Greg S. McCue. *Dark Knights: The New Comics in Context.* London: Pluto, 1993.

Bloom, Harold. *The Anxiety of Influence.* Oxford: Oxford University Press, 1973.

Boccassi, Ugo, and Anna Cavalli, ed. *Horrori di stampa: abracadario paurologico sul fumetto orrorifico e adiacenze racapriccianti.* Alessandria, Italy: WR, 1992.

Bollom, Brandon W., and Shawn M. McKinney. "Alphonse Maria Mucha: Posters, Panels . . . and Comic Books?" *International Journal of Comic Art* 7:1 (2005): 149–79.

Bongco, Mila. *Reading Comics: Language, Culture, and the Concept of the Superhero in Comic Books.* New York: Garland, 2000.

Bordoni, Carlo, and Franco Fossati. *Dal feuilleton al fumetto.* Rome: Editori Riuniti, 1985.

Botting, Fred. *Gothic.* London: Routledge, 1996.

Boudreaux, Madelyn. "An Annotation of Literary, Historic, and Artistic References in Alan Moore's Graphic Novel *V for Vendetta*." 13 August 2004. http://madelyn.utahgoth.net/vendetta/vendetta1.html. Accessed 8 January 2005.

Bradbury, Ray. *The Illustrated Man* (1951). New York: HarperCollins, 1997.

Brady, Matthew. "Top Shelf and Ormond Street Hospital Settle over Peter Pan in *Lost Girls*." *Newsarama* Forum. 26 October 2006. http://www.forum.newsarama.com/showthread.php?t=8897. Accessed 12 July 2007.

Brancato, Sergio. *Fumetti. Guida ai comics nel sistema dei media*. Rome: Datanews, 1994.

———. *Sociologie dell'immaginario. Forme del fantastico e industria culturale*. Rome: Carocci, 2000.

Brigg, Peter. *The Span of Mainstream and Science Fiction: A Critical Study of a New Literary Genre*. Jefferson and London: McFarland, 2002.

Bristow, Joseph, and Trev Lynn Broughton, ed. *The Infernal Desires of Angela Carter: Fiction, Femininity, Feminism*. London and New York: Longman, 1997.

Brooker, Peter. *Modernity and Metropolis: Writing, Film and Urban Formations*. Basingstoke: Palgrave, 2002.

Brooker, Will. *Batman Unmasked: Analyzing a Cultural Icon*. New York and London: Continuum, 2001.

Brunoro, Gianni. *Comicslexicon: prontuarietto essenziale dei più frequenti termini tecnici, concettuali e critico-informativi attinenti al fumetto*. Milan: Libreria dell'immagine, 1994.

Bukatman, Scott. *Matters of Gravity: Special Effects and Supermen in the XX Century*. Durham, NC, and London: Duke University Press, 2003.

Burbey, Mark. "An Interview with Alan Moore." *Comics Journal* 93 (1984): 77–85.

———. "An Interview with John Totleben." *Comics Journal* 93 (1984): 87–99.

———. "An Interview with Stephen Bissette." *Comics Journal* 93 (1984): 47–75.

Bussagli, Marco, ed. *XX secolo. Fumetto*. Milan: Electa, 2003.

Campbell, Eddie. "Alan Moore Interviewed by Eddie Campbell." *Eddie Campbell's Egomania* 2 (2002): 1–32.

———. *Alec: How to Be an Artist*. Paddington: Eddie Campbell Comics, 2001.

———. "Graphic Novel Manifesto." http://wasaaak.blogspot.com/2006/02/eddie-campbells-revised-graphic-novel.htm. Accessed 20 July 2006.

Cannon, Danny, dir. *Judge Dredd* [film]. Hollywood Pictures, 1995.

Canosa, Michele, and Enrico Fornaroli, ed. *Desideri in forma di nuvole: cinema e fumetto*. Pasian di Prato, Italy: Campanotto Editore, 1996.

Carney, Sean. "The Tides of History: Alan Moore's Historiographic Vision." *ImageTexT* 2:2 (2006). http://www.english.ufl.edu//imagetext/archives/v2_2/carney. Accessed 10 January 2007.

Carrier, David. *The Aesthetics of Comics*. University Park: Pennsylvania State University Press, 2000.

Carter, Angela. *The Bloody Chamber and Other Stories* (1979). New York: King Penguin, 1993.

———. *The Infernal Desire Machines of Doctor Hoffman* (1972). Harmondsworth: Penguin, 1992.

————. *Love* (1971). London: Picador, 1988.

————. *The Magic Toyshop* (1967). London: Virago, 1981.

————. *Nights at the Circus* (1984). London: Vintage, 1994.

————. *The Passion of New Eve* (1977). London: Virago, 1982.

————. *The Sadeian Woman: An Exercise in Cultural History* (1979). London: Virago, 2000.

————. *Shadow Dance* (1966). London: Virago, 1995.

————. *Shaking a Leg: Journalism and Writings*. London: Chatto & Windus, 1997.

————. *Wise Children* (1991). London: Vintage, 1992.

Catricalà, Maria, and Gianfranco Marrone, ed. *Come parla il fumetto e la multimedialità: atti del convegno tenuto a Roma il 19 novembre 1999*. Rome: Comic Art, 2000.

Ceserani, Remo. *Raccontare il postmoderno*. Torino, Italy: Bollati Boringhieri, 1997.

Chamberlain, Michael, and Paul Thompson. *Narrative and Genre*. London: Routledge, 1998.

Christ, Carol T., and John O. Jordan, ed. *Victorian Literature and the Victorian Visual Imagination*. Berkeley, Los Angeles, and London: University of California Press, 1995.

"Clause 28." *glbtq: An Encyclopaedia of Gay, Lesbian, Bisexual, Transgender, and Queer Culture*. http://www.glbtq.com/social-sciences/clause_28.html. Accessed 13 November 2004.

Colley, Linda. *Britons: Forging the Nation 1707–1837*. New Haven: Yale University Press, 1992.

Collina, Stefania, and Mauro Masera. *Teatro, cinema, fumetto, pubblicità*. Torino, Italy: Paravia, 1999.

Collins, Meredith. "History, Pornography, and *Lost Girls*." *ImageTextT* 3:3 (2007). http://www.english.ufl.edu//imagetext/archives/v3_3/lost_girls/collins.shtml. Accessed 20 July 2007.

Comic Book Artist 25 (June 2003). Special Edition: *America's Best Comics*.

Comics Interview 65 (1986). Special Edition: *Watchmen*.

Comics Journal 93 (1984). Special Issue: *Swamp Thing*.

Concina, Bruno. *Pensare il fumetto*. Argenta, Italy: Edizioni Trentini, 1999.

Coppin, Lisa. "Looking Inside Out: The Vision as Particular Gaze in *From Hell* (Alan Moore and Eddie Campbell)." *Image & Narrative* 5 (January 2003). http://www.imageandnarrative.be/uncanny/lisacoppin.htm. Accessed 24 March 2005.

Crafton, Donald. *Before Mickey: The Animated Film, 1898–1928*. Cambridge: MIT Press, 1992.

Crippen, Tom. "'Hey-Yoh!': A Review of *Lost Girls*." *Comics Journal* 278 (2006): 139–40.

Dagilis, Andrew. "The Freedom Cop." *Comics Journal* 129 (1989): 55–60.

Dalby, Richard. *The Golden Age of Children's Book Illustration*. London: O'Mara, 1991.

Dameson, Jim. "The Flâneur and Walter Benjamin." *Northwest Review* 38:3 (2000): 135–45.

Daniels, Les. *DC Comics: Sixty Years of the World's Favorite Comic Book Heroes*. London: Virgin, 1995.

————. *MARVEL: Five Fabulous Decades of the World's Greatest Comics*. New York: H. N. Abrams, 1991.

Davidson, Steef. *The Penguin Book of Political Comics*. New York: Penguin, 1982.

Day, Aidan. *Angela Carter: The Rational Glass*. Manchester: Manchester University Press, 1998.

De Abaitua, Matthew. "An Interview with Alan Moore." *The Idler* February–March 1998. http://www.idler.co.uk. Accessed 10 January 2003.

De Zordo, Ornella, and Fiorenzo Fantaccini, ed. *Le riscritture del postmoderno*. Bari, Italy: Palomar, 2002.

Dean, Michael. "Michael Dean Replies" [letter]. *Comics Journal* 284 (2007): 22.

Del Monte, Alberto, ed. *Il romanzo picaresco*. Napoli, Italy: ESI, 1957.

Di Liddo, Annalisa. "Transcending Comics: Crossing the Boundaries of the Medium in Alan Moore and Eddie Campbell's *Snakes and Ladders*." *International Journal of Comic Art* 7:1 (2005): 530–45.

Di Nocera, Alessandro. *Supereroi e superpoteri. Storia e mito fantastico nell'America inquieta della Guerra Fredda*. Rome: Castelvecchi, 2000.

Dierick, Charles, and Pascal Lefèvre, ed. *Forging a New Medium: The Comic Strip in the Nineteenth Century*. Bruxelles: VUB University Press, 2000.

Docker, John. *Postmodernism and Popular Culture: A Cultural History*. Cambridge: Cambridge University Press, 1994.

Donawerth, Jane. *Frankenstein's Daughters: Women Writing Science Fiction*. Syracuse: Syracuse University Press, 1997.

Draper, Ronald P., ed. *The Literature of Region and Nation*. Basingstoke: Macmillan, 1989.

Dubrow, Heather. *Genre*. London: Methuen, 1982.

Duff, David, ed. *Modern Genre Theory*. London and New York: Longman, 1999.

Duin, Steve, and Mike Richardson. *Comics Between the Panels*. Milwaukie, OR: Dark Horse Comics, 1998.

Eagleton, Terry, ed. *Raymond Williams: Critical Perspectives*. Boston: Northeastern University Press, 1989.

Eco, Umberto. "Quattro modi di parlare di fumetti." *Fucine Mute* 9, October 1999. http://www.fucine.com/network/fucinemute/core/index.php?url= sommario.php&t1=1. Accessed 30 January 2004.

———. *Apocalittici e integrati*. Milan: Bompiani, 1964.

———. *I limiti dell'interpretazione*. Milan: Bompiani, 1970.

———. *Il superuomo di massa*. Milan: Bompiani, 1970.

Eisner, Will. "Address: The Future of Graphic Narrative" [video recording]. *Festival of Cartoon Art Series*. Columbus: Shaw Video Services, 1989.

———. *Comics and Sequential Art*. Tamarac, FL: Poorhouse, 1985.

———. *A Contract With God and Other Tenement Stories* (1978). New York: DC Comics, 2000.

———. *Graphic Storytelling*. Tamarac, FL: Poorhouse, 1996.

———. *A Life Force* (1983). New York: DC Comics, 2001.

Eklund, Tof. "A Magical Realism of the Fuck." *ImageTexT* 3:3 (2007). http://www.english.ufl.edu//imagetext/archives/v3_3/lost_girls/eklund.shtml. Accessed 20 July 2007.

Eliot, T. S. "Tradition and the Individual Talent." In *Selected Prose of T .S. Eliot*. Ed. Frank Kermode. London: Faber and Faber, 1975. 37–44.

Ellison, Harlan, ed. *Dangerous Visions* (1967). New York: ibooks, 2002.

Ellison, Harlan, and Jacek Yerka. *Mind Fields: The Art of Jacek Yerka, The Fiction of Harlan Ellison*. Beverly Hills: Morpheus International, 1994.

Ellison, Harlan, and Richard Corben. *Vic & Blood*. New York: NBM, 1989.

Estren, Mark James. *A History of Underground Comics*. Berkeley: Ronin, 1993.

Faber, Michel. "Released at Last." *The Guardian* 5 January 2008.

Favari, Pietro, ed. *Le nuvole parlanti*. Bari, Italy: Dedalo, 1996.

Ferrero, Antonio. *Cinema e fumetto: saggi disinvolti su settima e ottava arte*. Cuneo, Italy: Primalpe, 2002.

Festi, Roberto, ed. *Fantascienza: ritorno alla terra. Il fumetto e la grafica di fantascienza come anticipatori di visioni*. Trento, Italy: Stampalith, 1999.

Fischer, Craig. "Blah-Blah... Fischer... Blah-Blah... Dean..." [letter]. *Comics Journal* 284 (2007): 19–22.

——. "Charmageddon! Or The Day Aleister Crowley Wrote Wonder Woman." *Iowa Journal of Cultural Studies* 6 (Spring 2005). http://www.uiowa.edu/~ijcs/comics/fischer.htm#. Accessed 10 October 2005.

——. "The Straw Man: A Review of *Lost Girls*." *Comics Journal* 278 (2006): 136–38.

Fishbaugh, Brent. "Moore and Gibbons's *Watchmen*: Exact Personifications of Science." *Extrapolation* 39:3 (1998): 189–98.

Fossati, Franco. *Dizionario del fumetto*, Milan: Mondadori, 1992.

Foster, Mark, dir. *Finding Neverland* [film]. Miramax, 2002.

Fowler, Alastair. *Kinds of Literature: An Introduction to the Theory of Genres and Modes*. Oxford: Clarendon, 1982.

French, Philip. "Jack the Knife." *The Observer* 10 February 2002.

Fresàn, Rodrigo. *Kensington Gardens*. New York: Farrar, Straus and Giroux, 2006.

Fresnault-Deruelle, Pierre. *Il linguaggio dei fumetti*. Palermo, Italy: Sellerio, 1989.

Frezza, Gino. *Fumetti, anime del visibile*. Rome: Meltemi, 1999.

——. *L'immagine innocente: Cinema e fumetto americani dall'origine*. Rome: Napoleone, 1978.

——. *La macchina del mito tra film e fumetti*. Scandicci, Italy: La Nuova Italia, 1995.

——. *La scrittura malinconica: sceneggiatura e serialità nel fumetto italiano*. Scandicci, Italy: La Nuova Italia, 1987.

Frye, Northrop. *Anatomy of Criticism* (1957). Princeton: Princeton University Press, 2000.

——. *Fables of Identity: Studies in Poetic Mythology*. New York: Harvest, 1963.

——. *On Culture and Literature*. Chicago and London: University of Chicago Press, 1978.

——. *The Secular Scripture: A Study of the Structure of Romance* (1976). Princeton: Harvard University Press, 2004.

Gaiman, Neil. *Coraline*. Illustrated by Dave McKean. New York: HarperCollins, 2002.

——. *The Day I Swapped My Dad for Two Goldfish*. Illustrated by Dave McKean. New York: HarperCollins, 1997.

——. "*Lost Girls*." Neilgaiman.com, Journal Section 19 June 2006. http://www.neilgaiman.com/journal/2006/06/lost-girls-redux.html. Accessed 10 January 2007.

——. *The Wolves in the Walls*. Illustrated by Dave McKean. New York: HarperCollins, 2003.

Gaiman, Neil, and Dave McKean. *Violent Cases* (1987). Amherst: Kitchen Sink, 1998.

——. *Signal to Noise*. Milwaukie, OR: Dark Horse, 1992.

Gasiorek, Andrzej. *J. G. Ballard*. Manchester: Manchester University Press, 2005.

Gehr, Richard. "Alan Moore's *Girls* Gone Wilde." *The Village Voice* 22 August 2006. http://www.villagevoice.com/books/0634,gehr,74247,10.html. Accessed 10 January 2007.

Geipel, John. *The Cartoon: A Short History of Graphic Comedy and Satire*. Newton Abbot, UK: David & Charles, 1972.

Genette, Gérard. *Palimpsests: Literature in the Second Degree*. Lincoln: University of Nebraska Press, 1997 (*Palimpsestes. La littérature au second dégré*, 1982).

———. *Paratexts: Thresholds of Interpretation*. Cambridge: Cambridge University Press, 1997 (*Seuils*, 1987).

———, et al. *Théorie des genres*. Paris, France: Seuil, 1986.

Giammanco, Roberto. *Immagini vignette visioni: Comics americani nel postmoderno*. Firenze, Italy: La Nuova Italia, 1991.

Gifford, Dennis. *Victorian Comics*. London: George Allen & Unwin, 1976.

Gilliam, Terry, dir. *Tideland* [film]. Capri Films, 2005.

Giordani, Mauro. *Alla scoperta della bande dessinée: cento anni di fumetto franco belga*. Bologna, Italy: Alessandro, 2000.

Golden, Catherine J., ed. *Books Illustrated: Text, Image, and Culture 1770–1930*. New Castle, DE: Oak Knoll, 2000.

Gordon, Ian. *Comic Strip and Consumer Culture, 1890–1945*. Washington: Smithsonian Press, 1998.

Gorla, Sandro, and Francesca Luini. *Nuvole di carta: viaggio nel mondo del fumetto*. Milan: Edizioni Paoline, 1998.

Goulart, Ron. *Comic Book Culture: An Illustrated History*. Portland, OR: Collectors Press, 2000.

———. *Comic Book Encyclopaedia*. New York: HarperEntertainment, 2004.

Gould, Ann, ed. *Masters of Caricature: From Hogarth and Gillray to Scarfe and Levine*. London: Weidenfeld and Nicolson, 1981.

Gravett, Paul. *Graphic Novels: Everything You Need to Know*. London and New York: HarperCollins, 2005.

——— "Alan Moore: The 'Lost' Interview." Paulgravett.com 13 January 2008. http://www.paulgravett.com/articles/116_moore/116_moore.htm. Accessed 20 January 2008.

Gravett, Paul, and Peter Stanbury. *Great British Comics: Celebrating a Century of Ripping Yarns and Wizard Wheezes*. London: Aurum Press, 2006.

Groth, Gary. "Alan Moore: Big Words Part I." *Comics Journal* 138 (1990): 56–95.

———. "Alan Moore: Big Words Part II." *Comics Journal* 139 (1990): 78–109.

———. "Alan Moore: Interview." *Comics Journal* 118 (1987): 60–72.

———. "Alan Moore: Last Big Words. Part III." *Comics Journal* 140 (1991): 72–85.

———. "Mainstream Comics Have, at Best, Tenuous Virtues." *Comics Journal* 152 (1992): 89–100.

———. "Pornographer Laureate. An Interview with Alan Moore." *Comics Journal* 143 (1991): 116–23.

Groth, Gary, and Robert Fiore, ed. *The New Comics*. New York: Berkeley Books, 1988.

Guerrera, Manfredo. *Storia del fumetto: Autori e personaggi dalle origini a oggi*. Rome: Newton Compton, 1995.

Guilbert, Xavier. "*Lost Girls* by Melinda Gebbie & Alan Moore." *Du9* February 2007. Translated December 2007. http://www.du9.org/Lost-Girls, 908. Accessed 20 December 2007.

Hale, Norman. *All-Natural Pogo*. New York: Thinker's Books, 1991.

Harvey, David. *The Condition of Postmodernity: An Enquiry into the Origins of Cultural Change*. Oxford: Blackwell, 1990.

Harvey, Robert C. *The Art of the Comic Book: An Aesthetic History*. Jackson: University Press of Mississippi, 1996.

———. *Children of the Yellow Kid: The Evolution of the American Comic Strip*. Seattle: Frye Art Museum in Association with the University of Washington Press, 1998.

Hasted, Nick. "He Does it with Magic." *The Guardian* 1 June 2000.

———. "Whatever Happened to Alan Moore?" *Comics Journal* 183 (1996): 107–12.

Hatfield, Charles. "A Review and a Response." *ImageTexT* 3:3 (2007). http://www.english.ufl.edu//imagetext/archives/v3_3/lost_girls/hatfield.shtml. Accessed 20 July 2007.

———. *Alternative Comics: An Emerging Literature*. Jackson: University Press of Mississippi, 2005.

Heer, Jeet, and Kent Worcester, ed. *Arguing Comics: Literary Masters on a Popular Medium*. Jackson: University Press of Mississippi, 2004.

Hobsbawm, Eric J. *Age of Extremes: The Short Twentieth Century 1914–1991*. London: Michael Joseph, 1994.

Hodnett, Edward. *Image and Text: Studies in the Illustration of English Literature*. London: Scolar, 1982.

Horn, Maurice. *Comics of the American West*. South Hackensack, NJ: Stoeger, 1977.

Horn, Robert E. *Visual Language: Global Communication for the 21st Century*. Bainbridge Island, WA: Macro VU, 1998.

Horrocks, Dylan. "Moore Morality." *Ultrazine: Alan Moore Special* 20 May 2003. http://www.ultrazine.org/ultraspeciali/UM018/horrocks/horrocks_eng.htm. Accessed 14 December 2004.

Hughes, Jamie A. "'Who Watches the Watchmen?' Ideology and 'Real World' Superheroes." *Journal of Popular Culture* 39:4 (2006): 546–57.

Hutcheon, Linda. *Narcissistic Narrative: The Metafictional Paradox*. London: Routledge, 1980.

———. *A Poetics of Postmodernism: History, Theory, Fiction*. London: Routledge, 1988.

———. *The Politics of Postmodernism*. New York: Routledge, 1989.

Inge, M. Thomas. *Anything Can Happen in a Comic Strip: Centennial Reflections on an American Art Form*. Jackson: University Press of Mississippi, and Randolph-Macon College, 1995.

———. *Comics as Culture*. Jackson: University Press of Mississippi, 1990.

Jackson, Kevin. "Old Moore's Ripping Yarns." *The Independent* 21 July 2000.

Jameson, Fredric. *Postmodernism or the Cultural Logic of Late Capitalism*. Durham: Duke University Press, 1991.

———. *The Cultural Turn: Selected Writings on the Postmodern: 1983–1988*. London and New York: Verso, 1998.

Jarman, Derek, dir. *Jubilee* [film]. Megalovision/Whaley-Malin, 1977.

Johnston, Rich. "Lying in the Gutters—Column 54." *Comic Book Resources* 30 May 2006. http://www.comicbookresources.com/columns/index.cgi?column=litg&article=2475. Accessed 20 June 2006.

Joyce, Simon. *Capital Offenses: Geographies of Class and Crime in Victorian London.* Charlottesville: University of Virginia Press, 2003.

Kavanagh, Barry. "The Alan Moore Interview." *Blather* 17 October 2000. www.blather.net/articles/amoore/index.html. Accessed 11 February 2004.

Kaveney, Roz. "Turn and Turn Again: Sinclair, Ackroyd and the London Novel." *New Statesman and Society* 9 September 1994: 39.

Keane, Brent. "Learning to Drive." *NinthArt* 24 March 2003. http://www.ninthart.com/display.php?article=528. Accessed 1 July 2004.

———. "*Skizz.*" *NinthArt* 28 June 2003. http://www.ninthart.com/display.php?article=327. Accessed 1 July 2004.

———. "*Supreme: The Story of the Year.*" *NinthArt* 15 August 2003. http://www.ninthart.com/display.php?article=637. Accessed 24 May 2004.

———. "*The Complete Ballad of Halo Jones.*" *NinthArt* 12 July 2003. http://www.ninthart.com/display.php?article=337. Accessed 1 July 2004.

Kelly, Walt. *Pogo: We Have Met the Enemy and He Is Us.* New York: Simon and Schuster, 1972.

Khoury, George, ed. *The Extraordinary Works of Alan Moore.* Raleigh: Tomorrows, 2003.

———. *Kimota! The* Miracleman *Companion.* Raleigh: Tomorrows, 2001.

Kibble-White, Graham. *The Ultimate Book of British Comics: 70 Years of Mischief, Mayhem and Cow Pies.* London: Allison & Busby, 2005.

Kidd, Kenneth. "Down the Rabbit Hole." *ImageTexT* 3:3 (2007). http://www.english.ufl.edu//imagetext/archives/v3_3/lost_girls/kidd.shtml. Accessed 20 July 2007.

Kitchin, Rob, and James Kneale, ed. *Lost in Space: Geographies of Science Fiction.* London: Continuum, 2002.

Klock, Geoff. *How to Read Superhero Comics and Why.* New York and London: Continuum, 2003.

Knoepflmacher, U. C. *Ventures into Childland: Victorians, Fairy Tales, and Femininity.* Chicago: University of Chicago Press, 1998.

Kreiner, Rich. "Messages from Hell." *Comics Journal* 173 (1994): 56–59.

Kubrick, Stanley, dir. *2001: A Space Odyssey* [film]. MGM, 1968.

Kumar, Krishan. *Utopia and Anti-Utopia in Modern Times.* Oxford: Blackwell, 1987.

Kunzle, David. *The History of the Comic Strip: The Nineteenth Century.* Berkeley: University Press of California, 1990.

Lacey, Nick. *Narrative and Genre: Key Concepts in Media Studies.* Basingstoke: Macmillan, 2000.

Lanier, Christopher. "Eric Drooker Unmasked." *Comics Journal* 253 (2003): 82–111.

Lawley, Guy, and Steve Whitaker. "Alan Moore." *Comics Interview* 12 (1984): 9–27.

Leigh, Mike, dir. *Life Is Sweet* [film]. British Screen/Channel 4 (UK), 1990.

Lent, John, ed. *Pulp Demons: International Dimensions of the Postwar Anti-Comics Campaign.* Madison-Teaneck, NJ: Farleigh Dickinson University Press; and London: Associated University Presses, 1999.

Levin, Bob. *Outlaws, Rebels, Freethinkers & Pirates: Essays on Cartoons and Cartoonists.* Seattle: Fantagraphics, 2005.

Liberati, Stefano. *L'arte dei fumetti 1986–1996.* Rome: Comic Art, 1996.

Live Action Cartoonists. "Have Markers, Will Travel: Live Action Cartoonists in the Age of Multimedia Performances and Online Comics." *International Journal of Comic Art* 5:1 (2003): 355–65.

Loach, Ken, dir. *Raining Stones* [film]. Channel 4/Parallax [UK], 1993.

———. *My Name Is Joe* [film]. Channel 4/Parallax [UK], 1998.

Lockhurst, Roger. *The Angle Between Two Walls: The Fiction of J. G. Ballard.* New York: St. Martin's, 1997.

Lucy, Niall, ed. *Postmodern Literary Theory.* Oxford: Blackwell, 2000.

Lupoff, Richard A., and Don Thompson. *All in Color for a Dime.* New Rochelle, NY: Arlington House, 1970.

Maffi, Mario. *Londra. Mappe storie labirinti.* Milan: Rizzoli, 2000.

Maitzen, Rohan. *Gender, Genre, and Victorian Historical Writing.* New York and London: Garland, 1998.

Malvern, Jack. "Comic Row Over Graphic Peter Pan." *The Times.* 23 June 2006. http://www.timesonline.co.uk/article/0,,2-2238812,00.html. Accessed 12 July 2007.

Marzola, Alessandra, ed. *Englishness. Percorsi nella cultura britannica del Novecento.* Rome: Carocci, 1999.

McAllister, Matthew P., et al., ed. *Comics and Ideology.* New York: Peter Lang, 2001.

McCloud, Scott. "Family Reunion: The Converging Futures of Comic Strips, Comic Books, and the Graphic Novel" [video recording]. *Festival of Cartoon Art Series.* Columbus: Shaw Video Services, 1995.

———. *Reinventing Comics.* New York: Paradox Press–DC Comics, 2000.

———. *Understanding Comics. The Invisible Art.* London: HarperCollins, 1994.

McCulloch, Fiona. *The Fictional Role of Childhood in Victorian and Early Twentieth Century Children's Literature.* Lewiston, NY: Edwin Mellen, 2004.

McHale, Brian. *Constructing Postmodernism.* London: Routledge, 1992.

———. *Postmodernist Fiction.* New York and London: Methuen, 1987.

McKean, Dave. *Dustcovers: The Collected Sandman Covers, 1989–1997.* New York: DC Comics, 1997.

———, dir. *Mirrormask* [film]. Script by Neil Gaiman. Jim Menson/Destinations, 2005.

McLaughlin, Joseph. *Writing the Urban Jungle: Reading Empire in London From Doyle to Eliot.* Charlottesville and London: University Press of Virginia, 2000.

McLeod, John. "Introduction: Measuring Englishness." In Rogers and McLeod, eds., *The Revision of Englishness.* 1–11.

Membery, York. "Stand Aside Marvel, the Victorian Superhero Lives Again." *The Observer* 12 May 2002.

Merino, Ana. "Women in Comics: a Space for Recognizing Other Voices." *Comics Journal* 237 (2001). http://www.tcj.com/237/e_merino.html. Accessed 15 October 2003.

Meyer, Susan E. *A Treasury of the Great Children's Book Illustrators.* New York: H. N. Abrams, 1997.

Micheli, Sergio, ed. *Parole e nuvole: Atti del Corso sulla* Letteratura per immagini *per insegnanti della scuola dell'obbligo. Facoltà di Lettere e Filosofia, Siena, novembre-dicembre 1982.* Rome: Bulzoni, 1985.

Miller, Frank. *Batman: The Dark Knight Returns* (1986). New York: DC Comics, 2002.

Millidge, Gary Spencer, and smoky man, ed. *Alan Moore: Portrait of an Extraordinary Gentleman.* Leigh-on-Sea: Abiogenesis, 2003.

Mills, Jonathan. "V for Verbal Violence." *NinthArt* 7 May 2001. http://www.ninthart.com/display.php?article=5. Accessed 1 July 2004.

Mills, Pat, and Kevin O'Neill. *Marshal Law: Fear and Loathing* (1987). London: Titan, 2002.

Mitchison, Naomi. *Memoirs of a Spacewoman* (1962). London: The Women's Press, 1985.

Moliterni, Claude, et al. *Il fumetto: Cent'anni di avventura.* Torino, Italy: Electa, 1996.

Moorcock, Michael. "Homage to Cornucopia." In Millidge and smoky man, ed. *Alan Moore: Portrait of an Extraordinary Gentleman.* 51–54.

———. *Mother London.* London: Scribner, 1988.

Moore, Alan. *Alan Moore's Writing for Comics.* Urbana, IL: Avatar Press, 2003. Originally published as "On Writing for Comics," *Fantasy Advertiser* 92–95 (1985–1986).

———. *Angel Passage* [CD]. Music by Tim Perkins. Re:, 2000.

———. "Behind the Painted Smile." In Moore and Lloyd, *V for Vendetta.* 267–76.

———. "Belly of Cloud." In Khoury, ed. *The Extraordinary Works of Alan Moore.* 162–67.

———. *The Birth Caul: A Shamanism of Childhood* [CD]. Music by David J. and Tim Perkins. Charrm/Locus +, 1995.

———. "The Birth Caul [essay]." *Locus,* 2001. http://www.locusplus.org. Accessed 21 July 2005.

———. "Bog Venus Versus Nazi Cock Ring: Some Thoughts Concerning Pornography." *Arthur* 1:25 (2006). http://www.arthurmag.com/magpie/?p=1685. Accessed 6 March 2007.

———. *Brought to Light* [CD]. Music by Gary Lloyd. Codex Records, 1998.

———. *From Hell. Book One: The Compleat Scripts.* Baltimore: Borderlands, 1994.

———. *The Highbury Working* [CD]. Music by Tim Perkins. Re:, 2000.

———. "A Hypothetical Lizard." In *Liavek: Wizard's Row.* New York: Ace, 1987. Also available at http://fourcolorheroes.home.insightbb.com/lizard. Accessed 25 March 2005.

———. *The League of Extraordinary Gentlemen Volume I: The Absolute Edition: Scripts.* La Jolla: America's Best Comics, 2003.

———. *The League of Extraordinary Gentlemen Volume II: The Absolute Edition: Scripts.* La Jolla: America's Best Comics, 2005.

———. "Light of Thy Countenance." In *Forbidden Acts.* New York: Avon, 1995. Also available at http://fourcolorheroes.home.insightbb.com/light.html. Accessed 25 March 2005.

———. *The Mirror of Love* (1988). Atlanta and Portland: Top Shelf, 2004.

———. *The Moon and Serpent Grand Egyptian Theatre of Marvels* [CD]. Music by David J. and Tim Perkins. Cleopatra, 1996.

———. "The Politics and Morality of Ratings and Self-Censorship." *The Comics Journal* 117 (1987): 35–36.

———. "Skizz—How He Came To Be." In Moore and Baikie, *Skizz.* 4–5.

———. *Snakes & Ladders* [CD]. Music by Tim Perkins. Re:, 2003.

———. *Voice of the Fire*. London: Gollancz, 1996.

———. *The Worm: The Longest Comic Strip in the World* [storyline]. Hove: Slab-O-Concrete Publications, 1999.

Moore, Alan, and Jim Baikie. *Skizz* (1983). London: Titan Books, 2002.

Moore, Alan, Steve Bissette, and John Totleben. *Saga of the Swamp Thing* (1983–1984). New York: DC Comics, 2000.

———. *Swamp Thing: Love and Death* (1984–1985). New York: DC Comics, 1990.

———. *Swamp Thing: The Curse* (1985). New York: DC Comics, 2000.

———. *Swamp Thing: A Murder of Crows* (1985–1986). New York: DC Comics, 2000.

———. *Swamp Thing: Earth to Earth* (1986–1987). New York: DC Comics, 2002.

———. *Swamp Thing: Reunion* (1987). New York: DC Comics, 2003.

Moore, Alan, and Brian Bolland. *Batman: The Killing Joke*. New York: DC Comics, 1988.

Moore, Alan, and Eddie Campbell. *The Birth Caul*. Paddington: Eddie Campbell Comics, 1999.

———. *From Hell: Being a Melodrama in Sixteen Parts* (1989–1999). Marietta: Top Shelf, 2000.

———. *Snakes and Ladders*. Paddington: Eddie Campbell Comics, 2001.

Moore, Alan, and Zander Cannon. *Smax #1*. La Jolla: America's Best Comics, 2003.

———. *Smax #2*. La Jolla: America's Best Comics, 2003.

———. *Smax #3*. La Jolla: America's Best Comics, 2003.

———. *Smax #4*. La Jolla: America's Best Comics, 2004.

———. *Smax #5*. La Jolla: America's Best Comics, 2004.

Moore, Alan, and Alan Davis. *Captain Britain* (1982–1983). New York: Marvel, 2002.

———. *The Complete D.R. & Quinch* (1983–1985). London: Titan Books, 2001.

———. *Miracleman Book 1: A Dream of Flying* (1982–1985). Forestville, CA: Eclipse, 1988.

Moore, Alan, and Steve Dillon. *Alan Moore's Time Twisters* (1986). London: Fleetway, 2000.

Moore, Alan, and Melinda Gebbie. *Lost Girls Book 1*. Marietta: Top Shelf, 2006.

———. *Lost Girls Book 2*. Marietta: Top Shelf, 2006.

———. *Lost Girls Book 3*. Maretta: Top Shelf, 2006.

———. "This Is Information." In *9-11: Artists Respond Volume 1*. Milwaukie, OR: Dark Horse Comics, 2002: 185–90.

Moore, Alan, and Dave Gibbons. *Watchmen* (1986–1987). New York: DC Comics, 1990.

Moore, Alan, Dave Gibbons, Rick Veitch, et al. *Across the Universe: The DC Universe Stories of Alan Moore*. New York: DC Comics, 2003.

Moore, Alan, and Ian Gibson. *The Complete Ballad of Halo Jones* (1984–1986). London: Titan, 2001.

Moore, Alan, Gene Ha, and Zander Cannon. *Top Ten vol.1* (1999–2000). La Jolla: America's Best Comics, 2001.

———. *Top Ten vol.2* (2000–2001). La Jolla: America's Best Comics, 2003.

———. *Top Ten: The Forty-Niners*. La Jolla: America's Best Comics, 2005.

Moore, Alan, and Peter Hogan. *Terra Obscura* (2003–2004). La Jolla: America's Best Comics, 2004.

Moore, Alan, Dave Johnson, et al. *WildC.A.T.S.: Homecoming* (1995–1996). La Jolla: Wildstorm/DC Comics, 1999.

Moore, Alan, Rob Liefeld, et al. *Judgment Day* (1997–2003). Miamisburg: Checker, 2003.

Moore, Alan, and David Lloyd. *V for Vendetta* (1981–1989). New York: DC Comics, 1990.

Moore, Alan, and Michael Lopez. *Voodoo: Dancing in the Dark.* La Jolla and New York: Wildstorm/DC Comics, 1999.

Moore, Alan, and Kevin O'Neill. *The League of Extraordinary Gentlemen vol. I.* La Jolla: America's Best Comics, 2001.

———. *The League of Extraordinary Gentlemen vol. II.* La Jolla: America's Best Comics, 2004.

Moore, Alan, and Bill Sienkiewicz. *Big Numbers #1.* Northampton: Mad Love, 1990.

———. *Big Numbers #2.* Northampton: Mad Love, 1990.

———. "Shadowplay: The Secret Team." In Joyce Brabner, ed. *Brought to Light: A Graphic Docudrama.* New York: Eclipse, 1989.

Moore, Alan, Chris Sprouse, et al. *Tom Strong Book 1* (1999–2000). La Jolla: America's Best Comics, 2001.

———. *Tom Strong Book 2* (2000–2001). La Jolla: America's Best Comics, 2002.

Moore, Alan, and Curt Swan. *Superman: Whatever Happened to the Man of Tomorrow?* (1986). New York: DC Comics, 1997.

Moore, Alan, and J. J. Van Ryp. *Another Suburban Romance.* Urbana, IL: Avatar Press, 2003.

Moore, Alan, Rick Veitch, et al. *Supreme: The Story of the Year* (1996–1997). Centerville, OH: Checker, 2002.

———. *Supreme 2: The Return* (1998–2002). Centerville, OH: Checker, 2003.

Moore, Alan, J. H. Williams III, and Mick Gray. *Promethea Book 1* (1999–2000). La Jolla: America's Best Comics, 2000.

———. *Promethea Book 2* (2000–2001). La Jolla: America's Best Comics, 2001.

———. *Promethea Book 3* (2001–2002). La Jolla: America's Best Comics, 2003.

———. *Promethea Book 4* (2002–2003). La Jolla: America's Best Comics, 2004.

———. *Promethea Book 5* (2003–2005). La Jolla: America's Best Comics, 2005.

Moore, Alan, and Bill Wray. "Come on Down." *Taboo* 1 (Fall 1988): 12–20.

Moore, Alan, and Oscar Zarate. *A Small Killing.* London: Gollancz, 1991.

Moretti, Franco. *Atlas of the European Novel 1800–1900.* London and New York: Verso, 1998.

Natov, Roni. *The Poetics of Childhood.* New York and London: Routledge, 2002.

Nevins, Jess. *A Blazing World: The Unofficial Companion to The League of Extraordinary Gentlemen, vol. II.* Austin: Monkeybrain, 2004.

———. *Heroes and Monsters: The Unofficial Companion to The League of Extraordinary Gentlemen.* Austin: Monkeybrain, 2003.

———. "Notes to *Top Ten*," 2001–2002. http://www.geocities.com/ratmmjess/annos.html. Accessed 10 April 2004.

Nyberg, Amy Kiste. *Seal of Approval: The History of the Comics Code.* Jackson: University Press of Mississippi, 1998.

O'Brien, Paul. "Article 10: Alan Moore's Magical Mystery Tour." *NinthArt* 27 July 2001. http://www.ninthart.com/display.php?article=80. Accessed 1 July 2004.

———. "Article 10: The Battle of Britain." *NinthArt* 4 February 2002. http://www .ninthart.com/display.php?article=215. Accessed 1 July 2004.

Orwell, George. *Nineteen Eighty-Four* (1949). London: Penguin, 1960.

Pagetti, Carlo. *Astolfo sulla luna: Utopia e Romance.* Bari, Italy: Adriatica, 1996.

———. *Il senso del futuro.* Rome: Edizioni di storia e letteratura, 1970.

———. "Vivere e morire a Londra." Introduction to Charles Dickens, *Il nostro comune amico* (*Our Mutual Friend*). Torino, Italy: Einaudi, 2002. v–xxiii.

Pagetti, Carlo, and Oriana Palusci, ed. *The Shape of a Culture.* Rome: Carocci, 2004.

Pagetti, Carlo, and Eric Rabkin, ed. *The Rise and Fall of Twentieth Century Formula Fiction. Textus* Special Issue 14:1 (2001).

Palusci, Oriana. *Terra di lei. L'immaginario femminile tra utopia e fantascienza.* Pescara, Italy: Tracce, 1990.

Pappu, Sridhar. "We Need Another Hero." *Salon.com* 18 October 2000. http://dir.salon .com/story/people/feature/2000/10/18/moore/index.html. Accessed 11 February 2005.

Parkin, Lance. *Alan Moore.* Harpenden: Pocket Essentials, 2001.

Peeters, Benoît. *Leggere il fumetto.* Torino, Italy: Vittorio Pavesio Productions, 2000.

Pellitteri, Marco. *Sense of Comics: La grafica dei cinque sensi nel fumetto.* Rome: Castelvecchi, 1998.

Perry, George, and Alan Aldridge. *The Penguin Book of Comics.* Harmondsworth: Penguin, 1971.

Petit, Chris, dir. *The Cardinal & the Corpse (or a Funny Night Out)* [film]. Performed by Alan Moore, Iain Sinclair, Driff Field. Channel 4 [UK], 1992.

———. *London Orbital* [film]. Text by Iain Sinclair. Film Four/Illuminations, 2002.

Pollicelli, Giuseppe. *Il fumetto è morto (e neanch'io mi sento troppo bene).* Rome: Mefisto, 1997.

Pugh, Martin. *Britain Since 1789: A Concise History.* Basingstoke: Macmillan, 1999.

Punter, David, ed. *A Companion to the Gothic.* London and New York: Longman, 2000.

Puszt, Matthew J. *Comic Book Culture: Fanboys and True Believers.* Jackson: University Press of Mississippi, 1999.

Raeburn, Daniel. *Chris Ware.* New Haven: Yale University Press, 2004.

Raffaelli, Luca. *Il fumetto: un manuale per capire, un saggio per riflettere.* Milan: Il Saggiatore, 1997.

Rey, Alain. *Les spectres de la bande: Essai sur la bande dessinée.* Paris: Minuit, 1978.

Reynolds, Richard. *Super Heroes: A Modern Mythology.* London: B.T. Batsford, 1992.

Rico, Francisco. *Il romanzo picaresco e il punto di vista.* Milan: Bruno Mondadori, 2001.

Robbins, Trina. *A Century of Women Cartoonists.* Northampton: Kitchen Sink, 1993.

———. *From Girls to Grrrlz: A History of Women's Comics from Teens to Zines.* San Francisco: Chronicle Books, 1999.

———. *The Great Women Superheroes.* Northampton: Kitchen Sink, 1996.

Rodi, Rob. "A World Saver and a Wanna-Be." *Comics Journal* 132 (1989): 52–55.

———. "Cruel Britannia: *The New Adventures of Hitler* and *From Hell.*" *Comics Journal* 142 (1991): 41–47.

———. "Oscar Winners." *Comics Journal* 167 (1994): 42–44.

———. "Super Fascists, Absolute Evil, and Wild, Wild Women." *Comics Journal* 109 (1986): 64–67.

Rogers, David, and John McLeod, ed. *The Revision of Englishness*. Manchester and New York: Manchester University Press, 2004.

Rose, Steve. "Moore's Murderer." *The Guardian* 2 February 2002.

Ross, Jonathan. "Jonathan Ross Meets Alan Moore." *The Idler* November 2001. http://www.idler.co.uk. Accessed 22 April 2003.

Rota, Valerio: *Nuvole migranti. Viaggi nel fumetto tradotto*. Mottola, Italy: Lilliput, 2001.

Sabin, Roger. *Adult Comics: An Introduction*. London: Routledge, 1993.

———. *Comics, Comix and Graphic Novels: A History of Comic Art*. London: Phaidon, 1996.

——— "Side by Side in the Fantasy League." *The Observer* 2 September 2001.

Salisbury, Mark, ed. *Artists on Comic Art*. London: Titan, 2000.

———, ed. *Artists on Comics Scripting*. London: Titan, 1998.

Sandifer, Philip. "Introduction: ImageSexT—A Roundtable on *Lost Girls*." *ImageTexT* 3:3 (2007). http://www.english.ufl.edu//imagetext/archives/v3_3/lost_girls/index.shtml. Accessed 20 July 2007.

———. "Review of *Lost Girls* by Alan Moore and Melinda Gebbie." *ImageTexT* 3: 1 (2006). http://www.english.ufl.edu//imagetext/archives/v3_1/reviews/sandifer.shtml. Accessed 20 January 2007.

Sani, Andrea. *Fumettopoli: Come nascono e come crescono le storie a fumetti*. Firenze, Italy: Sansoni, 1993.

Santala, Ismo. "Interview: Alan Moore." *ReadySteadyBook: A Literary Site* 23 October 2006. http://www.readysteadybook.com/Article.aspx?page=alanmoore. Accessed 12 February 2007.

Sarup, Madan. *An Introductory Guide to Post-Structuralism and Postmodernism*. Hemel Hampstead, UK: Harvester Wheatsheaf, 1993.

Savage, William W. *Comic Books and America, 1945–1954*. Norman and London: University of Oklahoma Press, 1990.

Schelly, Bill. *The Golden Age of Comics Fandom*. Seattle: Hamster, 1995.

Scholz, Carter. "In the Dark New Ages." *Comics Journal* 137 (1990): 59–64.

Semellini, Odoardo. *Fumetteria dello spazio*. Milan: Unicopli, 2001.

Sennett, Richard. *Flesh and Stone: The Body and the City in Western Civilization* (1994). London: Penguin, 2002.

Sennitt, Stephen. *Ghastly Terror! The Horrible Story of the Horror Comics*. Manchester: Headpress, 1999.

Shakespeare, William. *The Complete Works*. Ed. Stanley Wells and Gary Taylor. Oxford: Clarendon, 1997.

Shannon, Edward. "Victoria's Secret: *From Hell* Vol.1–4." *Comics Journal* 168 (1994): 47–48.

Sharrett, Christopher. "Alan Moore." *Comics Interview* 65 (1988): 5–23.

"Shazam! The Hero Breaks Down." *The Observer*, Weekend Section 2 November 1986.

Shelton, Gilbert. *The Complete Fabulous Furry Freak Brothers*. London: Knockabout, 2001.

Shindler, Dorman T. "Alan Moore Leaves Behind His *Extraordinary Gentlemen* to Dally with *Lost Girls*." *Sci Fi Weekly*. 7 August 2006. http://www.scifi.com/sfw/interviews/sfw13282.html. Accessed 10 July 2007.

Shirley, Ian. *Can Rock & Roll Save the World? An Illustrated History of Music and Comics.* London: SAF, 2005.

Silbermann, Alphons, and H. D. Dyroff, ed. *Comics and Visual Culture: Research Studies from Ten Countries / La BD et la culture visuelle: Traveaux de recherche réalisés dans dix pays / Comics und visuelle Kultur: Forschungsbeiträge aus zehn Ländern.* München, New York, London, and Paris: K.G. Saur, 1986.

Sillars, Stuart. *Visualisation in Popular Fiction, 1860–1960: Graphic Narratives, Fictional Images.* London: Routledge, 1995.

Sim, Dave. "Correspondence: *From Hell* Part 1." In Millidge and smoky man, ed. *Alan Moore: Portrait of an Extraordinary Gentleman.* 303–18.

———. "Correspondence: *From Hell* Part 2." In Millidge and smoky man, ed. *Alan Moore: Portrait of an Extraordinary Gentleman.* 319–29.

———. "Correspondence: *From Hell* Part 3." In Millidge and smoky man, ed. *Alan Moore: Portrait of an Extraordinary Gentleman.* 330–41.

Sinclair, Iain. "Jack the Rip-off." *The Observer* 27 January 2002.

———. *Lights Out for the Territory: 9 Excursions in the Secret History of London.* London: Granta, 1997.

———, ed. *London: City of Disappearances.* London: Hamish Hamilton, 2006.

———. *London Orbital.* London: Granta, 2002.

———. *Radon's Daughters.* London: Jonathan Cape, 1994.

———. *White Chappell, Scarlet Tracings.* London: Granta, 1987.

Singer, Marc. "Unwrapping the Birth Caul." In Millidge and smoky man, ed. *Alan Moore: Portrait of an Extraordinary Gentleman.* 41–46.

Skinn, Dez. *Comix: The Underground Revolution.* London: Collins & Brown, 2004.

Smith, Frank. "Moore's Marvel: The *Miracleman* Story." *NinthArt* 21 November 2003. http://www.ninthart.com/display.php?article=715. Accessed 1 July 2004.

smoky man, ed. *Watchmen: Vent'anni dopo.* Supervised by Sergio Nazaro. S. Angelo in Formis, Italy: Lavieri Editore, 2006.

Spiegelman, Art. *Comix, Essays, Graphics and Scraps.* Rome: Sellerio-La Centrale dell'Arte, 1999.

———. *Drawn to Death: A Three-Panel Opera* [performance]. Dir. Jean Randich. Music by Philip Johnston. Information at http://www.philipjohnston.com/drawn.htm. Accessed 30 April 2005.

———. "The Ephemeral Page Meets the Ephemeral Stage: Comix in Performance." *Theater* 33:1 (2003): 4–27.

Spielberg, Steven, dir. *E.T.: The Extra-Terrestrial* [film]. Universal, 1982.

———. *Hook* [film]. Amblin Entertainment/Tristar Pictures, 1991.

Stewart, Bhob. "Alan Moore: Synchronicity and Symmetry." *Comics Journal* 116 (1987): 89–95.

———. "Dave Gibbons: Pebbles in a Landscape." *Comics Journal* 116 (1987): 97–103.

Stone, Brad. "Alan Moore Interview." 22 October 2001. http://www.fortunecity.com/tattoine/sputnik/53/scifi/a_moore.htm. Accessed 2 September 2004.

Storey, John. *Cultural Studies and the Study of Popular Culture: Theories and Methods.* Athens: University of Georgia Press, 1996.

Strelka, Joseph P., ed. *Theories of Literary Genre*. London: Pennsylvania State University Press, 1978.

Strinati, Dominic. *An Introduction to the Theories of Popular Culture*. London and New York: Routledge, 1995.

Suvin, Darko. *Metamorphoses of Science Fiction: On the Poetics and History of a Literary Genre*. New Haven: Yale University Press, 1979.

Svankmajer, Jan, dir. *Neco z Alenky* (*Alice*) [film]. Channel 4/Condor Films, 1988.

Tantimedh, Adi. "Finding the *Lost Girls* with Alan Moore Part 1." *Comic Book Resources* 25 May 2006. http://www.comicbookresources.com/news/newsitem.cgi?id=7411. Accessed 10 January 2007.

———. "Finding the *Lost Girls* with Alan Moore Part 2." *Comic Book Resources* 26 May 2006. http://www.comicbookresources.com/news/newsitem.cgi?id=7420. Accessed 10 January 2007.

———. "Finding the *Lost Girls* with Alan Moore Part 3." *Comic Book Resources* 29 May 2006. http://www.comicbookresources.com/news/newsitem.cgi?id=7433. Accessed 10 January 2007.

Thompson, Kim. "Saga of the Swamp Thing." *Amazing Heroes* 39 (1984): 100–101.

Todorov, Tzvetan. *Mikhaïl Bakhtine. Le principe dialogique suivi des Ecrits du Cercle de Bakhtine*. Paris: Seuil, 1981.

Tondro, Jason. "*Angel Passage*: An Edition. Lyrics by Alan Moore." *International Journal of Comic Art* 5:2 (2003): 392–424.

Tropp, Martin. *Images of Fear: How Horror Stories Helped Shape Modern Culture (1818–1918)*. Jefferson, NC, and London: McFarland Classics, 1999.

Tucker, Lindsay, ed. *Critical Essays on Angela Carter*. New York: G.K. Hall, 1998.

Valenti, Kristy. "Interview with Melinda Gebbie (excerpt)." *TCJ.com* 28 February 2007. http://www.tcj.com/index.php?option=com_content&task=view&id=557&itemid=48. Accessed 29 November 2007.

Vallorani, Nicoletta. *Geografie londinesi: Saggi sul romanzo inglese contemporaneo*. Milan: Cuem, 2003.

Van Dijk, Teun A. *Discourse and Literature: New Approaches to the Analysis of Literary Genres*. Amsterdam: Benjamins, 1985.

Varnum, Robin, and Christina T. Gibbons, ed. *The Language of Comics: Word and Image*. Jackson: University Press of Mississippi, 2002.

Vollmar, Rob. "Discovering the Elephant: An Integralist Approach to Understanding Graphic Novels Part 1." *NinthArt* 6 October 2003. http://www.ninthart.com/display.php?article=679. Accessed 16 January 2004.

———. "Discovering the Elephant: An Integralist Approach to Understanding Graphic Novels Part 2." *NinthArt* 3 November 2003. http://www.ninthart.com/display.php?article=700. Accessed 16 January 2004.

———. "Discovering the Elephant: An Integralist Approach to Understanding Graphic Novels Part 3." *NinthArt* 15 December 2003. http://www.ninthart.com/display.php?article=734. Accessed 16 January 2004.

———. "Discovering the Elephant: An Integralist Approach to Understanding Graphic

Novels Part 4." *NinthArt* 12 January 2004. http://www.ninthart.com/display.php?
article=755. Accessed 16 January 2004.

Vylenz, Dez, dir. *The Mindscape of Alan Moore: A Psychedelic Journey into One of the World's Most Powerful Minds* [film]. Shadowsnake/Tale Produktion, 2003/2006.

———. "Interview with Melinda Gebbie." *The Mindscape of Alan Moore*, DVD 2.

Ware, Chris. *The Acme Library of Novelty*. New York: Pantheon, 2005.

———. *Jimmy Corrigan: The Smartest Kid on Earth*. New York: Pantheon, 2000.

Watkins, Gwynne. "The Brothers Freud: Alan Moore Talks About His 336-Page Fairy-Tale Porno." *Nerve.com* 3 August 2006. http://www.nerve.com/screeningroom/books/
interview_alanmoore. Accessed 12 December 2007.

Watson, Alasdair. "All Action." *NinthArt* 8 November 2002. http://www.ninthart.com/
display.php?article=425. Accessed 1 July 2004.

———. "Charming the Snake." *NinthArt* 14 December 2001. http://www.ninthart.com/
display.php?article=177. Accessed 1 July 2004.

Waugh, Patricia. *Harvest of the Sixties: English Literature and its Background 1960 to 1990*.
Oxford: Oxford University Press, 1995.

———. *Metafiction: The Theory and Practice of Self-Conscious Fiction*. London: Routledge,
1982.

Webb, Kate. "Seriously Funny: Angela Carter's *Wise Children*." In Lorna Sage, ed. *Flesh and the Mirror: Essays on the Art of Angela Carter*. London: Virago, 1994. 279–307.

Weiland, Jonah. "Gauging *Lost Girls* Reaction with Chris Staros." *Comic Book Resources*
15 September 2006. http://www.comicbookresources.com/news/newsitem.cgi?id=8374.
Accessed 10 January 2007.

Weiner, Stephen. *Faster Than a Speeding Bullet: The Rise of the Graphic Novel*. New York:
Nantier-Beall-Minoustchine, 2003.

Wells, Dominic. "Moore the Merrier." *The Times* 6 November 2002.

———. "It's Not Always Who Draws Wins." *Knowledge: The Times Critical Guide to the Cultural Week*, 25 February–3 March 2006: 9–11.

Westwood, Sally, and John Williams, ed. *Imagining Cities: Scripts, Signs, Memory*. London
and New York: Routledge, 1997.

Whitson, Roger. "Panelling Parallax: The Fearful Symmetry of William Blake and Alan
Moore." *ImageTexT* 3:2 (2007). http://www.english.ufl.edu//imagetext/archives/v3_2/
whitson/index.shtml. Accessed 20 July 2007.

Wiater, Stanley, and Stephen R. Bissette. *Comic Book Rebels: Conversation with the Creators of the New Comics*. New York: Donald I. Fine, 1993.

Williams, Raymond. *The Country and the City*. London: Chatto & Windus, 1973.

———. *Culture*. London: Fontana, 1981.

———. *Culture and Society, 1780–1950*. London and New York: Columbia University Press,
1958.

———. *People of the Black Mountains vol.1: The Beginning*. London: Chatto & Windus,
1989.

———. *People of the Black Mountains vol.2: The Eggs of the Eagle*. London: Chatto &
Windus, 1990.

Witek, Joseph. *Comic Books as History*. Jackson and London: The University Press of Mississippi, 1989.

Wolfreys, Julian. *Writing London: The Trace of the Urban Text from Blake to Dickens*. Basingstoke: Macmillan, 1998.

Wolk, Douglas. "*Lost Girls*." *Salon.com* 30 August 2006. http://www.salon.com/books/review/2006/08/30/moore/. Accessed 10 January 2007.

Wright, Bradford W. *Comic Book Nation: The Transformation of Youth Culture in America*. Baltimore: Johns Hopkins University Press, 2001.

Wullschlager, Jackie. *Inventing Wonderland: The Lives and Fantasies of Lewis Carroll, Edward Lear, J. M. Barrie, Kenneth Grahame and A. A. Milne*. New York and Detroit: Free Press, 1996.

INDEX